Before the Wars

Before the Wars

Churchill as Reformer (1910–1911)

Alan S. Baxendale

With a Foreword by Sir Martin Gilbert

Peter Lang Oxford

Peter Lang Ltd
International Academic Publishers
Evenlode Court, Main Road, Long Hanborough, Witney
Oxfordshire OX29 8SZ
United Kingdom

Alan S. Baxendale has asserted the right under the Copyright, Designs
and Patents Act of 1988 to be identified as the Author of this Work.

© Peter Lang Ltd 2011

All rights reserved.
No part of this book may be reprinted or reproduced or utilised
in any form, by any electronic, mechanical or other means,
now known or hereafter invented, including photocopying and recording,
or in any information storage or retrieval system, without the prior permission,
in writing, of the Publishers.

A catalogue record for this book is available from the British Library

Cover image: Sir Winston Leonard Spencer Churchill by Bassano, vintage print, 1911
© National Portrait Gallery, London

ISBN 978-1-906165-39-0

Every effort has been made to trace copyright holders and to obtain their permission
for the use of copyright material. The publisher apologises for any errors or omissions
and would be grateful for notification of any corrections that should be incorporated
in future reprints or editions of this book.

Printed in the United Kingdom
by TJ International

Contents

Foreword by Sir Martin Gilbert — vii

Author's Preface — xi

Acknowledgements — xiii

CHAPTER 1
Mr Secretary Churchill, 19 February 1910 — 1

CHAPTER 2
The Home Office and the Prison Commission:
Dramatis Personae — 9

CHAPTER 3
Treatment of the Gladstonian Legacy — 41

CHAPTER 4
Humanizing Convict and Local Prison Regimes:
Churchill's Initiatives — 65

CHAPTER 5
Young Offenders — 101

CHAPTER 6
Preventive Detention — 111

CHAPTER 7
Abatement of Imprisonment:
Draft Administration of Justice Bill, 8 April 1911 — 129

CHAPTER 8
The Royal Prerogative of Mercy: Churchill and the Judiciary   155

CHAPTER 9
Churchill's Penal Thought and Practice: An Assessment   165

Notes   175

Bibliography   213

Index   223

Foreword

Churchill was Home Secretary from February 1910 to October 1911, the shortest ministerial appointment of his career. It was also one of his most productive periods. The penal reforms he envisaged, and in many cases carried out, were a high point of his imagination and achievement. Alan Baxendale looks at the evolution of these reforms and examines the thinking that underlay Churchill's motives. His book is a study of enduring importance to our understanding of Churchill.

As a former civil servant, who from 1967 to 1985 was Chief Education Officer in the Home Office Prison Department, the author is well-placed to look at Churchill's working methods during his twenty-one months at the Home Office, and at his relationships with his staff – relationships that shaped his thinking and the nature of what he sought to do. 'All too often', Baxendale writes, 'Churchill's humanity in terms of prison management and sentencing tends to be overlooked.' It is not overlooked here, but examined with careful attention to detail, to motive, to method and to results, thanks to the author's archival research over many years, exploring in depth the Home Office records at The National Archives (formerly the Public Record Office). They have proved a treasure trove.

A Cabinet Minister who approaches a new ministerial position with a sense of the urgent need for reforms must work with and win over his senior officials and expert advisers. Baxendale shows how Churchill did this by enthusiasm, determination and a careful marshalling of the facts and arguments needed to make his case. Some of the most informative pages in this book centre on Churchill's relationships with his Permanent Under-Secretary of State, Sir Edward Troup, and the Chairman of the Prison Commissioners, Sir Evelyn Ruggles-Brise.

Ruggles-Brise had been Chairman of the Prison Commissioners for fifteen years when Churchill came to the Home Office. He, like Churchill, was a reformer, but they often disagreed on pace and method. The author writes of how Brise and his fellow Prison Commissioners had certain 'favourite ploys': to encourage Churchill 'not to be in such a hurry; to provide him with long and detailed accounts of existing policies, pointing out wherever possible the near congruency between them and the changes he wished to make, thereby undermining the case for change, or, at any rate, too much of it; stressing the hazards of encounters with the Treasury over money ....'.

The author shows how Churchill 'grew weary of the repeated use by his senior advisers of tactics of this kind'. The officials in their turn 'grew weary of the never-ending flow of Churchill's ideas, as well as his request for ever more information and unfeasible speed in the transaction of public business'. Brise, in bitterness, wrote privately to Churchill's predecessor as Home Secretary: 'I am sure of only one thing that he is not a great man, though an astute one and I do not think he has a future in English politics, but I may be wrong and often am.'

The pace and nature of the reforms that Churchill was able to push through during his short tenure of the Home Office, while not as great as he would have liked, or was given time for, were nevertheless remarkable. They included considerable improvements in prison conditions, drastic reductions in prison sentences, reducing solitary confinement from nine months to one month, the ending of many imprisonable offences including automatic imprisonment for non-payment of fines, and a halt to what he called 'purposeless congestion for petty offences'.

Churchill had no illusions about the ultimate reality of prison. As he told the House of Commons on introducing his reforms: 'We must not forget that when every material improvement has been effected in prisons, when the temperature has been adjusted, when the proper food to maintain health and strength has been given, when the doctors, chaplains, and prison visitors have come and gone, the convict stands deprived of everything that a free man calls life. We must not forget that all these improvements, which are sometimes salves to our consciences, do not change that position.'

Capital punishment was another issue on which Churchill took an unusual initiative. Although a supporter of the death penalty, he studied each capital murder case with enormous care, looking to see if there was any way at all that he could recommend a reprieve, in the light, perhaps, of what seemed to him a flaw in the prosecution case, or a weakness in the defence. Shortly before the outbreak of the Second World War, in a newspaper article about his time as Home Secretary, he wrote: 'Compassion wanders round the prison, seeking some window or loophole, however small, by which she can come to the aid of mortal suffering and fallible human retaliation.'

Fifty-five years after Churchill left the Home Office, Senator Robert Kennedy, who was then drafting a criminal justice bill for the United States, told me that he was looking for a statement by Churchill about the public attitude towards criminals. I was able to read to him over the telephone Churchill's statement to Parliament, which the Senator considered to be a high point of farsighted wisdom. Churchill told the House of Commons (on 20 July 1910): 'The mood and temper of the public in regard to the treatment of crime and criminals is one of the most unfailing tests of the civilisation of any country. A calm and dispassionate recognition of the rights of the accused against the State, and even of convicted criminals against the State, a constant heart-searching by all charged with the duty of punishment, a desire and eagerness to rehabilitate in the world of industry all those who have paid their dues in the hard coinage of punishment, tireless efforts towards the discovery of curative and regenerating processes, and an unfaltering faith that there is a treasure, if only you can find it, in the heart of every man – these are the symbols which, in the treatment of crime and criminals, mark and measure the stored-up strength of a nation, and are the sign and proof of the living virtue in it.'

This book shows in fascinating detail just how much we owe to Churchill in the evolution of our justice and prison system, and in our attitudes towards crime and punishment. It shows how he reached the conclusions he did, and how he acted to turn as many of them as possible into legislation and practice.

Sir Martin Gilbert
April 2009

Author's Preface

Historians of Winston Churchill's career customarily mention his innovations, whether realized or not, in prison treatment and sentences during his Home Secretaryship between February 1910 and October 1911. Little mention is made, however, of what motivated him, apart from what he himself conceded in an oft-quoted passage taken from his speech to the House of Commons on 20 July 1910. In this he drew attention to what Radzinowicz and Hood have subsequently described as 'the balance of considerations which should guide the penal system of a progressive country'.[1] Churchill's speech prompted me to try to identify the detailed thinking which underlay his motives.

My chosen approach has been to study the evolution of his thinking as it has survived in the documentary records of his Home Secretaryship held in the Home Office archive, together with other evidence, both primary and secondary. This evidence incorporates the exchange of views concerning specific prison treatment and sentencing issues in which Churchill engaged with his senior Home Office staff and His Majesty's Prison Commissioners in the course of their day-to-day transaction of criminal justice business.

These issues are still relevant today, given the ongoing debate about modification of the criminal justice system, the internal organization and management of the Home Office as its overseer and more particularly prison treatment and sentencing. Such matters are of perennial interest the world over and will remain so for as long as imprisonment retains its place in the table of sanctions for the punishment of crime.

More specifically, the book will hopefully shed light on Churchill as a person, a politician and a government minister by focusing on his working methods and his relationships with his staff. It acknowledges the positive and lasting influence he had on home affairs, which is well known through legislation which improved safety in the mines, secured the introduction of unemployment insurance, and improved the working conditions of shop assistants. All too often, however, Churchill's humanity in terms of prison management and sentencing tends to be overlooked. Instead, studies of this Home Secretaryship all too frequently concentrate on such ephemeral, not to say sensational, events as the siege of Sydney Street and the suppression of suffragettes and strikers.

Events of this kind may easily undermine the reputation of any Home Secretary, and Churchill's political opponents lost no time in using them as weapons against him. Churchill was never afraid to defend his conduct, however. Indeed, one has the impression that he rather enjoyed the battles whenever they were joined: he certainly usually gave as good as he got.

This book is also a by-product of a very different one on which I have long been engaged: a standard history of educational endeavour among prisoners detained in England and Wales. This is a self-imposed legacy of my service as Chief Education Officer in the Home Office Prison Department between 1967 and 1985. In the course of my research, it occurred to me to enquire what interest, if any, individual Home Secretaries over the years have taken in this aspect of prisoners' regimes. Once the legal obligation to provide prisoners with education facilities had been established, I found they almost invariably left the Prison Commissioners (or their predecessors or successors) to manage them, with little supervision. The sole exception, as this book hopes to prove, was Churchill. His interest lay not simply in education in its own right, but as a conjoined and integral part of prison regimes as a whole.

Considerations of this kind have stimulated me to discover what motivated him to amend the country's criminal justice system. His responsibilities as Home Secretary, of course, were many and varied. This book, however, confines itself to only two of them: prison treatment and sentences. Each of these subjects is replete with examples of what drove him to effect changes and of how those changes were initiated in the policies and practices he championed.

Acknowledgements

It is with pleasure that I record my gratitude to the following people and institutions for the valuable assistance they have freely offered.

To Professor Seán McConville, I am first and foremost indebted for supervising my research, for his advice on its interpretation, and for his thoughts on the drafting of its outcome. Our exchanges of view and his great patience have helped immensely with the organisation of the material I have accumulated over the years.

To my retired senior Home Office colleague, Terry Weiler, I am likewise indebted for his advice on the technicalities of Home Office and Prison Commission administration, on the wording of the earlier drafts of my text, and on sharing with me the burden of proofreading. With him I should also like to associate another of my retired Home Office colleagues, Kenneth Neale, who first interested me in the history of the prison system in England and Wales.

Further, I have much appreciated the help of two individuals who have provided me with their personal recollections. Sir John Ruggles-Brise kindly allowed me to visit his home, where I was able to inspect some of the library books and papers which had once belonged to Sir Evelyn Ruggles-Brise, Chairman of the Prison Commission (1895–1921). The bulk of Sir Evelyn's archive is now located in the Essex County Record Office, where the staff were very helpful to me in my exploration. Richard Waller is the son of Sir Maurice Waller, who became a Prison Commissioner when Winston Churchill embarked on his short-lived Home Secretaryship, and succeeded Sir Evelyn as Chairman of the Commission. Richard provided me with much valuable information relating to his father's career and access to what remains of Sir Maurice's private correspondence with Herbert Gladstone, whose private secretary he had been before he became a Prison Commissioner.

I also acknowledge the abundant assistance I have received from the staffs of the Shropshire County Record Office and the Public Record Office (Kew); the British, Bodleian, Churchill College and Home Office libraries; and numerous university and inns of court archive centres. These were invaluable in my attempts to track down the backgrounds of Home Office and Prison Commission staff, whose acquaintance I had made while working through Home Office papers.

I have also to record the experience I gained during eighteen years of service as Chief Education Officer in the Prison Department. I am indebted to colleagues in Prison Service institutions, and, of course, to prisoners themselves. In one way or another this accumulated experience has stirred my interest in prison history and it is reflected in what follows here.

Finally I wish most particularly to thank Sir Martin Gilbert, CBE, DLitt for the interest he has taken in the text of my book and for his encouragement and support in bringing it to a successful conclusion, as indicated in the Foreword of his own to its publication. With Sir Martin go, too, my many thanks to my Publisher and Commissioning Editor for their advice and help in matters of publication which have facilitated my understanding of what is involved in book production.

CHAPTER 1

Mr Secretary Churchill, 19 February 1910

The Path to Home Secretary

Following the Liberal Party's re-election in January 1910, Herbert Asquith made several alterations to his cabinet. The most significant of these was his appointment of Winston Churchill as Home Secretary in place of Herbert Gladstone, who had occupied the position since December 1905 and was now bound for South Africa to serve as its first Governor-General. Churchill's appointment came in recognition of his parliamentary contributions since May 1904, when he had deserted the Conservative Party, his contributions as a minister in the Liberal governments which had held office since December 1905,[1] and most recently his contributions to the Liberal Party's electoral campaign of January 1910.[2]

Churchill was delighted with his promotion. It enhanced his prospects of achieving even higher office. Like his father, Lord Randolph Churchill, whose egotism and ambition he replicated, he had the premiership in his sights. He was determined that what had eluded his father should not elude himself.[3] There was more to his delight than this, though. An important contributory element was the opportunity it afforded of realizing an ambition nurtured during his brief experience of imprisonment in the South African War (1899–1902), while serving as a newspaper correspondent attached to the British Army. Between 15 November and 12 December 1899, he was detained in the Model School at Pretoria, before escaping and eventually making his way to safety in Durban on 23 December.[4] While admitting to having no ground for complaint about his treatment in prison, he nevertheless found his days of captivity 'long, dull, and profitless'.[5] These opinions were still in the forefront of his mind at the time of his appointment as Home Secretary. Recalling a conversation she had with him at the time, Lady Violet Bonham Carter describes his experience of captivity as making him 'the Prisoner's Friend ... his mind ... seething with plans for lightening their lot by earned remissions of sentence while "in durance vile", by libraries and entertainment'. Quoting Churchill himself, she adds, '"They must have food for thought – plenty of books – that's what I missed most – except the chance of breaking bounds and getting out of the damned place – and I suppose I mustn't give them that."'[6]

These opinions, indeed, incorporated experience of prison treatment and sentences accumulated during his years in office since 1905. While serving as Parliamentary Under-Secretary of State at the Colonial Office, for example, issues of imprisonment and criminal justice in Britain's overseas territories regularly came before him for adjudication. Thus in 1907 the government of Natal State deported to St Helena twenty-five Zulus whom it regarded as ringleaders of prolonged disturbances in Zululand. The Colonial Office approved the deportation, albeit with much reluctance, but only on the understanding that the deportees were to be treated as political prisoners and not as common convicts. Their diet had to be generous, and Churchill made it his business to ensure that this was so. However, he discovered that it was more 'suited to the lowest animals than men'. The Governor of St Helena was taken to task about this, and informed that stone-breaking was not to be the prisoners' only employment. Once their allotted daily labour had been performed, they should be allowed to cultivate a small patch of land on which they could grow vegetables for their own use or for sale; or given the opportunity to make baskets, carve wood or make shoes; or encouraged to undertake light work. If any profit accrued from such activity 'the money should be given to them to buy any extra comforts they may wish'.[7]

Churchill's service at the Colonial Office also throws light on his interest in wider criminal justice. For example, there was a case involving a railway guard in Ceylon who was suspected of stealing a mail-bag. He had not been charged with theft because of lack of evidence, but had nevertheless been dismissed from his employment on the grounds of inefficiency. Churchill contacted the Governor and informed him that if such a proceeding were raised in the House of Commons it would be indefensible.

Power of summary dismissal had to be retained, but it should be used only 'for the express purposes for which it is reserved, namely for dealing with cases which are not within the cognizance of Criminal Courts, and never in substitution for regular criminal procedure'.[8]

Ceylon had a habit of generating questions of individual rights, and significantly it was to these particular issues that Sir Francis Hopwood, Permanent Under-Secretary of State at the Colonial Office, referred when he wrote to Churchill to congratulate him on his appointment as Home Secretary in 1910:

> Do try to inoculate it [the Home Office] with something like the 'quality of mercy'. Keep an eye on the sentences passed by fat-headed people and reduce them fearlessly whether they emanate from the Ermine or only the 'great unpaid'. If you feel such interest in the 'prisoner' as you felt in the wrongs of the 'personal case' when with us you have a most beneficent period of service before you.[9]

This was precisely what Churchill envisaged for himself at the Home Office.

After the Colonial Office, Churchill was promoted to the Presidency of the Board of Trade. As such, he was in charge of a government department for the first time, so had the opportunity to put many more of his ideas into practice. These included legislative and administrative measures to decasualize labour by a system of labour exchanges; to settle trade disputes; and to curb sweated labour. Of particular interest to him was preparatory work on a scheme of comprehensive, compulsory, contributary unemployment insurance. Churchill was responsible for the detail of this last measure, although Lloyd George, as Chancellor of the Exchequer, took the credit for it when he incorporated it into the National Insurance Act of 1911.[10]

Churchill's social thinking was defined by genuine compassion for society's less fortunate members. This facet perhaps derived from the misfortunes of his boyhood, the lack of care and concern for him displayed by his parents, their absence of interest and encouragement in his formal schooling, and their often bitter criticisms of him for failing to live up to their expectations. Left to fend for himself, it is not altogether surprising that he acquired a reputation for obstinacy, wilfulness, ill-discipline, ill-temper and social gaucherie; that he felt sold short in the knowledge and learning that were run-of-the-mill among his peers; and that, indeed, he believed he was inferior to them.[11] His friend, Wilfrid Scawen Blunt, quotes Churchill commenting to him on the condition and welfare of the poor in England as being 'worse off than the poor in any part of the East ... I would give my life to see them placed on a right footing in regard to their lives and means of living. That is what I am paid for and I really would give my life.'[12]

The legislative and administrative measures introduced while at the Board of Trade would be echoed later in Churchill's policies at the Home Office for prison treatment and related criminal justice practices. He would there become very conscious of the ills which would befall the King's Peace, a responsibility that lies heavy on the conscience and responsibility of every Home Secretary, if there were no, or an insufficient, uplift in the social condition of the country's ordinary working people.[13]

* * *

Mention has already been made of Wilfrid Scawen Blunt. He was but one of several contacts with the literary world pursued by Churchill at this time.[14] Churchill first met Blunt, a relative of the Leconfield Earls of Egremont and an old friend of his father, in 1903, and the two men developed a firm friendship of their own. Blunt's diary from this time chronicles their relationship. Blunt, a poet, diplomat and world traveller, like Churchill had undergone imprisonment. His custody, ordinary imprisonment with hard labour, had occurred in Ireland in early 1888 and lasted two months. The first part was served in Galway Gaol, a locally administered establishment where treatment was not unduly oppressive, but for the second period he was in Kilmainham Gaol, outside Dublin, which was administered by the central government. Here, his treatment was harsh. His offence was having publicly delivered a political speech in a prohibited district.

Blunt's diary entry for 5 September 1909 describes a leisurely afternoon meeting when he and Churchill discussed 'nearly all the great questions of the day'. In the course of doing so, Blunt mentioned to Churchill his experience of imprisonment, which provoked Churchill to declare: 'I am dead against the present system and if I am ever at the Home Office I will make a clean sweep of it.'[15] Blunt adds that he promised to send Churchill a paper on the system if ever that time should come.

John Galsworthy was of an altogether different stamp to Blunt. By 1910, he was a well-established novelist and dramatist. His work included the play *The Silver Box*, which illustrates the different ways in which poor and wealthy offenders are treated. *Justice* similarly portrays the bleak way the law treats the criminal, while *The Skin Game* chronicles the clash between the new rich and the old landed gentry.

Galsworthy was interested in prison reform, animal rights, alleviation of suffering and, in the particular case of his own profession, the abolition or modification of theatrical censorship. Sympathy for the less well-off in life, lifting at least some of the weight off the underdog, stands out in his analyses of these themes, but it was tempered by his legal training, a jurisprudence graduate of New College, Oxford, and a barrister of Lincoln's Inn, which enabled him to present his views in the form of well-argued briefs. This was of great importance in his pursuit of prison reform, where he had to convince senior civil servants and ministers of the validity of his arguments.

Galsworthy's influence on Churchill was profound, and had been at work long before Churchill was appointed Home Secretary. On 14 May 1909, for example, when looking into the relationship between capital and labour at the Board of Trade, Churchill wrote to Galsworthy, saying how much he 'admired and enjoyed' *Strife*, which depicts the clash of these opposing interests. 'It is a fine piece of work,' he said, 'which will long survive the silly chatter of the day.' In the same letter he informed Galsworthy that he had read 'with great sympathy' the latter's two articles of 1 and 8 May 1909 in *The Nation*, open letters to Herbert Gladstone, then Home Secretary, on the need to rid the prison system of solitary confinement in the initial stages of local and convict prison sentences. Churchill assured Galsworthy that he would 'talk to Mr Gladstone on the subject as soon as he returns to business'.[16] Thus began the close association between the two men in the field of prison reform.

Gladstone's Valedictory Advice[17]

When, on 19 February 1910, Churchill took up his appointment at the Home Office, his intention was to 'make a clean sweep' of the prison system of England and Wales. There is no evidence at this stage, however, that he had formulated precise measures for its replacement. The most that can be said is that he wished, after his own experience as a prisoner and under the influence of Blunt and Galsworthy, to humanize prisoners' treatment through such devices as lectures, concerts, access to a plentiful supply of varied reading material, and opportunities for meaningful employment, this last involving a reconsideration of the whole question of prisoners' separate confinement. The translation of all these ideas into detailed reality was to dominate his work at the Home Office in the criminal justice field.

On his arrival there, Churchill found Gladstone had provided him with a set of hand-over notes. They reflected a similar humanitarian outlook to Churchill's own, so he found them encouraging. They were also helpful in their indications, as far as practical administration was concerned, of what might be achieved by way of prison reform. With regard to prison business, Gladstone drew Churchill's attention to three issues. The first was that the Prison Commissioners were 'harassed' and he advised that they should be given 'some rest'. He did not go into any more detail, but probably had in mind their heavy workload implementing the provisions of the 1908 Prevention of Crime Act, which had established borstal detention for selected young offenders and preventive detention for recidivist professional criminals. They were also on the receiving end of voluminous parliamentary, public and press criticism of the prison treatment of members of the women's suffrage movement, who had been convicted of public order and related offences in pursuit of their political objectives.[18] One thing was certain, though, in spite of Gladstone's request that the Commissioners be given 'some rest': there would indeed be no rest for the weary in the Prison Commission while Churchill was Home Secretary.

The second issue concerned files on which Gladstone had minuted the need for changes in the prison system, which, in his opinion, could be effected 'very profitably without much trouble or difficulty'. Churchill was to discover these included lighter treatment for prisoners of conscience (e.g. the suffragettes); reduction, if not outright abolition, of separate confinement in the initial stage of convict and local imprisonment; and improved library facilities for all prisoners.

The final issue was the need to amend the 1898 Prison Act. This was essential because of the failure of the courts to use their power to classify into three divisions offenders whom they sentenced to local imprisonment. Gladstone had cautioned that legislative alteration of this matter was not something which could easily be undertaken. This was because it was bound up with the hard-labour element in sentencing, a contentious issue with political overtones. Nevertheless, the outgoing Home Secretary concluded, 'no doubt the department will direct attention to this in due course'.

Of all the matters Gladstone mentioned in his hand-over notes, however, sentencing policy and the different roles in this matter of the Home Secretary and his senior officials were destined to cause Churchill more concern than any of the others. Gladstone commented:

> The office [the Secretary of State's senior officials] presents, as a rule, the traditional view of treatment, which in most cases is quite right.[19] But they can't bring to bear the outside imported view of human nature and human society which necessarily belongs to the Home Secretary. It very often happens that examination of the sordid affairs of discreditable and useless people involves a great deal of time. But you will find that if you give this generously you will be repaid by being able to lift up not a few miserable creatures out of trouble and disgrace.

Churchill's Prison Reform Programme

There seems little reason to doubt that Gladstone's valedictory advice provided Churchill with the foundation of what was to be his prison reform programme. Principally, he formulated measures relating to milder treatment of convicted prisoners and a reduction in both the number of people sentenced to prison and the length of time they were to serve there.

Between February 1910, and July 1910 when he outlined his penal policy to the House of Commons, Churchill primarily concerned himself with humanizing prison treatment. Thereafter, until he exchanged the Home Office for the Admiralty in October 1911, he devoted most of his time to questions of sentencing.

Prisoners of conscience were treated less harshly and shorter terms of separate confinement were introduced for convict prisoners in the initial stages of their sentences. Both of these measures were at an advanced stage of consultation by his predecessor, and Churchill had to decide exactly how to proceed with them. However, his remaining measures for the amelioration of prison treatment were very much his own. These included lighter treatment for aged convicts, a special labour scheme for selected convicts, aid to discharged convicts, and lectures, concerts and improved library facilities for all prisoners.

His sentencing measures gave special consideration to young offenders sentenced to borstal detention and adult offenders sentenced to preventive detention. These were new sentences offered to the courts under the 1908 Prevention of Crime Act, pioneered by Gladstone, which came into operation on 1 August 1909. Churchill, therefore, was involved with them almost from their introduction and so was in a strong position to influence their practical application.

CHAPTER 2

The Home Office and the Prison Commission: Dramatis Personae

1910

Winston Churchill's thinking about prison treatment and sentences evolved and crystallized gradually in the course of his exchanges with senior Home Office staff and the Prison Commissioners. These exchanges reflect the deep concern which the staff of both institutions felt for the maintenance of traditional policies and precedents, and their reluctance to countenance change. Thus Home Secretaries who wished to initiate change found themselves confronted with a hard row to hoe. Herbert Gladstone, an older man than Churchill when he arrived at the Home Office and more experienced in the management of staff, had succeeded through persuasion.[1] This took time, five years in total, but he was a patient man. Churchill, on the other hand, was young, ambitious and keen to make a substantial name for himself rapidly. He feared he might not be in office long enough to achieve his ambition because of the political vagaries of the time.[2] He demanded instant action by his staff and had no compunction in adopting an autocratic stance when it suited his purposes. His senior officials and Prison Commissioners, accustomed to the gentlemanly management of Gladstone, found Churchill's style little to their liking. They had been accustomed to advising their minister but now found themselves being advised – and directed – by him. Thus their relationship with Churchill was occasionally uncertain or fractious. Indeed, this situation may well have contributed to the dissolution of the relationship towards the end of 1911, when Asquith moved Churchill from the Home Office to the Admiralty.[3] It is therefore appropriate at this stage to look into the responsibilities and organization of the Home Office and the Prison Commission during Churchill's Home Secretaryship, and to provide details of the major figures with whom he dealt throughout his tenure.

The Home Office[4]

Origins and responsibilities

The Home Office as Churchill found it in 1910 and as it remained until well into the twentieth century originated in 1782 when the Rockingham administration came into office on the fall of Lord North's government, following North's failure to reverse the secession of Britain's American colonies. Since 1689, Britain's domestic and foreign responsibilities had usually been transacted by two departments of state – the Northern and Southern – each headed by a secretary of state.[5] Foreign affairs were distributed between them on a geographical basis reflecting in origin the religious divisions associated with sixteenth-century diplomacy, but they both participated in the management of the nation's domestic business. In 1768 colonial issues were hived off to a third secretary of state, but he became unnecessary with the loss of the American colonies. The abolition of this post triggered a review of the distribution of business between the two traditional secretaries of state. As a result, the Southern Department became the Home Department, and the Northern Department was transformed into the Foreign Department. Shortly thereafter it became common practice to speak of their respective secretaries of state as 'Home Secretary' and 'Foreign Secretary' and of the departments themselves as 'offices'. The first Home Secretary was Lord Shelburne and the first Foreign Secretary Charles James Fox. Shelburne, as a peer, took precedence over Fox, as a commoner. This pre-eminence endured until very recent times, with the Home Secretary being considered the foremost of all secretaries of state. To reflect this, in this book he shall be *the* Secretary of State, while the others will be secretaries of state *for* whatever business their departments conducted.[6]

The Home Office as constituted in 1782 immediately inherited responsibilities associated with the Secretary of State's traditional function as Secretary to the King, relating to the sovereign's role as the executive arm of the constitution as it had been shaped from the early Middle Ages. Some of the more important functions included advising the King on the use of his prerogative powers, especially those relating to Mercy and the Sovereign's Peace, and conveying his instructions to the armed forces when the civil power asked for their help to maintain law and order in the community.[7] By Churchill's time as Home Secretary, however, these duties had been overlaid by a raft of miscellaneous ones enshrined in parliamentary statutes. These had started to accumulate after the French Revolutionary and Napoleonic Wars and did so in greater numbers from the middle of the nineteenth century. This addition of ever more responsibilities has continued to the present day. They originated in the growing industrialization of the country at a time when its population was fast rising, becoming increasingly mobile thanks to the spread of railways and improved road communications, locating itself in major towns and cities rather than villages and market towns, and giving birth to all manner of social problems. These highlighted the weaknesses of both traditional central and local government, and the demands of the population at large for greater participation in their own governance.

The outcome towards the end of the nineteenth century was well expressed in Sir William Harcourt's rumbustious account of his responsibilities as Home Secretary in Prime Minister Gladstone's second cabinet (1880–5). It was delivered in the course of an address at Glasgow on 26 October 1881, acknowledging the Freedom of the City conferred on him by the City Fathers.

> There is the criminal business of the whole country; all the magistrates, all the judges, for England and Scotland; all the judicial business. Then, Sir, there is naturalization. Then there is the class of business – which is, at times, more extensive than one could desire – called disturbances. Then there is a very particular class of business called burials. And there is vivisection, and the recorders and the magistrates, and the lunatics, and the asylums, and the habitual drunkards, and the factories, and the

mines, and the chimney sweepers, and hackney cabs, and the police, and explosives, and small birds, and tithes, and enclosures, and municipal corporations, and metropolitan buildings, and artisans' dwellings. And at the end of it is the business of the Channel Islands and the Isle of Man. And when you have spent a morning on light work of that kind there is about ten hours' sitting in the House of Commons, and after that it is supposed that I am desirous of engrossing a larger share of business than that which I have at present.[8]

The situation was just the same under Churchill. Indeed, if Sir Nicholas Faunt, a clerk in the office of Queen Elizabeth I's secretary, Sir Francis Walsingham, who wrote a treatise in 1592 on the Secretary's responsibilities, is to be believed, things had been no different in his day: 'cumber and variableness ... by reason of the variety and uncertainty of his employment'.[9]

Most of the legislation alluded to by Sir William, including the drafting of Bills, their passage through Parliament and their enforcement as legislation, became initially the responsibility of the Home Office, although whenever the business of any one of them attained sufficient significance to justify its status as a secretaryship of state in its own right or as a departmental ministry it was hived off accordingly, only to be replaced as often as not by some new item of business for which a location had to be found somewhere. The Home Office was, and is, the most convenient one to hand, 'the mother of departments', as it is sometimes known. Those subjects in Sir William's litany which have subsequently been hived off are easy enough to recognize. The recent transfer of functions to the Office of the Deputy Prime Minister and the creation of the Department of Constitutional Affairs are merely the latest examples of this tendency, i.e. at the time of writing.

Always at the centre of Home Office responsibilities, however, is criminal justice in its many manifestations: the great issues of liberty and authority, the rights and duties of the individual as against those of the general community, concepts beloved of political theorists and philosophers but deeply troubling to Home Secretaries and their staffs, who are accountable to Parliament for their application. They haunt the Home Office and convey its reputation, as a latter-day Home Secretary, Herbert Morrison, is said to have remarked, for 'corridors of dynamite'.[10] Unsurprisingly, then, politicians are often reluctant to step into the Home Secretary's shoes, for all the prestige attached to the appointment. Churchill, on the other hand, as we have seen, was delighted to be offered the post in 1910. However, as we shall presently discover, he was only too delighted to relinquish it at the end of 1911. 'The Home Secretary's Office', he wrote, as he reflected on it in 1939, 'is rightly considered a post of the highest dignity and honour, though it is certainly not one I would in any circumstances wish to occupy again.'[11]

Organization and staffing

The responsibilities of the Home Office in 1910 were distributed between four departments, or divisions, as they were coming to be called. These were the Industrial and Parliamentary; the Domestic; the Special; and the Criminal. The Industrial and Parliamentary Department concerned itself with legislation and its application with respect to factories, workshops, mines and quarries, and had its own statistics unit; additionally, it managed parliamentary returns and Bill business. The Domestic Department dealt with formal matters concerning warrants, appointments, licences, personnel matters and accounts. It also managed the all-important Home Office registry, the memory-bank of the institution through which every document received and dispatched could be traced, and where precedents and decisions were noted and classified. The Special Department was very small, established as recently as 1904 to deal with legislation relating to the employment of children, matters arising from the 1904 Licensing Act, and proposed legislation concerning aliens. It seems to have been created as a temporary measure, but ultimately it became more permanent, and was extended and renamed in a major Home Office departmental reorganization in 1912–13. The Criminal Department concentrated on its traditional roles connected with police and prison administration, and with the formulation and application of general criminal justice legislation. It, too, had a statistics unit, which compiled the country's judicial statistics. This department is at the centre of issues discussed in this book.[12]

About the time of Churchill's appointment as Home Secretary, there was a consensus among senior staff that this departmental organization was under heavy stress on account of the increasing volume of business to which it was subjected. Between 1889 and 1906, for example, the annual number of incoming papers increased from 50,224 to 62,624. By 1909 the figure had reached 71,153.[13] Incoming papers, of course, generated outgoing ones. Furthermore, Gladstone, as Home Secretary, calculated that between 1906 and 1909 the Home Office had been engaged in the passage of 42 Bills, 3 royal commissions, 19 select committees, 21 departmental committees, and 3 special commissions, all of which generated additional work on top of the increasing volume of routine business. This demanded more staff, but none was forthcoming.[14] The situation was described by Gladstone as one of 'very severe' strain 'under continuing self-sacrificing effort'. To this, he added: 'With rather a guilty conscience I must record my opinion that it has been too great. There has been constant risk of breakdown. Unless there has been a marked decrease in the volume and intensity of the work, some relief must be sought.'[15]

Thus it fell to Churchill to take action. A joint Home Office and Treasury committee was set up to look into the matter. It agreed that a new department might soon have to be established, but that immediately a modest increase of junior staff might suffice. Within two years, however, the nettle had to be more tightly grasped and a major departmental reorganization took place which resulted in the establishment of six departments in place of the existing four. Churchill, by then, was no longer at the Home Office, but he could claim to have set the reorganization in motion. It endured until the Second World War.[16]

With regard to the staffing of the four departments described above, each was headed in much the same way. The official in charge was a principal clerk (later known as an assistant secretary). He was supported by a senior clerk (later described as a principal)[17] and by one or more junior clerks (later classified as assistant principals). One senior clerk, S. W. Harris, served Churchill as a private secretary in support of his principal private secretary, Eddie Marsh, who had served him in this capacity in each of his previous ministerial posts and was destined to continue so serving him well into the future. The Parliamentary Under-Secretary of State, F. J. C. Masterman, and the Permanent Under-Secretary of State, Sir Edward Troup, each had the services of a junior clerk as private secretary. All twenty of these clerks belonged to the civil service upper or first division (later known as the administrative class). They were recruited through the civil service open competitive examination system and were almost entirely university graduates, usually well versed in the classics. The bulk of the routine work in these departments was undertaken by civil servants of the lower or second division (later known as the executive class). They, too, were recruited through a civil service open competitive examination from, on the whole, a background of Board, Grammar and Public School education.[18]

The business of these departments was coordinated by Sir Edward Troup, supported by the Legal Under-Secretary of State, Sir Henry Cunynghame, and two assistant undersecretaries of state, William Byrne and Ernley Blackwell. These four senior officials were set apart from their fellow twenty clerks because they constituted Churchill's immediate advisory team. Bracketed with them on prison and sentencing issues were the Prison Commissioners, more especially their chairman, Sir Evelyn Ruggles-Brise. Troup, Cunynghame and Byrne were university graduates and barristers, though Troup and Byrne had never practised. Blackwell, on the other hand, was not a graduate, but he and Cunynghame had practised as barristers before becoming civil servants. They were both recruited by the Civil Service Commission directly into the Home Office in the rank of assistant-under-secretary of state without being obliged to sit for the Commission's upper-division entrance examination.[19] The Commission was empowered to proceed in this way because of the nature of the legal requirements in respect of which the Home Office needed their specialist experience and expertise. Troup and Byrne had entered the Home Office after successfully negotiating the Commission's first-division entrance examination and had risen gradually through the Home Office hierarchy. As we shall see, Byrne and Cunynghame played little part in Churchill's reformation of prisons and sentencing practice. Conversely, Troup, Blackwell and Brise were integral to them.

Churchill, as Home Secretary, and Masterman, as Parliamentary Under-Secretary of State, constituted the political leaders of the Home Office and were accountable to Parliament for the effective and efficient management of its responsibilities. Masterman tended to concentrate on the industrial aspects,[20] but when Churchill considered it appropriate to do so he copied to him his criminal justice minutes and memoranda addressed to Troup, Blackwell and Brise, mainly, one supposes, to keep Masterman in the picture. There are few comments on them from Masterman, but in all probability conversations about Home Office business in general occurred between him and Churchill (otherwise he would not have been able to speak for Churchill in the House of Commons). Troup, Blackwell and Brise therefore constituted the principal Home Office senior personnel who worked with Churchill on his plans for reforming prison treatment and sentencing.

The Prison Commission

At this stage it is appropriate to introduce the Prison Commission and the operational prison scene in order to understand the stance of its chairman, Brise, in his discussions with Churchill and other senior Home Office officials about prison treatment and sentencing. Brise's views were largely conditioned by the day-to-day, face-to-face contact that governors and their staffs had with prisoners: the maintenance of order in the prisons; and how to balance the claims of character reformation and deterrent measures in custody to suppress and preferably reduce the volume of crime in the community. Caution, in his view, was required lest reformation should outrun deterrence.

Origins of the Prison Commission

Prior to 1898 there were two separately administered prison systems in England and Wales: the 'convict system' and the 'local prison system'. The former provided custody for prisoners serving sentences in excess of two years, under a regime known as penal servitude. The latter did the same for prisoners whose sentences were for less than two years. This was called ordinary imprisonment. Local prisons were so styled because before 1878 they were owned and controlled by local authorities, such as counties and boroughs. In addition to offering short-term imprisonment facilities for sentenced offenders, they detained people charged with offences who were awaiting trial or sentence, members of the armed services sentenced to ordinary imprisonment following trial by court martial, and persons imprisoned as debtors, or on civil process, or in default of sureties. In 1878, however, the central government took them statutorily into its ownership and control, and for this purpose appointed a board, known as the Prison Commission, to manage them in accordance with a detailed administrative code and, in relation to the prisoners, a detailed code of treatment, both of which were embodied in the statute itself.[21]

The precedent for this board was a similar one which had been statutorily established in 1850 to take over the powers, duties and codes of administration and prisoner treatment invested at the time in the management committees of the then three central government convict prisons and in the Home Office Superintendent of Convicts.[22] This earlier board was known as the Directorate of Convict Prisons.

Each board was constituted as a sub-department of the Home Office, had its own funds voted to it by Parliament that were discrete from the Home Office Vote, and in all day-to-day administration was virtually self-regulating. The legislation establishing each of these boards laid down the number of Commissioners and Directors, provided for the appointment of their respective chairmen, and regulated through the Home Office and Treasury the appointment of Commission and Directorate staff, and the appointment, grades, salaries and conditions of service of institution staff. Each board had the status in law of a body corporate with a common seal. The Commissioners and Directors were also required to report to Parliament annually on their stewardship of the prisons of England and Wales.

The two boards remained distinct, albeit under the same chairman, until 1898, when, following a recommendation by the 1895 Prison Department Committee, they were legislatively united into a single organisation whose members henceforward performed duties interchangeably in both local and convict prisons.[23] Shortly beforehand, their separate parliamentary funding had been administratively conjoined into one Vote. Thereafter it became customary to refer to the united Boards as the 'Prison Commission' and to its members as 'Prison Commissioners'. The 1898 Act, however, did not abolish the Directorate of Convict Prisons as a legal entity. For statutory reasons, the Directors were obliged to continue signing themselves as such when communicating on convict prisons and as Commissioners when doing likewise on local prisons. It was only in 1948, when the Criminal Justice Act of that year abolished convict imprisonment and the penal servitude sentence which underlay it, that the Directors of Convict Prisons were finally officially phased out.[24]

Headquarters organization[25]

At the time of Churchill's appointment as Home Secretary, the Chairman of the Commission was Sir Evelyn Ruggles-Brise, who had occupied the post since 1895, when he was selected for it by the then Home Secretary, Herbert Asquith. Brise was assisted by three Commissioners (Maurice Waller, Frederick Dryhurst and Captain Cecil Eardley-Wilmot), and by seven inspectors who were accountable to the Commissioners for the performance of their duties. In this way they differed from their predecessors, who, prior to the 1878 prison reorganization, operated as an independent team which made recommendations and offered advice to the Home Secretary on the management of the local prisons. The post-1878 inspectors were more in the nature of auditors of Commission policy and practice. Three of them were drawn from the ranks of serving governors and the remaining four were specialist inspectors: one was a medical inspector; one a lady inspector qualified additionally as a medical practitioner, one the chaplain inspector; and one the Commission's secretary (Basil Thomson).[26] The medical inspector was drawn from the ranks of serving prison medical officers and the chaplain inspector from the ranks of serving prison chaplains. The Commission also had the services of a medical advisor, Sir Horatio Donkin,[27] one of the country's leading physicians and an authority on mental illness. Other key officers were the building surveyor, the controller of accounts and stores and the keeper of the Convict Register. One or two clerks of works and thirty or thirty-one general clerks completed the Commission's headquarters staff of just under fifty members.

At first sight, the membership of the Board at Commissioner level seems unbalanced. Thus, only one Commissioner, Captain Eardley-Wilmot, recruited in 1890 from the British Army as deputy governor of Wandsworth Prison, had experience of governing and inspecting prisons. After experience as governor at Lincoln, Canterbury, Borstal and Parkhurst prisons, he was appointed a prison inspector in 1904, and became a Commissioner five years later. In the course of his career to that time he had served as secretary to the 1896 departmental committee to enquire into the education and moral instruction of prisoners in local and convict prisons. He had also been a member of the 1906 departmental committee on vagrancy, for which his experience of local prisons, which were awash at the time with prisoners committed for vagrancy and sleeping rough, well prepared him. He was the Board's key adviser on prison technical and operational matters, but was not alone as far as these issues were concerned. He and his fellow Board members were supported by a continuous flow of up-to-date information and advice from their inspectors, and not least from their secretary, whose experience bridged both the prison technology of Captain Eardley-Wilmot and the administrative skills of the remaining Commissioners. The latter were drawn from the most senior grades of the civil service and their specific role was to analyse the policy options available to the Home Secretary for the management and development of the prison system in England and Wales and to advise him accordingly.

Brise, Waller and Dryhurst over the years had served alongside one another as administrative-grade clerks in the Criminal Department of the Home Office, as well as alongside the Home Secretary's most senior officials. All three had served as private secretaries to Home Secretaries, and, in the cases of Brise and Waller, had been promoted directly to Prison Commissionships from private-secretary status. Dryhurst, whose civil service career had begun at the Post Office in 1882, had undergone a long spell as private secretary to the blind Henry Fawcett, Postmaster-General in Prime Minister Gladstone's second administration, before joining the Home Office as a junior clerk in 1889. For a short period he again served as a private secretary, this time to the Home Secretary, Herbert Asquith.

Following his promotion to a principal clerkship in 1903, he entered the Prison Commission as a Commissioner. Unlike Brise and Waller, he was not a university graduate, but like them he had entered the civil service through the open competitive examination for administrative clerkships. All three, it is clear, were well versed in the traditions and methodology of the Home Office, its ministers and senior officials, their caution in the transaction of business, their conservative stance towards change, and their sensitivity to public and parliamentary opinion where law and order were concerned. The chapters which follow will illustrate how this experience affected their responses to Churchill's proposals for changes in prison treatment and sentencing.

The scale of the Commission's responsibilities[28]

The Commission oversaw in each of the years between 1909–10 and 1911–12, which spanned in part Churchill's Home Secretaryship, six convict and fifty-six local prisons. In addition, it oversaw two state inebriate reformatories (in Warwick and Aylesbury prisons) and in 1910–11 and 1911–12 the first three borstal training institutions (Borstal itself, Feltham and the correctional borstal in Canterbury Prison). To this number of custodial institutions was added in 1911–12, under the 1908 Act, the preventive detention prison at Camp Hill on the Isle of Wight. Thus, in 1911–12 the Commission was overseeing sixty-eight penal institutions of one kind or another, into which were received under sentence 175,749 detainees, translating into an average daily population of 19,797.[29]

The approved parliamentary estimate for 1911–12 indicated that these establishments had a staff complement of 3,433, comprising 3,008 men and 425 women. The cost to the Exchequer of their pay, allowances and uniforms was £375,950. To arrive at the true cost of the prison system of England and Wales at this time, however, it is necessary to add the cost of running the Commission's headquarters, the upkeep of the prisons, building maintenance and extensions, and residual costs for convicts of an earlier time who had been transported overseas. Allowing for offsetting appropriations-in-aid, the parliamentary approved estimates for the Prison Commission in

1911–12 totalled £780,900. For this sum, the Chairman of the Commission under the Prison Act of 1877 was the accounting officer.

Institutional management[30]

The primary task of any prison is to contain the prisoners committed to its keeping. The staffing model for this purpose, embracing a culture of command and obligatory obedience, which evolved in the course of the nineteenth century, continues to this day, not only in the United Kingdom but in many countries around the world. It was derived from the armed forces, which accounts for its hierarchical structure. Prior to the findings of the 1895 Prison Department Committee, the structure was one of command and little else. The governor was in charge of the prison and directed its operations through a team of warders headed by a chief warder, under whom there were principal warders, warders and assistant warders.[31] Supporting the governor were a medical officer and a chaplain, one treating the prisoners' bodies and the other their souls. In the largest prisons the governor usually had the assistance of a deputy, and the medical officer and chaplain the help of supporting staff. Every local prison had a statutory visiting committee and convict prison a statutory board of visitors to adjudicate on serious cases of prison indiscipline, to hear prisoners' complaints, and, generally, to bring to the notice of the Home Secretary any matters of prison administration the committee or board considered worthy of his attention. The governor, medical officer and chaplain constituted the senior staff of the prison, their remuneration being graded according to the size of their prisons. In terms of direction, however, instructions came from the governor and were implemented through the warder grades. This was impressed on the prisoners by the uniform and badges of rank worn by the warders, by the arms they carried in the convict prisons (bayonets by the warders and cutlasses by the principal officers) and by a saluting system.[32] Orders and information from above were expected to be acted on immediately. The warders were responsible for the physical control of the prisoners. There was no question about what to do in cases of riots and indiscipline of any kind: the necessary procedures were put into effect at once and orders were obeyed to the letter.[33]

If life was hard for the prisoners, it is only fair to add that it was almost as hard for the warders. They were under a strict code of discipline and could be fined or dismissed for any breach they committed, however minor that indiscretion might be. They had no trade union to represent their interests and when they began to agitate for one shortly before the First World War the Home Office and Home Secretaries, including Churchill, strenuously resisted their attempts.[34]

Prison treatment: the onset of change

The military model for operating a prison lends itself well to the physical control of prisoners, if that is the exclusive object of the prison. Between the publication of the 1895 Prison Department Report and the outbreak of the First World War, however, exclusiveness of this kind in the role of the warders began to give way under the impact of additional duties being laid upon them. These required them to reduce the distance they had been accustomed to observe between themselves and the prisoners, in the interest of control, by obliging them to play a part in the reformatory treatment for prisoners recommended in the report. This was especially the case in the newly founded borstals, whence it spread to the newly founded preventive detention prison at Camp Hill. Its further spread was delayed by the intervention of the First World War but resumed thereafter, gradually finding its way into the adult prison establishments. Interchange of staff between borstals and prisons, particularly at the governor level, eventually became, as it has since remained, established practice in the Prison Service. It reflects a strong belief in imprisonment at its best as a training experience for those subjected to it. For staff set in authority over them, service in both young and adult offender establishments provides a variety of experience which is an important consideration in the development of their careers.

The warders (or prison officers, as they have officially been called since the 1920s) thus found themselves having to fulfil a difficult role. On the one hand they had to maintain distance between themselves and the prisoners in the interests of control. On the other they were obliged to come closer to them as individuals in the interests of their reformatory treatment. In attempting to fulfil this dual role they felt they were increasingly at risk between 1895 and the First World War. The Commissioners at the time were sensitive to this, and evidence of their sensitivity will reveal itself in their discussions with Churchill and his Home Office senior officials about the amelioration of the prisoners' treatment. However, the Commissioners were gradually coming round to the view that, while at all cost control over prisoners must be maintained, force was not the only means to this end. They therefore decided to develop more extensively the embryonic system of privileges for prisoners as rewards for good behaviour inherited from previous years. The more good behaviour guaranteed control, the less would be the need for force.[35] This has since become the calculus underlying discipline in the prison system of England and Wales to this day. Nevertheless, it has left prison staff of all grades, including governors, uneasily poised between their two roles: command (force) when something seriously goes wrong in the day-to-day life and work of the prison, and management (privileges) when all is sweetness and light. Hardly surprisingly, the same uneasy situation is experienced by prisoners. This is a gap which has never been wholly bridged.

Churchill was in at the beginning of this dilemma, which helps to explain the caution of the Commissioners in the face of his desire to make faster progress with ameliorating prisoners' regimes. Against his background of military training, Churchill must have known the risks just as well. It is therefore interesting that in the first phase of his Home Secretaryship he concentrated on issues concerning prisoners' regimes, while in the second phase his interest was focused on legislative measures to abate the use of imprisonment as a penal sanction. This suggests that in dealing with prisoners' regimes he sensed he had ameliorated them as far as he prudently could if he was to carry with him his senior Home Office officials, the Commissioners, prison staff and the public. Given the attitudes and circumstances of the time, it is likely that he considered any more radical action would be resisted for fear of undermining the control essential to the maintenance of law and order in the prisons. He then thought it best to proceed by concentrating on modifying the sentence structure on which imprisonment is based.

Policy-making: relationships within the dramatis personae

Churchill's stance

McCallum Scott, Churchill's friend, admirer and first biographer, writing in 1905, described him as being 'probably the most hated man in British politics', with the exception of Joseph Chamberlain.[36] Churchill had entered the House of Commons under the banner of the Conservative Party, but within five years he had crossed the floor to the Liberals. It was to this event that Scott was alluding, because it earned Churchill the immediate enmity of his former party. This antipathy proved to be far more enduring than either Scott or Churchill could have imagined, with the memory of it being kept alive by further changes in Churchill's party allegiances over the next forty years. Churchill was simply his own man: he did not fit conveniently into any of the established parties during his long life in politics. Only midway through the Second World War could it be said that he and the Conservative Party finally became anything like reconciled with each other.

Churchill's explanation of his 1904–5 'apostasy' was delivered to a meeting of working men and women on 6 June 1904 in north-west Manchester. 'When I worked in association with the Conservative Party I was what was called a Tory democrat. I belonged to the more Liberal and progressive section of the Tory party.' He added he was in this respect following in the footsteps of his father, Lord Randolph Churchill, who, in his endeavours to convert the Conservative Party 'into an active Liberalizing force', had fallen out with the Tory leadership over such issues as administrative reform, licensing reform, financial retrenchment and wider social questions, and had gone down in the struggle.[37] Churchill, in short, as an act of filial piety, was intent on raising his father's 'tattered flag'. What is more, he chose to do so by copying his father's tactics, gathering around himself a group of like-minded Members of Parliament who made it their business to act as a ginger group within the main parliamentary Conservative Party, in the process destabilizing the party leadership.[38] They championed points of view which were at variance from those of the leadership relating not only to social questions but to the controversial way in which the Conservative Government was bringing the Boer War to a close; its reluctance to concede self-government to the defeated Boer republics; its army reforms; and the danger it presented to the continued maintenance of free trade in the face of Chamberlain's championing of tariff reform.

Although the Conservative leadership had seen off Lord Randolph and his Tory democracy, there was some residual sympathy for him among the Conservative rank and file, partly because he did not desert the party. For his son, however, there was no affection, because he did just that. He had bitten the hand that had originally fed him, and that, for most Conservative politicians, was unforgivable. He was accused of being unprincipled, irresponsible, excitable, given to chopping and changing his views on the questions of the day, a careerist, inordinately ambitious for ministerial preferment, and so on. When, after only five years in Parliament, he was appointed a junior minister in Campbell-Bannerman's Liberal administration, President of the Board of Trade three years later in Asquith's first administration, and, two years after that, in Asquith's second government, Home Secretary, the Conservative Party inside and outside Parliament concluded that its reading of his character was fully justified. In its role as the opposition party it was determined to exploit every opportunity it could to undo both him and the ideas and policies for which he stood.

He was also exposed to risks outside politics. He could not help being born into the ducal Marlborough family, but that family was, and had long been, plagued with financial extravagance and other scandals. It was held in low repute even within the narrow boundaries of the aristocracy, to say nothing of its poor standing among the wider public. Prime Minister Gladstone's verdict on the family, uttered in 1882, said it all: 'There never was a Churchill from John of Marlborough down that had either morals or principle.'[39] It was a verdict which resonated until well into the twentieth century. Some of this distaste inevitably rubbed off on Churchill, who for his part only made matters worse for himself by the blistering nature of his language inside and outside Parliament to belabour the House of Lords for obstructing the will of the House of Commons. His behaviour branded him within the social class from which he originated as a traitor and a fomenter of class war.

Such issues were embarrassing for Churchill, but they do not seem to have troubled him unduly. He stuck to his guns and in parliamentary and more public debate gave as good as he got, and sometimes gave the impression that he enjoyed the contest.[40] One would have expected him to be hotly challenged, for example, on his prison treatment reforms, given their controversial nature, but this was not the case. On the other hand, he was challenged on his sentencing proposals, especially his penchant for using the Royal Prerogative to change sentences handed down by the courts. In this situation, however, it is important to bear in mind that throughout his Home Secretaryship he enjoyed on the whole the good will of his cabinet colleagues, although they were often sorely tried by the frequency and length of his contributions on subjects outside his own portfolio, and the impression he conveyed that he had solutions for every problem under discussion.[41] Above all, he had the backing of the Prime Minister; and, in David Lloyd George, the Chancellor of the Exchequer, possessed a powerful friend at court. Churchill and Lloyd George were the driving rods of social reform in the Cabinet, although they had different approaches to policy. Churchill favoured a top-down approach, one of betterment within the country's inherited social structure, while Lloyd George was more radical, altering the structure from the bottom upwards. Between these contrasting approaches, however, there was enough common ground for them to form a formidable partnership.

In so far as Churchill had real problems in formulating and bringing to fruition the changes he wished to make in the country's prison and sentencing arrangements, they were located in the Home Office itself and in the Prison Commission. This being so, it will be helpful to turn now to the relationships within those institutions.

Sir Evelyn Ruggles-Brise's stance[42]

Brise was born at Spains Hall in Finchingfield, Essex, in 1857. He was the second son of Sir Samuel Ruggles-Brise, an Essex landed proprietor with aristocratic connections who served as Member of Parliament for East Essex from 1868 to 1884. Following an education at Eton, where he was a contemporary of Herbert Gladstone and had a distinguished scholastic career, he entered Balliol College, Oxford. In 1877 he achieved second-class honours in Moderations and in 1880 graduated with first-class honours in Literae Humaniores. At Balliol he came under the influence of the idealist philosopher T. H. Green, whose *Lectures on the Principles of Political Obligation*, especially the one concerning 'The Right of the State to Punish', would in due course influence his attitude towards the treatment of prisoners.

In 1881 he entered the civil service after a successful performance in the open competitive examination for upper-division clerkships, in which he achieved sixth place in the pass list. After some delay, while he made up his mind about his posting, he accepted a junior clerkship in the Home Office, where in 1884 he was appointed assistant private secretary to the Home Secretary, Sir William Harcourt (Liberal), and a year later became his principal private secretary. Thereafter, he served the three succeeding Home Secretaries in this capacity: R. A. Cross (Conservative), Hugh Childers (Liberal) and Henry Matthews (Viscount Llandaff, Conservative), to whom he owed his promotion in 1892 to a Prison Commissionership occasioned by the retirement of Admiral Hornby, one of the founding Commissioners under the 1877 Prison Act. In 1895, during Lord Rosebery's short-lived Liberal administration, Herbert Asquith, then Home Secretary, appointed Brise, now aged thirty-seven, Chairman of the Prison Commission and Directorate of Convict Prisons (as well as British delegate to the 1895 Paris International Penitentiary Congress).

This promotion came about because of the retirement from these posts of Major-General Sir Edmund Du Cane, who had also served as Surveyor-General of Prisons and Inspector-General of Military Prisons since 1869. Sir Edmund's retirement coincided with the outcome of a Prison Department Inquiry Committee on the condition of the prison system in England and

Wales. Its Chairman was Herbert Gladstone, First Commissioner of Public Works and recently Asquith's parliamentary under-secretary of state at the Home Office. Asquith had appointed the committee in response to widespread public and parliamentary criticism of the prison system as it had been managed by Du Cane during his twenty-six years of responsibility. Among the committee's many recommendations were two which Churchill was to inherit, as mediated by Herbert Gladstone, his immediate predecessor as Home Secretary: less harsh and unfeeling treatment for prisoners; and new sentences for young offenders and persistent serious offenders.[43]

Brise's biographer records that when Asquith's intention to appoint him successor to Du Cane was communicated to him (in what Brise described as 'a most charming letter from Mr Asquith to whom I was personally unknown at the time') the news was so unexpected that it came 'as a thunderclap to myself and all my colleagues and even to the House of Commons itself'.[44] Brise intimated that Asquith may have been motivated by the evidence which he, Brise, had given to the Prison Department Inquiry. He declared:

> My own position was one of extreme difficulty. It was my strict duty to defend my Chief and my department and at the same time to intimate in a diplomatic way I was not in favour of the existing system. I sincerely hope that I discharged this difficult task without prejudice to the colleagues with whom I was working and without endorsing the clamour of the Press, which I had reason to believe was largely dictated by personal motives. I had, of course, no idea what effect my evidence might produce on the Tribunal before whom I sat.[45]

Brise managed to balance his criticisms of the system in his evidence by indicating where he agreed with it. At any rate, Asquith, in his 'charming letter', expressed his confidence in Brise as a man who would devote himself 'to carrying out the many changes and reforms which had been advocated in the Report of Mr Gladstone's committee'.[46] In the course of so doing, as the following chapters will indicate, his philosophy of prison treatment revealed itself. At this stage, however, it is important to be clear on one or two general points which conditioned his relationships with his fellow Commissioners and his colleagues in the Home Office and the prisons.

On a personal level, Brise was very different from his predecessor. He was, for example, far more consultative with his fellow Commissioners, his governors and the Home Office senior officials, and a great deal more diplomatic in his dealings with the various Home Secretaries to whom he was accountable.[47] Unlike his predecessor, he was not a military man, nor had he risen to the Chairmanship of the Commission after years of virtually exclusive experience in managing convicted offenders in custody. He brought to the task a vision founded largely on reflection about theories of human conduct imbibed from his study of the classics and of Europe's leading philosophers, such as Hobbes, Locke, Spinoza, Rousseau, Bentham, Mill, Darwin and Spencer, all of whose theories were mediated to him through his teachers at Oxford, most notably Green and Benjamin Jowett, Master of Balliol.[48] He was very much in touch with current ideas about penal practice and its rationale in the United Kingdom and abroad through his regular attendance as the British delegate to the quinquennial International Penitentiary Congress, where he was a much-admired participant.[49] He took a great interest in the newly emerging discipline of criminology, and was ready to support research into the causes and treatment of crime and to view criminals as individuals rather than as an amorphous mass. In some respects these interests did not endear him to his Home Office colleagues. They poured scorn, for example, on Brise's support for one of his prison deputy medical officers, Charles Goring, aided by Carl Pearson, a biometric eugenicist, whose researches suggested the existence among some offenders of inherited mental and physical characteristics. In Brise's opinion, these findings underlined the need for greater classification among prisoners and the development of a variety of treatments for dealing with them.[50]

This example is indeed a reminder that no matter how tactful he was in his dealings with his colleagues in the Home Office, regardless of the fact that he was on a par with them in terms of seniority, academic background and recruitment, he could not always secure acceptance of his proposals for developing the prison system. He was constrained by the historic traditions of the Home Office and by its cautionary attitude towards change of any kind, as well as by its sensitivity to press reaction and parliamentary questions about penal matters, which it went to great lengths to monitor and to speculate on what lay behind them.[51] Not that Brise himself wanted to make revolutionary changes in the prison system; but he did want to take it forward along the lines of the 1895 Prison Department Committee Report. Nevertheless, he wished to proceed cautiously, believing there were limits to change because of the need for the system to exemplify deterrence, without which there might well be a collapse of the hierarchical social order of the day, to say nothing of his own place in it by virtue of his family background. Of course, he had also to live with a fact of life: he was in charge of a system institutionally run by governors, chaplains, medical officers and warders, many of whom had been recruited, trained and gained experience in the policies and practices of his predecessor. These men's opinions could be changed only over a long period of time. He, too, his senior colleagues in the Commission and the Home Office, indeed the public at large, had all imbibed the penal philosophies of those years, and while room had now to be made for new approaches to the country's criminal justice problems, they found it difficult to free themselves from the traditions of former times. They were all living through a time of transition: a caution was their watchword as they approached the hazards which lay ahead.

Account has to be taken here of the fact that, between Asquith's departure from the Home Office in 1895 and the arrival there of Herbert Gladstone in 1905, the two Conservative administrations of Lord Salisbury (1895–1902) and A. J. Balfour (1902–5) showed little interest in penal matters, certainly after the passing of the 1898 Prison Act, which marked the legislative reaction of the Government of the day to the recommendations of the 1895 Prison Department Committee's recommendations.[52] It was fortunate, therefore, given Brise's interest in proceeding with their implementation, that in due course two Home Secretaries appeared on the scene to breathe new life into them. Gladstone, who had been Chairman of the Prison Department Committee and draughtsman of its report, was determined to ensure that the recommendations were more fully implemented. Churchill, who shared his predecessor's views, was equally determined not only to put his shoulder to the wheel but to introduce and implement novel reforms of his own, and greatly to accelerate the pace of their introduction.

Churchill and Brise, as the following chapters will show, had their differences, often sharply edged. Brise and the Commissioners, of course, knew full well that at the end of the day they would have to accommodate the minister's wishes, but they fought tenaciously to ensure that in the process of decision-making their viewpoints were taken fully into account. At the time, indeed they were able to thwart changes which Churchill wished to introduce into borstal sentencing and some aspects of adult sentencing, but there is little doubt that, had he remained longer at the Home Office, he would have fought to reclaim his lost ground.[53] Their favourite ploys were: to encourage the Home Secretary not to be in such a hurry; to provide him with long and detailed accounts of existing policies, pointing out wherever possible the near congruency between them and the changes which he wished to make, thereby undermining the case for change, or, at any rate, too much of it; stressing the hazards of encounters with the Treasury over money for more staff and additional accommodation; and deprecating the influence on policy of 'outsiders' like Wilfred Scawen Blunt and John Galsworthy, who, however well meaning, they represented as lacking the knowledge of prison and sentencing problems available to 'insiders' like themselves.[54]

Churchill, for his part, gave them a fair hearing, and where he thought that compromise could be helpful he adjusted his attitude accordingly. But he was not to be thwarted on what he had set his heart and mind to achieve, and he grew weary of the repeated use by his senior advisers of tactics of this kind. The officials, in their turn, grew weary of the never-ending flow of Churchill's ideas, as well as his requests for ever more information and unfeasible speed in the transaction of public business. Brise summed up his irritation in the following extract from a personal letter he wrote to his friend Gladstone, by this time Governor-General of South Africa, about his experience of working for a year under Churchill's Home Secretaryship:

> We are still groaning under the domination of WSC. I could tell you stories of him which would make your hair turn white! but I must be silent on paper from the traditional loyalty of a public servant to his Chief. I am only sure of one thing that he is not a great man, though an astute one and I do not think he has a future in English politics, but I may be wrong and often am.[55]

Churchill, despite his differences with Brise, nevertheless had a high regard for him, describing him in a speech to the House of Commons as 'one of the foremost reformers of this country, whose efforts in dealing with useful offenders have admittedly proved very valuable'.[56] Moreover, he sympathized with and understood the difficulties with which Brise had to contend when addressing his responsibilities, as indicated in the following extract from a letter he wrote to Galsworthy, who was critical of the prison system under Brise's management and who, like Churchill, wanted a more radical and accelerated approach to its reformation:

> But in Sir E. Ruggles-Brise we have a man who for ten to twelve years has stood forward at the head of the movement for Prison Reform. It is to his personal exertions and largely through his own contributions in money and subscriptions from his personal friends that the noble institution of the Borstal System has been erected, is being expanded, and must ultimately cover practically the whole ground. I well remember how, at a time when a current reaction seemed to be threatened, and when the 'No Pampering for Convicts' cry made itself heard, he cheerfully faced the prospect of abruptly terminating an official career full of achievement and high promise. I think he quite realizes the value to all the movement with which he has been associated of the external driving power which your thought and actions provide. At the same time the man who is laboriously dealing with intractable facts and small resources may be pardoned a temporary feeling of irritation when he is overtaken and surrounded on all sides by the airy and tenuous clouds of sentiment and opinion ... We must not expect much regeneration from a system largely devoid of sympathy; but it seems to me that effort, spontaneous, constant, increasing and increasingly rewarded is perhaps one of the most hopeful themes for reflection.[57]

One of the interesting features of these two tributes which Churchill paid to Brise is the emphasis he placed on Brise's reform of the arrangements for managing young offenders in custody. Adult offenders in local and convict prisons are not mentioned. As the following chapters will show, the full weight of Churchill's criticisms of the prison system and, by association, of the Home Office senior officials and the Prison Commissioners fell upon the arrangements for managing adult offenders. Churchill saw good possibilities for further development on the young offender site of the system because of the new foundations being laid in that area. A young offender system made possible the implementation of novel regime philosophies. The problem confronting Churchill, by way of contrast, lay in the adult offender system where the inherited foundations were inadequate to take the strain of new and radical regime developments. They did not inhibit regime change altogether, but they cramped and confined the possibilities. However, building a brand-new prison made possible in such an institution the opportunity to try out new regime ideas on a more extensive scale. It was for this reason that the eyes of adult imprisonment reformers were focused at the time on the new prison being built at Camp Hill on the Isle of Wight. In the event, although this lies outside the scope of this book, Camp Hill made possible experimentation, the results of which were to have significant influence on adult prison regimes in the inter-war years. Both Churchill and Brise would be justified in claiming a share of the credit for those later advances.[58]

Ernley Blackwell's career

As has been said, Ernley Blackwell was the only one of Churchill's senior Home Office officials who did not have a university education. Born in St Andrews, Scotland, in 1868, a son of James Hay Blackwell, Surgeon-Major of the Honourable East India Company, he attended Glenalmond College, one of Scotland's leading public schools, from 1880 to 1887.[59] In 1889 he was admitted to the Inner Temple where he was clearly a student of ability, winning a scholarship worth a hundred guineas for prowess in real property law. His call to the Bar followed in 1892 and in 1906 he was recruited into the Home Office as an assistant under-secretary of state.

Blackwell's post at the Home Office was a newly created one. It was part of the outcome of the inquiry into the mishandling of a criminal justice case involving a certain Adolph Beck who had been wrongly convicted and imprisoned. The Criminal Justice Department of the Home Office was not the only agency at fault, but it was criticized for its examination of prisoners' petitions, 'an ancient and non-legislative function of the office which derived from the Home Secretary's responsibility for seeing that justice was done and exercising the Crown's prerogative of mercy.'[60] The department in this instance failed to detect a miscarriage of justice arising from a mistaken case of identity; this, inter alia, led to Beck's wrongful imprisonment. Beck was pardoned and offered compensation of £2,000 (later increased to £5,000). His case was a severe setback to the reputation of the department. To avoid any repetition, it was felt that the department needed the service of a good practising barrister, a person of seniority to relieve the pressures on existing senior staff. One of his responsibilities would be to advise the Home Secretary on how to reply to prisoners' petitions, whether or not to recommend the King to grant mercy under his prerogative, there being no Court of Criminal Appeal in existence at the time. A post reflecting such a brief was eventually agreed upon with the Treasury and in due course it was offered to Blackwell.

Over time, he took on other responsibilities, particularly where legal drafting was required (evidence of this will shortly unfold in his role as chairman of Churchill's Imprisonment Abatement Committee). He was very exacting in his interpretation of the law and in his grasp of what the consequences would be of the introduction of new law for established legal practices and precedents. His thorough examination of cases involving the death penalty and his advice to Home Secretaries on whether to recommend Mercy, for example, are probably what he is remembered for most nowadays. Gladstone, in commending him to Churchill in 1910, declared that Blackwell had 'devoted himself to criminal work. His appointment greatly strengthened the work of the department ... you can implicitly rely on his accuracy and the soundness of his law.'[61] *The Times*' obituarist made much the same point: 'Under his guidance, the Department was in safe hands, for he was a man of shrewd judgment and great integrity, and of judicial temperament, capable of holding the scales fairly between undue severity and undue leniency in the revision of sentences.'[62]

There was, indeed, another outcome of the Beck case: the emergence in 1908 of the Court of Criminal Appeal.[63] It was empowered to correct convictions wrongfully reached in the technicalities of legal procedure at Assize and Quarter Sessions. The court's scope for action was therefore limited and had little impact on the number of prisoners' petitions, especially those which sought reductions in sentence lengths or raised questions involving the suitability of the sentence. All these matters continued to remain part of 'the ancient and non-legislative functions' derived from the Royal Prerogative of Mercy as exercised on the recommendations of the Home Secretary.[64]

Blackwell's appointment as Legal Assistant Under-Secretary of State took place in 1913 on the retirement of his predecessor, Sir Henry Cunynghame. He continued to serve in the post until his retirement in 1933. Honoured with a CB in 1911 and KCB in 1916, he died in 1941.[65]

Sir Charles Edward Troup's stance

Sir Edward Troup was Permanent Under-Secretary of State in the Home Office during Churchill's Home Secretaryship. He was the anchorman of the ministry, coordinating the full span of its responsibilities, and through his hands were routed all matters of significance emanating from and proceeding to the Home Secretary. His minutes to the minister, reviewing all the information and advice on the formulation and interpretation of policy and on questions requiring decision, were rounded off by his own recommendations. These constituted the final word of the Home Office as a government department on which the Home Secretary would base his decision. Troup ensured that business at all levels was properly conducted within the established legalities and administrative procedures. This placed him fairly and squarely within the traditions of the Home Office, but he realized that time and circumstances did not stand still and that changes had to be made from time to time. His concern here was to control the pace and extent of change, particularly in relation to the maintenance of law and order, the 'King's Peace', and with respect to the effectiveness and efficiency of all available measures to deter crime.

Troup had joined the Home Office in 1882 at a time when deterrence was equated with harsh and unfeeling treatment for prisoners and when sentences, even for very minor offences, were severe. The 1895 Prison Department Committee had advocated ameliorations and a range of useful educational and employment activities for prisoners to focus their minds on betterment in their lives and to help them on their return to the community. The Prison Commissioners, in light of the committee's recommendations, had started to initiate changes of this kind, but their advances had been few and cautious, for they too were motivated by the same conservatism as characterized the Home Office. Nor was there sufficient interest in these matters among the Conservative governments of the time to encourage the Home Office and the Prison Commission to provide a more stimulating version of prison reform.

All that changed in 1905 when the Liberal Party came to power and installed two Home Secretaries, Herbert Gladstone and Winston Churchill, who were determined to advance prison reform. This, in its turn, required the Home Office officials and the Prison Commissioners to reconsider their attitudes, especially as both Home Secretaries presented them with proposals (previously it had been the other way round). This was a novel situation which the bureaucrats did not find easy to digest. It will presently be shown how Troup deployed his knowledge and skills, protective of his minister, devising ways of reconciling his ideas and requirements with customary Home Office ideology, including formulating a compromise between the Home Office and the Prison Commission. One of the most interesting features of these reconciliations was the way the Commissioners and the Home Secretary's senior officials developed useful solutions to difficult policy issues when Churchill, a sterner and more rough-hewn taskmaster than Gladstone, pressurized them to rethink their points of view.

Sir Edward Troup's career

When Troup retired as Permanent Under-Secretary of State at the Home Office in 1922 after forty years' continuous service, during which he had toiled in every rank from junior clerk upwards, Sir Ernley Blackwell said of him, 'what the Home Office is today Sir Edward has made it'.[66] This was no exaggeration. So deep had he laid its foundations that in 1961 Sir Austin Strutt, himself a senior Home Office official, claimed that Blackwell's statement still rang true.[67]

In view of Troup's role in the making of the Home Office during the late nineteenth and early twentieth centuries, it is strange that, apart from a brief mention of him in the 2004 *New Oxford Dictionary of National Biography*, no major study of him has appeared. He left behind no memoir of his own,[68] and little information seems to have survived about him even among those who knew him well and committed their few recollections of him to paper. For an insight into Troup the official we must rely on his minutes and correspondence as they have survived among the official papers of the Home Office at the Public Record Office. The following chapters will explore this resource in so far as it relates to prison treatment and sentencing managed in the Criminal Justice Department of the Home Office during Churchill's Home Secretaryship. The papers throw light on Troup's attitude to the business coming before him and hint at the personality of the man himself.

Troup was born in Huntley, Aberdeenshire, in 1857, the son of the town's 'independent' minister. Following his education at a parish school, he entered Aberdeen University where in 1876 he graduated in the degree of MA with first class honours in mental philosophy and second class in classical literature. In July 1880 he sat and passed the entrance examination for admission to the Upper Division Clerkship of the Home Civil Service and was offered and accepted a junior clerkship in the Home Office. He did not in fact take up the offer until the end of 1882. This was because he was a Domus Exhibitioner at Balliol College, Oxford, from 1880 to 1883, although, by the end of the Michaelmas Term, 1882, he had completed the studies which qualified him for the University's Ordinary BA degree. This was conferred on him in June 1883. By that time he had been in post at the Home Office from the end of 1882.[69]

On his arrival at the Home Office, he served first in the Criminal Department. Promoted to a senior clerkship in 1886, he took on additional responsibility for parliamentary business in 1887, and in 1888 he qualified as a barrister of the Middle Temple. In 1896 he became a principal clerk, a post which carried with it the headship of the newly created Parliamentary and Industrial Department. Seven years later he was promoted to an assistant under-secretaryship of state, which carried responsibility for police and criminal business. Promotion to the Permanent Under-Secretaryship of State, on the recommendation of the Home Secretary, Herbert Gladstone, followed in 1908, together with a knighthood. Troup was the first member of the Home Office staff recruited through the civil service open entrance examination system and brought up, as it were, in the Home

Office to achieve this promotion. 'It adds much to the value of the promotion,' he wrote to Gladstone, 'that it is from you I receive it ... Please accept the thanks which I feel much more strongly than I can express.'[70] In 1912 Aberdeen University conferred on him an honorary Doctorate of Laws, and in 1918 he was awarded the KCVO. He retired in 1922.

The foregoing recital of Troup's promotions does not really do justice to the breadth of his experience in the Home Office. His responsibilities included: the reconstruction of the criminal part of Judicial Statistics and his editorship for a time of its publication; updating of the Home Office Registry, 'the mainspring of the office', as Home Secretary Sir William Harcourt described it;[71] and overseeing Home Office parliamentary business – Home Office Bills, Private Members' Bills, keeping an eye on Bills of other government departments of consequence to the Home Office, Provisional Order Bills, bye-laws, debates, parliamentary questions and so on. He also served on a variety of committees, and chaired others, for example the 1893 committee on the identification of habitual criminals, and the 1920 committee dealing with cremations.[72] It would appear, too, that at some stage he served as a private secretary, although to whom is not clear. In short, he had all-round experience of all aspects of Home Office business by the time he was appointed Permanent Under-Secretary of State. It comes as no surprise, therefore, to find Gladstone on leaving the Home Office commending him to Churchill in generous terms. He described him as 'an admirable official. The closeness and accuracy of his work can always be relied upon and there is no greater authority in the country on all matters relating to criminal administration.'[73]

Other colleagues who knew him well shared these sentiments. Sir Harold Scott, for example, recalling his own arrival at the Home Office as a junior clerk in 1911, mentions that 'Troup's code of accuracy, finish and integrity permeated the whole Department [the Home Office]. We knew that nothing slip-shod would escape his eye: to get his approval was a rare honour.'[74] Sir Laurence Guillemard, who entered the Home Office as a junior clerk in 1886, somewhat earlier than Scott, remarks that Troup 'had already shown the ability and industry which marked him out as a future under-secretary of state'.[75] Sir Harold Butler, who in 1908 also entered the Home Office as a junior clerk, pays tribute to Troup's industry and to the pains he took to ensure that his junior clerks were properly trained to acquire a high standard of alertness and efficiency. To this end, Troup interviewed them frequently, no matter how busy he was.[76] *The Times*' obituarist, who commented on Troup's Home Office work generally and drew particular attention to his service during the First World War, provides a succinct summary of him as 'a civil servant of exceptional character and ability, to whom the public of his day owed much and of whom, largely through his own modesty, it knew little'.[77]

Unfortunately, while these accounts give us valuable information about the official, they tell us little about the man. Sir Harold Scott comes closest when he describes Sir Edward as 'a rather silent heavy Scot, with little sense of humour'.[78] Lucy Masterman, wife of C. F. G. Masterman, labels Troup 'deaf' and 'disillusioned', although she qualifies this by saying that he was also 'kindly'.[79] These portraits, however, are at variance from the impression one forms when reading his official minutes and memoranda. Furthermore, in a rare newspaper article he wrote following his retirement, he certainly does not come across as 'disillusioned', 'silent', or 'heavy'.

> There is no part of my time at the Home Office of which I had pleasanter recollections than the eighteen months when Mr. Churchill was my chief and Mr. Masterman his Parliamentary lieutenant ... Mr. Masterman sat in the room adjoining mine, and the door between them was often opened, and a talk with the most refreshing of colleagues about the last Suffragette attack on personal liberty or about the chief's latest exploit sent me back to my pile of official papers with the feeling of having been out of doors on a breezy morning.[80]

Lucy Masterman, drawing from her husband's diaries, also called Troup 'the wisest and sanest of Permanent Secretaries', and thought the Home Office officials generally were 'uncommonly better than those at the Local Government Board – keen, far more reasonable about Parliament, and altogether a higher type and a better standard'.[81] Additionally, in the article where she labelled Troup 'deaf', she recalls him saying that Churchill was 'the first great Home Secretary since Asquith [1892–5]. He brings ideas into the office.'[82] In other words Troup recognized the Home Secretary as a harbinger of change. His own role was to harmonize that change with the traditional outlook of the Home Office, and, in the process, as Permanent

Under-Secretary of State, to protect his Minister when parliamentary gales began to blow, as they had a habit of doing with Churchill. This demanded great sense and coolness on Troup's part, which was aptly demonstrated, for example, by his role in helping to defuse the Newport dock strike of 1910, and by his restraining influence, not always successful, however, as demonstrated by the Siege of Sydney Street. In the event, as this study will show, he played his hand with skill, although, according to Lucy Masterman, he qualified his 'first great Home Secretary since Asquith' verdict on Churchill with the remark that 'He drives me crazy sometimes.'[83] However, in his 1925 newspaper article he declares there were usually happy endings. 'Once a week or perhaps oftener Mr. Churchill came down to the office, bringing with him some adventurous and impossible project: but after half an hour's discussion something was evolved which was still adventurous but no longer impossible.'[84]

Home Office papers sometimes confirm this, but, as this study proceeds, they also reveal that the discussions could last a great deal longer than thirty minutes and that they were by no means always amicable.

CHAPTER 3

Treatment of the Gladstonian Legacy

'Greater elasticity in the local prison system'[1]

The 1898 Prison Act provided three types of treatment (known as divisions) for convicted offenders detained in local prisons in England and Wales. Its purpose was to give effect to the principle of classification, 'a commonplace of penology', as the Prison Commissioners termed it, a process acknowledging 'the nature of the offence and ... the antecedents of the offender'. If a court failed to order an offender to be placed in a particular division, or specified that the offence carried 'hard labour', the offender was automatically located in the third-division, where treatment was rigorous.

Prisoners in the second division were treated virtually identically, except that they were considered to be 'less criminal', so were deemed in need of protection from further contamination in the interests of their reformation. The courts made little use of second-division sentencing, but the Prison Commissioners were able to counteract this by using what was known as the 'star' system of prisoner classification. Thus, they were able administratively to separate the less criminal from the more so. Nevertheless they regarded this practice as being inferior to judicial classification.

The first division was restricted to prisoners of conscience, such as those who objected to compulsory education for children on religious grounds, or to compulsory vaccination. Prison treatment in this division was generous by usual custodial standards. Prisoners could have their own food delivered to them, work in their own trades and professions where this was environmentally possible and receive proper payment for their services. They were also allowed extra visitors, and could take part in normal conversations. The suffragettes campaigned strenuously to have the benefits of this division conferred on them, because they regarded their offences as conscience-based. The problem posed by their cases, however, concerned the means by which they exercised their consciences: causing public disorder and damaging property, thereby breaking the criminal law. In the view of the Commissioners, 'the elasticity for which the Prison Act of 1898 provided the means' had not been secured. Shortly before leaving office, Gladstone indicated to his senior officials how he wanted this matter to be resolved.[2] Doubtless they would have drawn Churchill's attention to it in due course, but in the event they were pre-empted by Wilfrid Scawen Blunt, who alerted Churchill to it immediately on his arrival at the Home Office.[3]

He did this by fulfilling his promise to send Churchill a paper on imprisonment if ever Churchill should find himself Home Secretary. Churchill arrived at the Home Office on 19 February 1910. Blunt wrote his memorandum on 24 February and sent it to Churchill under a covering letter the next day. Prompted by this document, Churchill addressed a minute on 28 February to Sir Edward Troup (Permanent Under-Secretary of State at the Home Office since 1908) indicating that he wished to prescribe 'a special code of regulations dealing with the treatment of political prisoners in His Majesty's Prisons'.[4] His minute made no mention of the suffragettes, but that he had them in mind may be inferred from his definition of a political prisoner (as he called such a one at this stage, as 'a person who has committed an offence, involving no moral turpitude, with a distinct political object'. He envisaged the prisoner's punishment taking the form of restraint on his or her liberty, without, however, the enforcement of conditions calculated to degrade or humiliate dignity or self-respect. He suggested that such prisoners might, on payment, have their food sent in from the outside, wear their own clothes, be excused compulsory work, and be freed from hair-cutting and 'any unnecessary interference with usual habits'. He considered, moreover, that political prisoners 'should be allowed access to all books which are found in a good public library, and without restriction to number, subject only to reasonable convenience'.

Such prisoners, however, were *not* to have their own way in all matters. They should not be allowed, for example, to receive 'daily or weekly newspapers, or contemporary publications dealing with political affairs'.

As far as their correspondence and visits from friends were concerned, he considered they should be regulated 'entirely by State policy', extended or contracted to any degree from day-to-day, 'as the Secretary of State may order'. His minute concluded by asking Troup how these practices might be effected, whether legislation would be required or whether administrative devices would suffice.

Churchill's minute was primarily concerned with 'political prisoners', and what he recommended for their treatment largely tallied with what Blunt had to say about the matter in his memorandum. Blunt, however, took the subject further, recommending a wholesale reconstruction of prison treatment generally. Some of his proposals, as we shall see, had a bearing on Churchill's later measures. Nevertheless, there was one practice on which Churchill disagreed fundamentally with Blunt: he was not prepared to abandon the forcible feeding of prisoners who went on hunger strike to obtain treatment from which they were barred by Prison Rules.[5] Churchill may have wanted to make 'a clean sweep' of the prison system, but, whereas Blunt started with a vision of 'across-the-board' reformation, Churchill preferred to tackle particular issues as he identified them in the course of his day-to-day departmental activities.

When replying to Churchill's minute,[6] Troup explained he had taken counsel with Sir Evelyn Ruggles-Brise (Chairman of the Prison Commissioners since 1895).[7] Brise had expressed the view that it was unwise to make distinctions in prison treatment dependent on offenders' political motives. Troup concurred, adding, 'if political motive is admitted in extenuation of a minor offence, it is difficult to resist the application of the same principle to graver offences, and even to political murders, which are the worst of all murders'. Moreover, in a reference suggesting he had in mind the 1898 Prison Act, he stated that the creation of another sentencing division to give effect to Churchill's wishes would be possible only with further parliamentary legislation. This, however, could be bypassed, as Brise had suggested, by using the power conferred on the Home Secretary under the Act to make rules for the governance of prisons. Churchill, therefore, would be able 'to grant ameliorations or privileges to a particular description of prisoners (i.e. to individuals coming within the description)'. Troup advised that no reference at all should be made to political motives in describing the prisoners for whom the ameliorations were intended. His suggestion was that the prisoners should be described only as '(in the Second Division) who are persons of good antecedents, and who have been convicted of offences which do not involve dishonesty, cruelty, or indecency, or serious violence'. Such words would, he thought, cover the prisoners Churchill had in mind. With regard to the ameliorations and privileges themselves, he considered they should be qualified to the effect that they should 'not be in excess of any privilege conferred on prisoners in the First-Division' and that '(if merely for parliamentary purposes)', they ought to be enumerated in the Rule as 'any amelioration of treatment in regard to food, the wearing of prison clothing, hair-cutting, cleaning of cells, employment, books, visits and letters (and otherwise) provided etc.'

He concluded by saying that, if Churchill was content with this advice, a draft Rule based upon it could be prepared for his consideration, which would then have to be laid before Parliament for thirty days before it could come into operation.

On 7 March, Churchill responded to Troup's suggestions.[8] He revealed that by now the Home Office files dealing with all of these issues had caught up with him, and disclosed that they were being dealt with by Gladstone up to the time of his departure from the Home Office. Gladstone had placed on record his view that in the second division there should be two groups of prisoners, with separate Rules for those not guilty of 'offences not involving dishonesty, cruelty, indecency or serious violence, and whose conduct in prison is satisfactory'. He had also recommended that the Prison Commissioners rather than the courts should be responsible for allocating prisoners to treatment under these Rules.[9] Churchill recorded in his minute that he agreed with Gladstone, although his opinion was 'formed under entirely different conditions', and thanked Troup and Brise for their efforts.

He accepted it was dangerous and undesirable to regulate prison treatment on the basis of the motive underlying the offence – 'the Courts alone must be the judge of that' – and was pleased with the suggested description of the group of prisoners eligible for ameliorations and privileges. Nevertheless, he laid down that their visits and correspondence should be 'absolutely at the discretion of the Prison Commissioners acting under instructions of the Secretary of State. Complete isolation from the outside world is an essential point in regard to any prisoner who commits an offence with a political object.'

He concluded with an instruction that a Rule should be drafted on the lines proposed by Troup, bidding him, however, to check with the legal authorities that what was being put in hand was in no way beyond his ministerial powers or likely to involve the Home Office in a dispute with the courts.

Churchill's Prison Rule 243A

In paragraph 43 of their Annual Report to Parliament for 1909–10, the Prison Commissioners reported the new Rule in the terms Churchill had announced to the House of Commons on 15 March 1910.[10] 'I feel,' he then said,

> as did my predecessor, that Prison Rules which are suitable to criminals who are guilty of dishonesty or cruelty, or other crimes implying moral turpitude should not be applied inflexibly to those whose general character is good and whose offences, however reprehensible, do not involve personal dishonour. I propose, therefore, to give power to the Prison Commissioners, under the direction of the Secretary of State, to mitigate in such cases the conditions of prison treatment which are generally regarded as of a degrading character, and, in order to effect this, I propose to lay upon the Table the following Rule, which will acquire statutory force in the ordinary manner:

> In the case of any offender of the second or third division whose previous character is good and who has been convicted of, or committed to prison for, an offence not involving dishonesty, cruelty, indecency, or serious violence, the Prison Commissioners may allow such amelioration of the conditions prescribed in the foregoing Rules as the Secretary of State may approve in respect of the wearing of prison clothing, bathing, hair-cutting, cleaning of cells, employment, exercise, books, and otherwise. Provided that no such amelioration shall be greater than that granted under the Rules for Offenders of the First Division.

It will be observed that between 7 March, when he authorized the drafting of the Rule, and his announcement of it in the Commons on 15 March,

Churchill extended its benefits to prisoners in the third division who fell within the category concerned, as well as to those in the second division. Presumably this was to cover persons sentenced by the courts to third-division treatment who, in the opinion of the Commissioners, were more suitable for the second division and whom they could reclassify by means of the 'star' system. Gladstone, in a letter to Churchill of 16 March, expressed his satisfaction that Churchill was acting on his proposals, but ventured to doubt whether the extension of the changes to the third division was necessary.[11]

Churchill subsequently issued further instructions to the effect that suffragettes and passive resisters alike should be treated under the Rule, and enlarged the specification of the ameliorations to be permitted.[12] The Commissioners mentioned them, albeit summarily, in paragraph 44 of their 1909–10 Annual Report. Expressed more fully, the prisoners concerned were to be allowed to wear their own clothes, to be searched by a special officer, to be exempted from hair-cutting and bathing requirements, to receive first-division food – to be specially provided if it was paid for – to do their own work, to exercise mornings and afternoons in association, to have a supply of books, to receive letters and visits once a fortnight, and to have their cells cleaned for them. The Commissioners disliked the idea of prisoners being allowed to have their own food, but Churchill's view prevailed that suffragettes should be denied the opportunity of an 'excuse for contumacy'.[13] Significantly, nothing was said in the Rule about forcible feeding. Churchill, indeed, went on record, declaring, 'There is to be no squeamishness as to forcible feeding in the case of persons who refuse either to eat food which they have supplied themselves or to take prison diet.'[14]

Blunt's reaction to Churchill's Rule was one of satisfaction. 'It is everything I could have wished, and I went to Eccleston Square [Churchill's home in London] to congratulate and found him alone. He is quite thorough about the reforms and said he would have liked to adopt the whole of my programme only public opinion was not ready for it yet.'[15] Blunt, however, had misread the Rule, for he went on to say that, in addition to having full power to mitigate prison treatment, the Home Secretary had the power 'to put all prisoners with a good character (and that will include political prisoners) in the first class of misdemeanants'. This latter reading was incorrect. The first-division continued to be reserved for first-class demeanants, prisoners not deemed to be criminal prisoners within the meaning of the 1865 Prison Act.[16] The suffragettes had been charged with or convicted of breaking the criminal law. Gladstone, Churchill, their Home Office senior officials and the Prison Commissioners, and Government as a whole adhered rigidly to the axiom that no one had any right to claim exemption from the criminal law on the basis of political motivation for the commission of illegal conduct.[17]

While it is true that suffragettes and passive resisters failed to achieve first-division status during their imprisonment, they nevertheless obtained a considerable number of ameliorations in the second division. These ameliorations left them not far short of first-division prisoners in terms of privileges. In this respect, Churchill was a realist. He recognized, as he informed Blunt, that public opinion imposed limitations on what might be possible. And yet he remained optimistic, as he commented to Galsworthy in a letter of 11 March 1910,[18] while he was formulating the Rule.

His new Rule earned him much credit and encouraged him to pursue his intentions. The *Spectator*, in its issue of 30 July 1910 (pp. 158–9), commenting on Churchill's speech to the House of Commons on 20 July 1910 when he outlined his penal policy, warmly supported his general approach, describing it as sound and reasonable. It also wished him 'all possible success in his attempts at prison reform'. *The Times*, in a leading article on 23 July 1910 (p. 11), was similarly complimentary: 'a scheme marked by a rare combination of good sense and imagination'.

Convict prisons: separate confinement[19]

Prior to the 1850s, the principal sentence available to English and Welsh courts when dealing with people convicted of offences meriting terms of imprisonment in excess of two years was transportation, in the main to the Australian colonies. When these territories refused to accept any more of the mother country's convicts, the Imperial Government had to devise a plan whereby it absorbed them into custody in England and Wales for the whole of their sentences. Thus was born the new sentence of penal servitude.[20]

Penal servitude, like transportation, was a three-staged sentence. In the first stage, the convict spent a period in solitary confinement; in the second, a period of associated labour in a public works prison; and in the third, a period in the free community under a police-supervised licence ('ticket-of-leave'), which lasted until the end of his sentence. The prisoner was liable to be recalled into custody during this final stage if he breached the terms of his licence.

When the sentence was first introduced, convicts were not classified according to their degrees of criminality. But by 1905 a system of classification had evolved which divided them into three classes. 'Stars' had never previously been convicted, or were not habitually criminal, or were not of 'corrupt habits' spent the first *three* months of their sentence in separate confinement. 'Recidivists' had been previously sentenced to penal servitude, had records which showed they had been guilty of grave or persistent crime, or had had their licence revoked or forfeited under a previous penal servitude sentence. They spent the first *nine* months of their sentence in separate confinement. Finally, 'intermediates' either had clean records but were considered unsuitable for the 'star' class, or had been previously convicted, but not of an offence serious enough to merit their inclusion in the 'recidivist' class. They spent their first *six* months in separate confinement.[21]

Progression through the second stage of the sentence was based on a system whereby convicts acquired privileges of a minor nature to encourage good work and behaviour, the whole process being based on accumulating prescribed totals of marks. These marks also controlled access to sentence remission of up to one-third for females and one-quarter for males.

This remained the standard for convict classifications until 27 November 1909, when Gladstone authorized the Prison Commissioners to standardize the length of separate confinement at three months for *all* convicts, irrespective of their classifications.[22] What is more, this was to be implemented in the local prisons where the convicts were committed, rather than, as before, in the few so-called collecting prisons. It was hoped that this would allow the authorities to give closer attention to individual prisoners' needs. Gladstone stressed the importance of special supervision – mental, moral, educational and industrial – for them; and second periods of exercise at the discretion of their respective medical officers, who would recommend for transfer to public works prisons convicts found to be suffering under the conditions of separate confinement. The appointed date for the inauguration of these new arrangements was 1 April 1910, to give the Prison Commissioners time to iron out any logistical problems.[23]

Gladstone's authorization of these changes brought to a close a campaign waged by John Galsworthy who, in a two-part open letter to the Home Secretary published in *The Nation* on 1 and 8 May 1909, urged 'the complete abandonment of this closed cell confinement save where it is rendered necessary by the conduct of the convict or [local] prisoner after his arrival in prison'.[24] Galsworthy cited support for his plea in paragraphs 76 to 80 and 52 and 53 of the Report of the 1895 Prison Department Committee.[25]

His letter occasioned a public and parliamentary furore. Gladstone could not ignore it, for he had been that committee's chairman, author of its report, and signatory to its recommendations. Moreover, other ministers had expressed an interest in Galsworthy's letter. Churchill, then President of the Board of Trade, told Galsworthy he had read his letter to *The Nation* 'with great interest and sympathy', and that he would talk to Gladstone about its message as soon as the latter, who was unwell at the time, returned to business.[26] In the event, the Prison Commissioners, heavily pressurized by Galsworthy, carried out the review that ultimately resulted in Gladstone's policy, as outlined above.[27]

If the senior officials at the Home Office believed that Gladstone's policy was an end to the matter, though, they were soon to be disabused of that notion. Churchill, on taking up his post at the Home Office, immediately started to question the practice.

Galsworthy was happy that the length of separate confinement had been reduced to three months for all male convicts, but he really wanted the practice to be abandoned altogether. Churchill's arrival at the Home Office suggested that this goal might yet be achieved. Fortified by his earlier correspondence with Churchill,[28] he lost no time in contacting him again. The date of his letter is not certain, but Churchill's reply is dated 24 February 1910, and it could not have been more encouraging. 'I greatly admire the keen and vigorous way in which you are driving forward a good cause,' he wrote. 'I am in entire sympathy with your general mood. I have not yet had time to examine the question, but I have given instructions for it to be brought before me with the least possible delay; I shall welcome an opportunity of discussing the subject with you.'[29] Indeed, on the same day Churchill wrote to Galsworthy, he also wrote to Brise. He asked Brise to supply, 'in compendious form', 'the main arguments against the total and immediate abolition of separate confinement as part of our ordinary Penal Code. I should be ready to discuss this matter with you early next week.'[30] The urgent tone of this memorandum may in part have reflected Churchill's reaction to Galsworthy's play, *Justice*, which had opened at the Duke of York Theatre in London on 21 February 1909. Both Brise and Churchill were present for this performance.[31]

Brise's reply was dated 25 February and passed to him by Troup on the following day. Its immediacy could be taken as an indication that Brise was seeking to limit the influence that the play, and the public's response to it, may have had on Churchill. In its condemnation of separate confinement, *Justice* may have persuaded the new Home Secretary to press for total abolition of the practice, something Brise was set against.

The play highlights the detrimental effects of separate confinement on the personality of an offender under separate confinement in the initial stage of a penal servitude sentence. He paces up and down in his cell, unable to see out of the window because it is out of his reach, beats madly against the door of his cell, and reacts convulsively to the slightest noise. *The Times* described the convict's predicament as 'a thing of real horror'.

Justice was received with widespread acclaim by the general public, the press and Galsworthy's fellow playwrights and authors, although the theatre critic of *Blackwell's* magazine took issue with some scenes that were 'too painful to be witnessed'. He urged Galsworthy to follow the lead of the classical Greek dramatists: 'he should employ a like reticence'.[32] Galsworthy himself said the play 'made a great sensation, especially in parliamentary and official circles'. Churchill, he claimed, viewed it sympathetically, Brise with a sinking sensation: 'his eyes were observed to start out of his head, according to an eye-witness.'[33]

Brise was riled by what he considered to be Galsworthy's inaccurate portrayal of separate confinement, 'propaganda', and believed it interfered with what the Commissioners were trying to do by way of prison reform. Their policy was one of '*festina lente*': dramatic gestures were taboo.[34] His reply of 25 February to Churchill[35] therefore methodically outlined seven reasons why the initial period of separate confinement should not be abolished. The first was that it was legally required in the 1905 Prison Rules. Second, it was advisable, allowing for such alleviations as 'chapel, exercise, interesting labour, books, and, if required, scholastic education', as a period of 'recueillement' for persons brought directly from what had probably been a criminal life. Third, it was generally preferred by first offenders, or non-criminals, who dreaded association at a public works prison, and disliked by the criminal or recidivist men, to whom association with 'old pals' at convict prisons was probably welcome. Fourth, Brise contended that, with the safeguards in use (medical care and observation), it was not damaging to mind or body for much longer periods than those now in force, and did not destroy 'moral fibre', as was alleged by Galsworthy.

Brise's fifth reason was the real heart of his case. Separate confinement accentuated the penal aspect of the sentence. The law did not admit that a sentence of penal servitude or ordinary imprisonment should be nothing more than 'deprivation of liberty'. Parliamentary Acts and Prison Rules sanctioned by Parliament prescribed the method of imprisonment. Experience had shown that a progressive stage system, with treatment varying from a lower to a higher stage, including a period of cellular confinement within the lower stage, had a reformatory and deterrent effect. It was therefore wise and reasonable, as well as being consistent with a humane prison system. To overturn these arrangements after a century of experience would be bold, but Brise *would* advocate it *if* he were convinced that the current system caused unnecessary suffering, was mentally or physically injurious, or affected in any way the moral fibre of a prisoner.

His sixth reason was that, from the point of view of discipline, the immediate association of men fresh from the outside with their fellows was ill-advised. Finally, he claimed that separate confinement for short periods increased the rigour of imprisonment. Subject to safeguards, however, this was not cruel or inhumane. The rigour of a penal system had to be relative to the character of the race. 'A flabby, soft, system', he contended, 'is good enough for a flabby soft people: what is good enough in a foreign system is not good enough here to restrain violence and strong impulses, either for liberty or lawlessness.' His implication was that the ameliorations of recent years had gone down the 'flabby, soft' road, and now it was time to stop.

As for initial separate confinement in local prisons, Brise opined that, while the law differentiated between ordinary imprisonment with hard labour and that without, there must logically be a corresponding difference of treatment. To the retention of this difference, he was strongly opposed. If it were removed, however, he would favour reducing the period of separate confinement in local prisons from twenty-eight days to fourteen.

As has been said, Brise's seven-point defence of separate confinement was handed to Churchill by Troup, who added some comments of his own.[36] He stated that, generally speaking, he agreed with Brise, and drew Churchill's attention to two of the seven points in particular. Separate confinement was an important penal element in a penal servitude sentence, the more so because the conditions of penal servitude had been so much ameliorated over the years that the sentence was in danger of becoming attractive if further ameliorations were implemented. Confinement and deprivation of luxuries must always be hard to bear for people who were accustomed to activity and to the enjoyments of life. On the other hand, for the great majority of convicts, their supply of food, clothing, shelter, warmth and light work was far better than they enjoyed outside. Some prisoners saw the improvement in their circumstances that these privileges conferred as being worth the loss of beer, tobacco, female company and personal liberty. It was already possible to come across men who deliberately *sought* penal servitude and others who were indifferent to it. If conditions improved, the number of people who liked, or at least did not fear, penal servitude would surely increase, and crime would therefore increase too.

Furthermore, emphasizing Brise's third reason, separate confinement operated most severely on old convicts who hated separation and wanted to return to their pals on the public works. The comparatively innocent offender preferred it to association. It was therefore an element in punishment which, to some extent, favoured the unfortunate and disadvantaged the hardened criminal. However, Troup conceded, if it involved cruelty, unnecessary and useless suffering, it should be abolished, regardless of the consequences.

Troup concluded by pointing out that the abolition of separate confinement would be expensive, as new workshops for associated work would have to be built and more staff employed. Moreover, and this was a shrewd comment, he considered it would be 'singularly unfortunate' if Gladstone's recent decision on the future of separate confinement were to be reversed before it had been given even a trial, and at the moment when Galsworthy had put on the stage a *caricature* of prison cells and separate confinement. 'Everyone would imagine that the Secretary of State had been influenced by Mr Galsworthy's play and that we admitted the truth of his representation of "solitary confinement", warned Troup.

Churchill replied to Troup in a lengthy memorandum on 7 March.[37] He stated he did not propose to come to any decision about reducing the length of convict initial separate confinement below the new limit due to come into operation on 1 April 1910, but he wished to give the matter 'a more generous consideration'. At the same time he shared a preliminary view with them, declaring he was 'impressed with the importance of making the first period of prison life a severe disciplinary course of interposing a hiatus between the world the convict has left and the public works gang which he is soon to join'. To aid his 'more generous consideration', he asked Brise and Troup to provide him with a formidable volume of information about convict crime: the scale of it in recent years; the numbers and types of offence and the different lengths of sentence involved; the number of ameliorating measures in prison treatment introduced over the last twenty years as bearing on the severity of punishment; and the prevalence of recidivism. He also asked them for an account of the 'ticket-of-leave' system, and in so doing afforded them a further glimpse of how his mind was grappling with the problem of recidivism. 'What voluntary and philanthropic associations are there', he asked, 'for sustaining ex-convicts at this juncture? The high percentage of men who come back again and again to penal servitude is the most tremendous and terrible fact which confronts the Prison Commission.'

In putting this question, Churchill left Brise and Troup to ponder a philosophical problem at the root of criminal behaviour:

> Only two explanations are possible: First, the existence of a special and very rare type of human being, not insane, but criminal by nature; or, secondly, that the present system degrades a man in his character, and in the eyes of his fellows, to an almost hopeless level. Neither theory is comforting. If the first be adopted, it is clear we are only punishing disease. If the second, that we are aggravating criminality.

It took time for Home Office senior officials and the Prison Commissioners to assemble all the information Churchill had requested. During this interval, however, consideration of separate confinement did not lie dormant. Both Galsworthy and Brise used the period to lobby Churchill further on their respective views. Their opinions certainly influenced Churchill when he received the information he had requested in dribs and drabs at the end of March and during April 1910. He took time to absorb both statistics and opinions, and finally made his decision about the future of separate confinement only on 27 May.

In a letter to Churchill of 8 March 1910, Galsworthy pleaded again for an end to separate confinement and the silence associated with it. He accepted the need for convicts to be held under a disciplined, even Spartan, regime, but insisted they should be allowed to live a more natural life within it.[38] In a further letter of 17 March, he contended that the original purpose of separate confinement – to prevent mingling and contamination among convicts – had long been weakened by the introduction of classification. Furthermore, the three months' separate confinement under the proposed Gladstone reform could hardly prevent contamination during three years' subsequent custody in associated labour.[39] He then advanced one or two ideas for improving convict regimes, citing some of the facilities already available in borstal institutions, and commented approvingly on possibilities he and Churchill seem to have discussed privately together a short time previously. These included assistance to convicts at the time of their release from custody, especially helping them into employment.[40] In passing, he expressed sorrow that the Home Office thought his presentation of separate confinement in *Justice* was unfair. He had striven to be 'scrupulously fair', drawing on what he had seen of the practice on visits to prisons during Gladstone's Home Secretaryship and he stood by his presentation.[41]

In his reply of 11 March, Churchill was sympathetic to Galsworthy's plea, but gently cautioned him on what was possible by way of further reform: 'The whole process of punishment is an ugly business at the best.' Nevertheless, he remained hopeful:

> Amid the cross-currents of the present situation, I am trying to use what lights I have to explore the whole subject of prison administration, and if I have the time I daresay I shall get to one or two conclusions of my own. We must not expect much regeneration from a system largely devoid of sympathy; but it seems to me that effort, spontaneous, constant, increasing, and increasingly rewarded, is perhaps one of the most hopeful themes for reflection.[42]

Soon after this exchange of letters between Churchill and Galsworthy, Brise made his concerns explicit. He was worried that the Gladstonian policy on the length of convict initial separate confinement and the logistics of implementing it might be destabilized. He therefore wrote once more to Churchill on 21 March with a view to championing the status quo.[43]

This letter was in part yet another attack on Galsworthy's *Justice*, which Brise believed was unfair because it generalized about separate confinement on the basis of a single case. Moreover, Brise contended that the horrors depicted in the play could not happen in a convict prison because 'in practice no Governor would allow a miserable specimen like Falder [the convict in the play] to stay for twenty-four hours in separate confinement.[44] Even if the Medical Officer disagreed, he would take him out on his own responsibility and report to the Commissioners.' He protested that he never doubted the sincerity and depth of Galsworthy's conviction about separate confinement, but went on to ask whether it was possible to present a prison scene on the stage in a way that would not mislead. Here he made a very sound point about prison administration. It is, he argued, 'a long continuous exercise of discretion, variation and differentiation on the part of governors, chaplains, medical officers etc. This cannot be shown on the stage. The essence of a good Prison System is that the authority on the spot shall be wise, humane, reasonable, and, with all this, a good disciplinarian.' He hoped and believed that prison officers possessed these qualities and were encouraged to exercise them. The system itself had to be consistent while at the same time being flexible. He argued that even 'the cleverest and most truth-loving playwright' would be hard pressed to render all of this accurately.[45]

Brise attached to his letter a draft circular memorandum to governors of all local prisons which after 1 April would have the custody of convicts for the initial three months' separate confinement. It prescribed the nature of the new regime for separately confined convicts, one in which there would be not only no impairment of mental and physical health, but, if possible, an improved 'morale' from the spiritual, educational and industrial influences which would be brought to bear on each individual case.

By 29 March, Churchill had clearly received at least some of the data he had requested from Brise and Troup, because on that day he minuted the file:

> please keep a copy of these interesting returns. The increase of certain crimes is a very disquieting picture. I have been accustomed to relying so much on the general tendencies of science and civilization, and the constant mitigation of at any rate the harshest conditions. These great powers must be subject to some countervailing influences very deep-seated in their character.[46]

Other elements of the requested information, however, did not reach him until later. They came in a memorandum from Brise dated 18 April and addressed to him through Troup.[47] Attached was an enclosure dated 15 April detailing the ameliorating reforms that had been introduced over the last twenty years, which also explained 'hard labour' in local prisons and alluded to the question of aid to convicts on their release from custody. It bears a comment from Churchill indicating he read it on 27 May, the very day that he issued his ruling on the future of initial separate convict confinement. A further comment enquires, 'Conversation. Could this not be extended?' This suggests he may have discussed the document personally with Brise, took a favourable view of it, and indicated he would like to see *further* amelioration put in hand.

What most disturbed Churchill in Brise's presentation, however, were the statistics of crime, especially those relating to recidivism. With reference to the number of convicts in custody on 31 December each year, for example, he commented there had been a 25 per cent increase between 1899 and 1908, compared with a 40 per cent decrease between 1889 and 1898. This tied in with his comment to Brise and Troup in his memorandum of 7 March 1910 concerning the high percentage of offenders who repeatedly returned to penal servitude.[48]

Brise attributed these figures to 'the sterner measures' taken under Acts concerning the prevention of crime from 1863 onwards, which tightened the control and supervision of convicts discharged from penal servitude, and to greater police efficiency in the identification of criminals partly via the fingerprint system. Troup also offered these explanations, and added another: the disappearance of the longer terms of penal servitude, which meant habitual offenders go in and out of custody more frequently, so adding to the total number of penal servitude terms in the records. He concluded, by way of reassurance, 'if allowance be made for these things I do not think there is any ground for holding that the number of habitual criminals (in the sense of convicts who have had one or more previous sentences of penal servitude) is increasing'.[49]

Brise quoted figures to show that of 2,312 convicts in Dartmoor, Portland and Parkhurst prisons, about 1,340 were convicted of house-breaking, larceny and other offences against property. About half of these had no previous sentences of penal servitude, but 370 had one such sentence, about 180 had 2, 120 had 3, 60 had 4, 6 had 5, and 3 had 6. These were the source of recidivism, but were they, as Churchill had also suggested, people who had been degraded by the prison system and were now so hopeless that the state was either punishing 'disease' or 'aggravating criminality'.[50]

Brise here stated he could not see how the prison system, which had been invented primarily for the punishment of crime and the protection of the community, could be expected to exist only for the purpose of a person's moral reformation: 'The reform of man is incidental to the prison system, but is not its primary or essential condition.'

By way of strengthening his arguments, Brise resorted to involving Churchill in the emerging discipline of criminology, citing the collapse of the Lombrosian doctrine of the criminal-born and the teachings of fellow criminologists such as Maudsley who quoted degeneracy as a cause of crime. He drew attention to a widespread belief of criminologists in the Western world at the time, notably Professor Tarde, that recidivism, growing rapidly and readily, was not a bad sign. On the contrary, it showed that 'la criminalité se localise en devant une carrière'.[51] In short, there was an irreducible minimum, a sort of hopeless residuum, in all civilized communities. To this, Brise added it was his belief that this group would be reduced with each generation, to which 'most desirable end' he believed the prison service was 'contributing its share, both by the efforts made to reclaim the young, and by the general encouragement given to every possible reforming influence among the older population'.

By way of conclusion, Brise referred to a recent conversation with Churchill in which the latter had indicated he was thinking of reducing the length of initial convict separate confinement to one month for first or 'star' offenders. If this were to be the case, Brise again asked that such offenders should be given the option to remain in separate confinement for up to three months or even longer for their own protection. Nevertheless, given Gladstone's draft regime, he thought that 'no one could maintain that injury to mind or body would be likely to ensue'.

Churchill's determination, 27 May 1910, and the new Rule[52]

Given Churchill's concern about the size of the prison population, the nature of the crimes committed, and especially the frequency with which so many offenders left prison only repeatedly to return there, he could not have found Brise's invocation of contemporary criminological theory too reassuring. He was already familiar with the concept of a social residuum.[53] It had influenced his thinking on the need for government intervention to ameliorate the life and work of the country's least favoured members. He was not inclined to settle for a residuum as a permanent feature of society, as has been seen in his policies when he was President of the Board of Trade, and he meant to continue in the same vein at the Home Office. Severe measures had clearly not paid off in terms of reduced offending. The vision of betterment portrayed in the 1895 Report was still a long way from realization. In Churchill's terms, more forward movement within its recommendations was required if it were to play its part more effectively in the programme of social improvement that was gradually unfolding in the policies of the Liberal Government, of which he was himself now a distinguished member. His determination of 27 May reflected all of these considerations:

> I should like it [i.e., separate confinement] to be reduced as from 1 July [1910] in all cases to one month, except in the case of recidivists, i.e. more than two previous sentences of Penal Servitude, when three months may if considered desirable be ordered.
>
> Provided that any prisoner (not being a recidivist) applies to remain in (or return to) separate confinement he may (subject to health, discipline, or convenience) be permitted to do so up to three or upon a second application up to six months in all.

Churchill's determination defined recidivists as prisoners with more than two sentences of penal servitude. This was contrary to the statutory definition: any convict '(a) who has previously been sentenced to penal servitude or whose record shows that he has been guilty of grave or persistent crime; or (b) whose licence, under a sentence of penal servitude, has been revoked or forfeited'.[54] Brise was therefore duty bound to report this matter to Churchill, and this he did in a memorandum of 9 June, addressed to Troup.[55] He pointed out that if Churchill's definition were substituted for the current statutory one the great majority of convicts hitherto classified as recidivists would be excluded. This in turn would make 'impossible' the accommodation situation in convict prisons. These prisons were already short of 700 cells in relation to annual commitments. It had been possible to meet the shortage thus far by keeping convicts in local prisons under the inherited periods of three, six and nine months' separate confinement. Gladstone's determination envisaged some 400 convicts being added to the population of the convict prisons, but such an increase could possibly be met by moving an identical number back to local prisons for the last twelve months of their penal servitude, although even this had to be managed by consent if discontent and possibly disorder were not to result. If Churchill's definition were used, some 200 convicts would be added. It 'would only be practicable to find room in convict prisons for this higher number by removing back to local prisons men with as much as two years and over to serve, which, in the case of men under sentences of three years (about 50 per cent of the whole) would mean they would spend only a few weeks in a convict prison, thus reducing only to a nullity in their cases the penal servitude system'.

Brise informed Troup that, in a discussion with Churchill, he had been asked to what extent it would be practicable for the Commissioners to carry out the Home Secretary's wishes. Accordingly, he now put forward their recommendations. They ideally wished to introduce a version of Gladstone's determination. They proposed a Rule, the draft of which was embodied in the memorandum, restricting separate confinement to one month for the 'stars', two months for the 'intermediates', and three months for the 'recidivists' as this term was defined in the 1905 statutory Rule. If this change could be made cautiously and gradually, permissive in its operation, and (in the words of Churchill's determination) subject to considerations of 'health, discipline, or convenience', then, they believed, they could see their way to meeting at least some of Churchill's wishes. They added that they were not in favour of shortening the period of separate confinement any further. They regarded the three periods of separate confinement as 'a necessary and essential preliminary of a sentence of penal servitude, and would regard any further limitation as a serious weakening of the necessary deterrence of the law'.

In forwarding Brise's memorandum to Churchill on 10 June, Troup minuted sourly: 'My personal view is that the whole change is retrograde, but I agree it is as well to keep up the distinction between the three classes – "Star", Intermediate", and "Recidivists".' He went on to discuss whether this should be done with or without a new parliamentary Rule.[56]

Churchill dissented from Brise's and Troup's submissions. On 14 June he minuted to Troup that he was content with the current statutory definition of the recidivist classification. 'Let them [the recidivists] have three months and the rest one,' he wrote. 'I did not contemplate the intermediate class having two months; nor do I approve it. Proceed by making a new Rule; but the change is to be made operative from the date of laying. A [parliamentary] Question should be arranged.'[57]

On 16 June Brise submitted a draft of the new Rule requested by Churchill and sent a memorandum concerning it to the Home Office, explaining it would be impracticable to give effect to the Rule from the date of laying because of logistical problems. Here he was alluding to moving convicts and local prisoners from one institution to another, and completing the building of workshops for their employment. He indicated that, as far as possible, the new Rule would be made retrospective and steps would be taken at once to remove those who had served periods of separate confinement longer than those now being laid down. All the same, the Commissioners would be grateful if they could be given time to carry out the administrative exercise involved.[58]

On 18 June Troup minuted to Churchill that the Commissioners should certainly be given the time they needed to manage their logistical problems. Churchill readily agreed, adding that the reduced periods of separate confinement should not apply generally until the new Rule had lain the required time on the table. Nevertheless, he stated he saw no reason why in any cases where it could be brought into operation before that time the prisoners concerned should not have the benefit of it.[59] Even so, he was not satisfied with Brise's new Rule and accordingly put forward one of his own, 'to be taken as a guide'.

> The period of separate confinement should not be prolonged for prisoners classed as 'Stars' and 'Intermediates' beyond one month, and for those classed as 'Recidivists' beyond three months, except subject to the approval of the Secretary of State in special cases of discipline and administrative necessity or except at the request of the Convict himself in which cases subject to considerations of health, discipline, and convenience when a further period not exceeding three months may be permitted. A period of separate confinement may be at once terminated or reduced in any case upon medical advice having regard either to the Convict's physical or mental condition.[60]

On 23 June Brise suggested one or two small drafting changes in Churchill's text and advised that arrangements would be made for bringing the new Rule into operation from 1 August 1910. At this point, Troup brought his own drafting skills to bear on both the text and Brise's emendations, and put it into its final form. Churchill approved it on the same day, commenting, 'It clearly reserves to the Secretary of State power to deal with exceptional cases. And all ordinary cases can be dealt with by the Commissioners in his name.'

This final form of the new Rule read as follows:

> The period of separate confinement which convicts will undergo at the beginning of their sentences shall not be prolonged for prisoners classed as 'Stars' and 'Intermediates' beyond one month, nor for 'Recidivists' beyond three months, except in special cases of disciplinary or administrative necessity.
> In such cases or where a Convict may himself prefer separate confinement to association on Public Works, a further period may subject to the approval of the Secretary of State, be permitted, not exceeding three months, provided always that any period of separate confinement may be at once terminated or reduced upon medical advice having regard to the Convict's physical or mental condition.
> The Rule numbered 8 (a) and (b) made by the Secretary of State on the 21st January, 1905, is hereby revoked.[61]

On 1 July Troup asked whether Churchill wanted to lay the Rule at once or after the speech he was due to deliver to the House of Commons on 20 July. 'It would be best, I should think,' he suggested, 'to explain it before it is published: and it makes no difference to the time the actual change takes place.' Churchill minuted: 'Yes, after the speech.' Troup accordingly gave instructions on 20 July for the Rule to be laid before both Houses of Parliament.[62]

In the course of his speech to the Commons on 20 July, Churchill announced the changes he had decided to make.[63] He paid tribute to Gladstone for the preparatory work he had undertaken, and acknowledged how the matter had been brought to the attention of the public 'by various able writers in the Press and exponents of the drama'. He had already privately thanked Galsworthy for his input,[64] and did so again in a letter of 30 July:

> There can be no question that your admirable play bore a most important part in creating that atmosphere of sympathy and interest which is so noticeable upon this subject at the present time. So far from feeling the slightest irritation at newspaper comments assigning to you the credit for prison reform, I have always felt uncomfortable at receiving the easily-won applauses which come to the heads of great departments whenever they have ploughed with borrowed oxen and reaped where they have not sown. In this case I can only claim a personal interest which has led me to seek the knowledge of others.[65]

Churchill was certainly being generous here, for, while Galsworthy had played a part, the Home Secretary's own had been much more significant. He had succeeded in changing established attitudes towards prison treatment in a few short months at the Home Office.[66]

CHAPTER 4

Humanizing Convict and Local Prison Regimes: Churchill's Initiatives

Aged Convicts

While investigating initial separate confinement for convicts, a number of ideas occurred to Churchill for further humanizing their regimes. One of these concerned the treatment of aged convicts. His attention had been drawn to this issue by a newspaper account of a sentence of eight years' penal servitude for house-breaking imposed on an offender by the name of White, alias Smith. Churchill sent the clipping to Troup, and asked him to provide a 'special report' on what exactly lay behind the case.[1]

The report recorded that White had been born in London in 1837, making him seventy-three years old when convicted. He had a string of previous convictions against his name, his first from 1859. His most recent sentence was his tenth, and his eighth of penal servitude, in a criminal career which included stealing, robbery with violence, and housebreaking. His most recent offence was failing to report to the police when under licensed release from penal servitude, and keeping a brothel.

Having learned all this from a Metropolitan Police report, on 22 March 1910 Troup commented: 'An absolutely worthless specimen of humanity ... When he has served three years, the remainder of his time might perhaps be converted to preventive detention – if he is physically fit for the work.'[2] The medical officer at Wormwood Scrubs, where White was detained, reported he was suffering from chronic bronchial catarrh, weakness of heart and the general effects of old age. His mental condition, on the other hand, was normal. The likelihood was that he would have to be detained in the prison hospital during the winter months.

Churchill, replying to Troup on 23 March, made no observations on White's criminal record, but concentrated instead on the humanitarian aspect of his prison treatment:

> The case may also be cited as the total failure of the most terrible sentence of imprisonment to effect the slightest reform upon the criminal. The sentence has been reduced from eight to six years since I saw it first. Even now it is severe. He is old, weak, and failing. It is quite useless keeping him under punishment. I should like him to go to preventive detention at once. How can this be done?

Troup's reply of 30 March insisted that the transfer could not take place because the new preventive detention prison on the Isle of Wight was not yet ready for occupation. In any case, White had not yet served the required preliminary three years' penal servitude. He continued:

> I think it cannot be too clearly put that there is a class of criminals who cannot be reformed or in any way influenced by any form of punishment. Some of them are definitely weak-minded like the weak-minded class at Parkhurst; others are intellectually normal, but are so constituted morally that neither kindness or severity has any permanent effect on them. You may alter prison treatment in any way you like – whether in the direction of leniency or severity – and it will have no more effect on their character than it would have on a congenital idiot or on a lunatic ...
> What is wanted is an entirely separate system for these hopeless cases. For those who are definitely 'weak-minded' such a system might easily be established: but the great difficulty in the cases of the morally imbecile is to distinguish and separate them. The only test I know of is that he again and again reverts to a form of crime which is certain to bring him back to prison speedily.

Churchill, unsurprisingly, then asked Troup on 1 April what he would suggest should be done with 'these old weak-minded probable life-sentences' (the Home Secretary was here bracketing White's case with a similar one which had since come to his attention). Troup thought it unlikely that either of the two men could earn his own living, 'even if he would'. This meant that the alternative to prison was the workhouse. For the convict, the workhouse had the advantage that he could go out whenever he liked and try his hand at some more house-breaking. On the other hand, prison was 'probably more comfortable with somewhat better medical attendance'. Troup could see no advantage in releasing the two men, but thought their cases might be noted for consideration after, say, two years. By then, their circumstances might have altered: for example, they might no longer be fit to commit even minor offences.

Churchill was far from satisfied with Troup's attitude. He wanted action, and to this end asked Troup on 3 April to produce some statistics. He wanted to know how many aged convicts there were with substantial periods of their sentences still to serve. 'It is clear', he declared, 'that the ordinary Prison Rules require some modification in the case of those whom there is no chance to reform, and no need to deter. It is the class and not the special cases which attract my attention.' A further request to Troup was made on 8 May for a statement from Brise to set out 'effective mitigation of the conditions under which these aged recidivists who will probably not survive their sentences are to be held. The punitive element should be largely excluded from their confinement. Cannot a special class be formed? It will not be very numerous.'[3]

Brise replied on 26 May. He enclosed a return of 'senile convicts' in Parkhurst Prison which showed how they were being treated.[4] The governor and medical officer provided additional information about each of them – age, length of sentence still to run, offence, character while in prison, ailments and whether they were hospitalized or fit for 'light work'. The governor added in general terms the nature of their regimes. Of course, this detailed the situation only at Parkhurst: 'senile convicts' were held in other prisons, too.

Brise's view was that it was undesirable to segregate these convicts from the rest of the inmates. This was because in many cases they showed 'proficiency and keenness at their work and would resent being taken off it'. On the other hand, if a convict were certified unfit for ordinary labour through age or infirmity, or if he had passed the age for ordinary convict prison treatment, 'it should be made the practice to congregate this class at Parkhurst with injunction that the ordinary prison regime should not apply'. He contended that this largely followed the practice at Parkhurst anyway, as the information supplied by the governor indicated. Even so, he thought there was still scope for 'special ameliorations', such as association in day rooms on wet days, special diet – rice puddings and softer food than the ordinary – and iron bedsteads in place of plank beds. He suggested, too, that they might be given the option of finishing their sentences at local prisons, where they would be near their relatives. There would be accommodation problems to be overcome before these arrangements could be implemented, but he would undertake to look into ways and means of overcoming them.[5]

Brise, for all his caution where ameliorated convict treatment was concerned, was here expressing a willingness to go along with Churchill's wishes. Troup, on the other hand, when forwarding Brise's proposals, expressed at best only grudging support:

> It is hardly the proper function of a prison to provide a home of rest for these aged sinners. We should be justified in turning them out and letting them go to the harder conditions which many workhouses provide: but they do less harm if kept in prison. And on the whole it seems best to retain them and even to increase their comforts.[6]

Churchill did not reply to Brise's proposals and Troup's comments until 19 June. He brusquely brushed aside Troup's mention of the workhouse as being irrelevant to the business under discussion. 'I am not concerned', he wrote, 'with any arguments relative to the treatment of aged paupers. They are not under my supervision. It is clearly our duty to suppress unnecessary and purposeless suffering.' As for Brise's proposals, he confessed they did not wholly meet his requirements, which he therefore now set out more fully.

Where it was clear from the age of the convict and the remaining length of his sentence that he was physically feeble, not dangerous and had little prospect of surviving the sentence, his confinement, subject to good conduct, should be free, as far as possible, from penal conditions. Warming to his theme, Churchill set out more precisely what he wanted Brise and Troup to do:

> I have decided, then, in principle to establish a special class with special relaxation and indulgencies. They will be our 'Old Guard'. I am inclined to think they can be much more conveniently handled, if they are brought together in one or, at the outside, two places in our convict prisons. Parkhurst is clearly indicated. Let me have a nominal roll of all convicts who will be over 72 years of age by the time they are discharged. This will give us the maximum numbers to be dealt with. Propose me then a plan in detail with relaxations for dealing with this class at one or two centres.[7]

On 8 August Brise submitted for Churchill's scrutiny the draft regulations for the 'aged convict' classification, together with a nominal roll of fifty-three convicts for inclusion in Churchill's 'Old Guard'. They were drawn from nine different prisons – Chelmsford, Dartmoor, Dorchester, Exeter, Gloucester, Lewes, Parkhurst (the majority), Stafford and Aylesbury. Brise envisaged concentrating them all in Parkhurst.[8] His regulations provided for members of the 'Old Guard' to live within the general convict community of their prison rather than in segregation from it. Their cells, however, would have better natural light by means of clear glass windows that could be opened widely, rather like the windows of cells reserved for tubercular convicts. Time would be needed to make the necessary alterations, but Brise indicated that every effort would be made to carry out the work as quickly as possible. Every cell would be equipped with a proper hospital bedstead in place of the usual plank bed, and a chair instead of the usual stool, with arms to it 'in such cases as it seems desirable'. There would be some latitude with regard to clothing; braces, shoes or light boots would be permissible. Food would be supplied to them in accordance with a specially compiled scale of dietary.

Each able-bodied convict would be expected to employ himself during the prison's usual working hours in some useful occupation, either in the workroom or out of doors, as arranged by the governor and medical officer. Ample opportunity for exercise would be provided, unrestrained by the usual period laid down in the Rules for convict prisons and, within reasonable limits, would be optional for the individual. 'Quiet conversation' would be allowed, regimented walking round the ring would not be strictly observed, and seats would be provided in the exercise yard. Finally, a day room would be made available, part being arranged for indoor employments and part provided with benches or chairs for those unable to work and for those who usually worked out of doors but had retreated inside because of inclement weather.[9]

On 17 August, having considered Brise's draft regulations, Churchill was pleased to minute on the file: 'Excellent. This entirely carries out my wishes. I am very much obliged to the Prison Commissioners for the care with which their humane regulations have been framed.'[10]

Parkhurst soon settled into being the normal location for aged convicts.

An incentive labour scheme for selected convicts

Another of Churchill's plans for improving the regimes of convict prisons concerned arrangements for employing the convicts more meaningfully. To this end, he laid before Brise on 28 March 1910 a novel proposition:

> Voluntary effort of a severe character ought to form an essential part of our prison system, and it should be rewarded by marks and consequent remissions wholly additional to the existing scale. Any convict serving a sentence of three years or more whose conduct has been exemplary for a certain substantial period, should be allowed to volunteer for 'strenuous labour'.[11]

He envisaged (in the early, experimental stage of the scheme, while evaluation was taking place) that some hundred convicts would voluntarily be involved. They would be mustered into a special class or classes on a convenient basis, would wear 'an entirely different dress, more like a uniform than the convict's garb', and would be employed exclusively on piece-work. The type of work would have to be carefully considered, with regard being paid to their different social backgrounds, ages and physiques, and their diets would have to be sufficient to maintain 'full healthy vigour', although no material comforts should be allowed. Through this, they could earn their freedom, 'to be regained much earlier by an unceasing and sustained effort of goodwill'. This effort would be recorded in the marks they earned 'while they remained in the class at the rate of an additional 25 per cent remission'. Nor was this all. Subject to whatever restraints were required to ensure their safe custody, they would be permitted to receive visits and letters much more freely than convicts under the normal regime of penal servitude.

The most interesting feature of this scheme, reflecting Churchill's experience as President of the Board of Trade, when he had introduced labour exchanges, was that assistance would be given 'to find situations for such men as might need them' after release. He envisaged their release being conditioned by parole rather than licence, supported by 'a special certificate of their character which it is my hope might gradually obtain a certain value'. Churchill was here expressing his concept of custody not just as an end in itself or some sort of ostracism, but as an integral element of social policy more widely conceived. He wrote, 'Since it is of the highest importance in social policy to secure the return to conditions of honourable citizenship of any criminal who is in earnest to do better, special arrangements should be made by means of a money grant both to employers and workmen in certain selected firms for the employment of paroled men.'[12]

Churchill concluded his memorandum by admitting his scheme involved 'difficulties and obstacles enough which do not require to be stated'. If it was impractical, it would 'fall to the ground in the mere process of construction'. He asked Brise to explore it further.

Brise set out his views on Churchill's scheme in a fifteen-page letter.[13] He explained the existing system of convict employment and the rewards attached to it, the operational difficulties he anticipated in the proposed scheme, and the manner in which he thought Churchill's objectives could be attained 'without a too great disturbance of the existing system or of the fundamental principle of *uniformity* of treatment'. He was broadly sympathetic to Churchill's point of view, but, as we shall see, with as little disruption to the status quo as possible (in keeping with the Prison Commission's *festina lente* attitude to change where prison treatment was concerned).

Under the existing 'marks' arrangements, Brise noted, convicts who completed an ordinary day's work were awarded six or seven marks, while those who completed a strenuous day's labour were awarded eight, thus exemplifying, 'in theory', Churchill's proposals. Marks, in addition, were related to remission. Thus, to earn marks securing remission on one hundred days, a convict receiving six marks a day would complete his whole sentence; if he received seven a day, he would complete his whole sentence less thirteen days; if he received eight a day, he would complete it less twenty-five days. Piecework, too, wherever possible, was adopted, but in 'shops, quarries, farms, and buildings' it was impossible to allot work by the piece.

Brise stressed that much consideration and ingenuity had been devoted over many years to devising suitable work for convicts of different backgrounds, ages and physiques, with diets to match – all matters to which Churchill had referred in his proposals. Furthermore, he warned that allowing prisoners to earn more letters and visits, not to mention reduced sentences, 'must be adopted with great caution'. After all, these were crucial weapons in the armouries of the prison authorities for the maintenance of order and obedience.

Brise was right to be cautious, as Churchill's scheme undoubtedly posed serious difficulties for prison managements. Chief among these was the required expansion of convict classification. Brise explained this well:

> Each [existing] stage and each [existing] classification involves differential treatment and the strain on the staff, both discipline and clerical, is already enormous. More than this, I believe that the existence in the midst of a large convict population of a new special class of 'strenuous' labourers, specially dressed, earning greater privileges and more remission, would, apart from the difficulty of administration, cause resentment and dissatisfaction among the body of convicts, for nothing is more jealously watched than the earning of privileges, and nothing gives rise to so much anger and fighting on the works as a sense of injustice, which develops to a point of ferocity in the mind of a low-type convict when he sees his fellows enjoying privileges and marks of distinction from which he thinks himself unjustly excluded.[14]

Brise also doubted that the scheme could succeed, even if it were located in a specially built, equipped and staffed prison. He argued that suspicion and jealousy would be aroused among those who viewed it as an encroachment on free labour and even as a reward for crime. He was also sure that it would be impossible in an existing convict prison to recognize this new standard of labour as being harder, more strenuous or more deserving of reward than existing ones.

This litany of difficulties should not be interpreted as a total condemnation of Churchill's scheme, because Brise admitted that all was not well with the 'marks' system. Under the existing arrangements, virtually every convict received eight marks a day, the only exception being the obviously idle or the misbehaved. 'Given', Brise argued, 'the limitations of the class from which our discipline and instructing officers are recruited, and of the conditions of life in prison, nothing else can be expected.' He thought it would be too much to expect the staff concerned to have to operate a new system of such complexity that 'the tyro and the less robust man and the sick man, the old and the young, would all have to be gauged by different tests'. Worse, if the rewards and privileges were to go only to the strenuous, chiefly 'old lags' and men with previous experience of prison would inevitably be rewarded.

Brise, though, was far from completely negative. At this point, he made proposals which did not identically match Churchill's, but were nevertheless directed to the same end. They borrowed from the 'special merit' award in borstals. This complemented the ordinary borstal 'marks' scheme, and recognized particularly good conduct and demeanour on the part of the inmate.[15] It facilitated progress towards 'stage' and remission and carried certain other privileges. He thought it could equally be applied to longer-sentenced convicts in respect of special industrial performance. However, he did not envisage its extension to convicts serving sentences of less than four years, for whom the current 'marks' system leading to one-quarter remission served its purpose well. In any event a further shortening of their sentences 'would make instruction to a man in any trade practically worthless'. A convict serving a sentence in excess of four years, on the other hand, would be eligible after completing his first two years to earn 'special merit' marks at the rate of thirty a month. Once he had accumulated 360 marks, he would be eligible to be considered for promotion to the long-sentence class at the start of his fourth year. (In the existing situation this class could not be reached in under seven and a half years.) It was valued because it carried such privileges as a special dress code, extra gratuity which could be spent on dietary 'comforts' or additions according to taste, conversation at exercise, and special employment in a position of trust, if one were available.

Furthermore, subject to continued exemplary conduct, there was an automatic increase in the amount of remission equal to three months for each year. So a convict serving a sentence of five years could obtain his release in three years and six months, rather than the existing three years and nine months. On a sentence of six years, a convict would serve four years instead of the existing four years and six months. On an eight-year sentence, he would serve five years instead of six.

Turning to Churchill's suggestions for helping convicts who had participated in the scheme to find employment on their discharge, Brise commented that this raised the question of aid generally to convicts at the time of their release. This, he declared was currently unsatisfactory. Until it was rectified, it would not be possible to implement Churchill's employment assistance proposals. He then outlined a plan for updating existing arrangements for aid to convicts on their release which involved a substantial injection of public money and an enlarged role for the state in its administration. These were novel propositions for the time, and he indicated to Churchill that he would provide the Home Secretary with a more detailed exposition in due course.

Troup, again, poured cold water on Brise's idea.[16] He thought it would not encourage strenuous hard labour as such or give special remission for hard work. The hours and conditions of labour would be the same. The standard for earning full marks would remain the same too. Brise's scheme therefore merely allowed much greater remission on all long sentences. All truly long sentences would be reduced to little over half of their full term. Reductions on this scale would be met with public contempt. There had already been significant reductions in sentence lengths and Troup believed that no more should be carried out, certainly not 'in an indiscriminate manner'. If there was to be any reduction, he believed it should be allowed only after an examination of the merits of each case, and with some attempt at standardization, with remission granted only where the sentence leaned on the side of severity. He doubted whether judges would be able to remember the arithmetic of the proposed new calculations and feared some of them would disregard them altogether or even increase their sentences to be on the safe side.[17]

After reading both Brise's version of his scheme and Troup's observations, Churchill commented: 'The "merit marks" plan goes some part of the way to meet my wishes. Does it sufficiently embody the principle of a definite act of "volunteering"? That is the mainspring. The advantages of the new proposal are considerable. I should like to discuss them with you.'[18] Brise's plan for aid to discharged convicts, however, clearly appealed to Churchill, who wrote: 'I will take immediate steps to deal with this. I do not expect difficulty in getting £5,000 a year from Treasury. They had better be addressed at once officially on the subject. Proceed meanwhile with your plan. I presume you will issue a circular to the Societies affected and then arrange a conference. I will help at each stage. This ought not to take more than a month to settle.'

Against Churchill's comments there is a handwritten note by Brise to Troup which reads: '1. "Merit Marks!" This, I understand from our recent interview with the Secretary of State, is reserved for future consideration. 2. Aid-On-Discharge. Draft letter to Treasury submitted to him 22.4.10. I will await further instructions.' With that, Churchill's incentive labour scheme for selected convicts was subsumed into a general scheme for aid to convicts on their release from custody.

Aid to discharged convicts[19]

If there was one feature of imprisonment which concentrated Churchill's mind more than any other, it was recidivism, the frequency with which offenders repeatedly returned to custody.[20] He was determined to confront it.

He believed that more humanitarian treatment and more purposeful employment for prisoners throughout their sentences could contribute to the solution, especially if these measures were supported by more effective arrangements to enable prisoners to integrate successfully into the free community on their release. His proposal for an incentive labour scheme was designed to test this belief with selected convicts.[21] Our concern here is exclusively with aid to and supervision of discharged convicts as elaborated during Churchill's Home Secretaryship, a project in which he, his senior officials and the Prison Commissioners were all in substantial agreement and consequently were able to contrive new arrangements remarkably quickly.

Prior to Churchill's Home Secretaryship there were no systematic arrangements for aiding convicts on the completion of their sentences. That was not to say, however, that on their discharge they had no means of obtaining the necessities of life. They were entitled to receive the gratuities they had earned by their labour and conduct in the course of ploughing their way through the progressive stage system of convict treatment on which penal servitude sentences were structured. These were eventually paid to them either through the police, who supervised them during the licensed periods of their release, or at the places to which they went following their discharges.

Gratuities bore no relation to the value of the work convicts had performed. They were based solely on the degree of industry apportioned to the marks which monitored the convicts' performance. Convicts were not allowed to spend any of their gratuities during their sentences, so these accumulated in order to constitute a cash fund payable to them on discharge. The most that could be earned was £6, although the average was less, because a very long sentence was needed to accrue the maximum and by 1910 shorter sentences predominated.[22]

Individual convict prisons, unlike individual local prisons, had no discharged prisoners' aid societies, but, as Brise explained in his memorandum to Churchill of 14 April 1910, this situation had recently improved because certain metropolitan discharged prisoners' aid societies had started to take an interest in aid to discharged convict prisoners.[23] These were The Royal Society, Wheatley's Mission, the Church Army, the Salvation Army and the Catholic Aid Society.[24] A practice was emerging whereby the 'prospects' of a convict were taken shortly before his release. This enabled him to affiliate himself to a specific society on his release. There were, however, snags in this procedure. Convicts were not obliged to place themselves under the direction of *any* of the societies. A convict who did 'naturally' chose one where he had 'the best chances of receiving his gratuity as a lump sum'. The Commissioners tried to check this practice to stop convicts squandering their gratuities as soon as they were released, but they found 'great difficulty in doing so'. Another weakness of the procedure was that few societies kept records of the convicts with whom they dealt.

Brise therefore concluded that Churchill's scheme was doomed to failure unless the whole question of aid to and supervision of released convicts was addressed.

Brise first suggested that a central government association should be set up to oversee discharged convicts during the licensed periods of their release and to take over their monitoring from the police.[25] He envisaged this association being modelled on the Borstal Association, a semi-official central agency which oversaw aid to and supervision of borstal detainees released on licence. Its expenses were met in part from voluntary subscriptions and in part from public funds. It acted under the presidency of the Home Secretary and the vice-presidency of Brise himself. The central association he was suggesting for dealing with released convicts on licence would differ in that it would be financed wholly from public funds. He thought the day-to-day work of the association should be managed by an executive committee to include representatives of the five existing societies. An office would be required and a permanent staff. Every convict would be interviewed in his prison at intervals before his discharge by a representative of the society he had chosen and, following his release, it would be mandatory for him to present himself at the association's office. Reporting to the police would be discontinued except for convicts who refused offers of assistance and were likely to be a danger to the community. The association would assign such convicts to the police for supervision. Convicts who were considered to be 'special merit' cases, with a special record from their prisons (a reference to the selected convicts Churchill had in mind for his incentive labour scheme), would receive the attention of the association's central office 'with a view to rehabilitating them in honourable employment'.

Brise put the cost of all these suggestions at about £5,000 per annum, and, as has been noted, Churchill gave them his backing and undertook to raise the funds required. Brise, for his part, stressed his suggestions at this stage were preliminary thoughts; more work would have to be done, on which he would report in due course. Churchill encouraged him to proceed along the lines he had indicated and to think in terms of an early conference with the five societies to secure their cooperation.

Brise's continuing work soon led to the presentation of his final suggestions to Churchill.[26] These confirmed the original proposals: thus, the central association's president would be the Home Secretary and its vice-president Brise himself. It would operate through a council comprising representatives of the central government and the five societies. Brise informed Churchill that he had discussed these proposals with the societies, and that they were willing to cooperate.

At this point, however, he also introduced an entirely new suggestion: the proposed central association should become an umbrella organization for aid and supervision not only for released convicts but also for released preventive detention prisoners (once the Isle of Wight prison became operative) and for the Borstal Association. A uni-part organization would thus become tri-partite. Brise justified this extended format because of the need, as he saw it, to maintain 'a close nexus between the three branches [released convicts, preventive detention prisoners and borstal inmates] as there will be a necessary correlation between them, and it will be possible to follow the cases up from the beginning. In this way, confusion and overlapping will be avoided and careful record will be kept of each case from the beginning.'[27]

Brise envisaged released borstal inmates continuing to be managed by the Borstal Association and its agents in accordance with their established administrative and financial practice. Convicts, for their part, would have their cases examined while they were still serving their sentences, and each on his release would be required to present himself to the association's office. With full knowledge by this time of his circumstances and of the resources available to the participating societies, the association would then hand him over to the responsible care and charge, if possible, of one of the societies, or to one of the association's general team of agents. If the released convict remained 'obedient to orders and conducted himself well, he would be excused from reporting to the police'. Failure in these respects would invoke the penalties attaching to breaches of his release licence. Interestingly, Brise did not specify these procedures for those released from preventive detention, but the implication of his memorandum is that they would apply to them equally.

Brise conceded that officially controlled, publicly funded aid on discharge was revolutionary and of great importance, but he believed it to be the only means of improving the existing system and therefore reducing crime.

To effect all of his suggestions would not be cheap. There would have to be a central office and staff (both superintending and clerical), and a staff of agents throughout the country who would discharge a quasi-police duty in reporting failures, and aid-society duties in searching for employment. He estimated that this would cost £4,000 a year with respect to released convicts, to which would have to be added a further £2,000 for maintenance, clothes and tools, making a total of £6,000, or £1,000 more than he had earlier predicted. But there was more. This made no provision for released preventive detention inmates, whose needs Brise estimated at £1,000 per annum. The requirements of released borstal inmates were already covered and funded; but Brise was obliged to point out that their funding would have to be increased as their number increased. The likelihood was that the greater part of the increased cost would have to be borne by the Exchequer, because voluntary sources were unlikely to contribute much more than they currently did. As a result of all this, Brise now estimated the total cost of the scheme at £10,000, double his original estimate. He suggested that this figure be put to the Treasury.

Brise probably anticipated that the Treasury would baulk at this request, so he cited savings currently being made in the Commission's parliamentary-approved estimates for gratuities payable to convicts on their release. (There had over the years been a substantial fall in the gratuities paid to discharged convicts, on account of a decline in their number and the prevalence of shorter sentences.) Nothing, however, was being paid to any of the societies working with discharged convicts, and Brise contrasted this with the financial provision made available for discharged local prisoners – £12,631 for gratuities and £3,234 to the societies which worked with them. 'The old idea', he explained, 'was that the gratuity was sufficient to maintain a man when searching for employment on discharge, and no financial support has hitherto been given to the societies aiding convicts:

and it is this system which, in the opinion of the Directors [Commissioners] is inadequate, and has become still more so since the three years' sentence was introduced with the corresponding lesser gratuity.'

As has been mentioned, Churchill did not envisage any difficulty securing £5,000 for his scheme.[28] However, £10,000 was an entirely different matter.

When the Treasury received the bid it was aghast. It promptly sought to quash it, using detailed arguments about rising costs over the years in particular items of prison expenditure, and concluded that the Prison Commission's proposals should be postponed 'to a more convenient season'. These objections were conveyed to Churchill in a personal letter from the Financial Secretary.[29] It set out typical Treasury arguments that most of the cost could be met by making economies elsewhere. Churchill refuted these with ease, pointing out inter alia that the Prison Commission had a statutory duty to £2 to every prisoner discharged at the end of a local prison sentence, and that if the Commission exercised this duty to the full without regard 'to an almost harsh economy', it would spend nearly £500,000 on discharged prisoners. Moreover, when actual costs over the years, as opposed to parliamentary-approved estimates, were taken into account, the Prison Commission could show additional savings in the performance of its responsibilities. 'I cannot feel, therefore,' Churchill added, 'when our actual expenditure is so enormously below our legal powers, that any just charge of profuseness can be sustained.'

The Home Secretary then explained precisely why his proposals for dealing with aid to convicts were so important:

> The awful fact which forces itself upon the attention of anyone who studies our prison statistics is the hopeless regularity with which convicts return to Penal Servitude. I have discovered that of the convicts discharged during the years 1903–04–05 three out of every four are already back in Penal Servitude. It is this terrible proportion of recidivism that I am anxious to break in upon. It is clear that the existing attempt at reform, aid-on-discharge, and police supervision fail together to enable or encourage a convict to resume his place in honest industry. A supervision more individualised, more intimate, more carefully considered, more philanthropically inspired, is necessary; and for this purpose I propose to weave all the existing Prisoners' Aid Societies [i.e., currently involved with discharged convicts] into one strong confederacy, to

sustain them with funds on a larger scale than they have hitherto had at their disposal, to place them in contact with individual convicts long before these are again thrown on the world, and only to use the ordinary methods of police supervision cases which are utterly refractory. Sir Evelyn Ruggles-Brise tells me that he is prepared, in order to meet the Treasury wishes, to advise the gradual discontinuance of the 'Gratuity' system to the extent of about £2,000 a year.

Churchill indicated, however, that Brise could not put the cost of the treatment of each convict on discharge under the proposed new system at less than £6 a head. Furthermore, when the preventive detention institutions were full, as they might be in two or three years' time, the cost of after-care of their inmates would not be any lower. 'For the present,' he added, 'an additional £7,000 will enable me to carry out the plan I have in view. But it would not be frank to conceal from you the fact that three years hence, should the Preventive Institutions begin to operate, this expenditure will rise to £10,000 a year.'

The Treasury seems to have been convinced. In the Prison Commission's published 'Parliamentary Estimates for 1911–1912' there duly appeared under the sub-heading for 'Gratuities to prisoners and charities' the sum of £24,000, an increase on the provision for the previous year not of £7,000 but of £7,500! The way was now clear for Churchill's conference with representatives of the discharged prisoners' aid societies concerned to go ahead.

The conference, Tuesday, 19 July 1910, and establishment of the association

At the very end of his letter to the Financial Secretary, Churchill earnestly pressed for a favourable reply without delay. 'Our time may be short,' he wrote, alluding to the constitutional crisis then threatening to terminate the life of the Government, 'and I am most anxious to begin my negotiations with the various Prisoners' Aid Societies concerned.' In the event, the Government's life was spared until later in the year because of the death of Edward VII, on 6 May, and a declaration of a six months' truce among the political parties to give his successor, George V, time to settle into his reign.[30]

There was, however, another reason at this stage for Churchill's wish to press ahead quickly with his conference: a looming House of Commons debate in which Churchill would have to defend his stewardship of the Home Office, and especially his responsibility for the Prison Commission. Clearly, therefore, it would be to his advantage to be able to report a favourable outcome to his negotiations with the aid societies. Such an outcome would turn on his being able to tell them the Home Office had secured from the Treasury the necessary funds for the proposed new association. Fortunately for him, Churchill received Treasury approval of the funds just in time for the conference which took place on 19 July, but only just in time for the Commons debate on the very next day.

Churchill was accompanied to the conference by his parliamentary under-secretary of state (Masterman), Troup and Brise. The Royal Society, St Giles's Christian Mission (Wheatley's) and the Catholic Aid Society each sent a representative; the Salvation Army two representatives; and the Church Army three and what are described in the minutes as 'one or two others.'[31] The Borstal Association was represented by its head, Wemyss Grant-Wilson.[32]

Churchill opened the conference with a powerful speech in which he stressed the importance of the work the suggested central association could undertake and the availability of a substantial contribution from public funds towards its establishment and operation. The societies welcomed the proposals (a tribute to Brise's preliminary discussions with them) and Churchill was able to give them assurances on various points of detail which concerned them. When closing the meeting, he was able to announce he would formally invite the societies to join the association. The societies promised to reply favourably to his invitation, subject to the formal agreement of their respective management committees.

The very next day, Churchill appeared in the Commons to defend his stewardship of the Home Office. The day after that he issued a minute to his advisers and to Brise, beginning with the injunction 'it is important that departmental action should follow hot foot upon the Parliamentary announcement made last night'. He then itemized six themes on which he required action, one of which reads: 'Let us proceed at once to form the central agency. The sooner that body meets for the first time the sooner the machinery can be devised. Propose me the personnel.'[33] Everything then proceeded swiftly.

In a letter of 8 September to Troup, for Churchill's attention,[34] Brise informed him that a preliminary meeting of the central association had been held on 6 September, attended by all the societies concerned. Provisional agreement was reached involving the establishment of a general council comprising all these societies,[35] having as its officers the chairman of the Prison Commission as chairman, Wemyss Grant Wilson as vice-chairman and Basil Thomson (secretary of the Prison Commission) as secretary. Agreement had also been reached on the council's office, which for the time being would be the same as the Borstal Association's at 15 Buckingham Street under the immediate direction of Alexander Paterson, a member of the executive of the Borstal Association and destined in due course to become a Prison Commissioner. The date from which the association, its council and office were to operate would be 1 January 1911. Brise declared the proceedings of the association in its preliminary meeting had been 'characterized by much friendliness and harmony between the different bodies and there is every prospect of a successful co-operation'.

In a further letter to Troup dated 29 October, for Churchill's attention, Brise submitted for approval procedural details for carrying out the objectives of the association and for handling court hearings involving convicts who misbehaved while released under licence. Brise's letter concluded by requesting the assistance of the Home Office in securing the concurrence of the police authorities throughout the country to all of these arrangements.[36]

Radzinowicz and Hood justly commend Churchill's efforts to assist discharged convicts: 'it cannot be denied that the movement to forge a system of after-care worthy of a modern, prosperous state, and in tune with its developing social conscience, had at last begun to take root'.[37]

Lectures and concerts for prisoners

Although Churchill was clearly concerned with the issues discussed thus far, nothing was more dear to his heart than measures to occupy and stimulate the minds of convicts and local prisoners. They were his antidote to the 'long, dull and profitless days' he associated with imprisonment as he had known it when he was a captive of the Boers.[38] So it is no surprise that early in April 1910 he addressed Brise on these matters: 'Will you kindly consider among the different points which we are examining whether some regular system of lectures should not be introduced into the prison? And will you make me some proposals on this head showing the scale and manner you think action might be taken, and its probable cost.'[39]

Brise's reply of 18 April[40] indicated that lectures, 'addresses' and musical presentations were already occasional features of some convict and local prison regimes and he enclosed copies of the Commission's standing orders to governors which regulated the procedures to be followed. He then described to Churchill how these events had made their way into prison regimes and the current arrangements for dealing with them. He termed them 'of comparatively recent origin', a reference, perhaps, to a recommendation in the 1895 Report designed to enhance the humanitarian contribution to the reformation of prisoners' behaviour.[41] Subsequently, a further departmental committee reviewed the arrangements then in place (for the management of which in each convict and local prison the chaplain was responsible) relating to prisoners' education and moral instruction, including the circumstances under which lectures 'could be introduced with advantage to the prisoners and without impairment to prison discipline.'[42] The outcome was a conservative recommendation: the members declared they were 'of opinion that the possibility of benefiting even a few prisoners should not be given up without a fair trial, and we recommend that the experiment be tried in, say, two convict, and in three or four local prisons.'[43] Upon this recommendation, between 1896 and 1910, the Commissioners constructed an ever-widening range of lectures and some concerts. These events, however, were kept under very strict and detailed central control in convict prisons. In local prisons, oversight of them was delegated to their visiting committees, which, nevertheless, were required to keep the Prison Commissioners informed in some detail of what they were doing.[44]

Churchill's intervention, therefore, was hardly breaking new ground. Significant, however, was his suggestion that the activities be 'regular', rather than occasional. As we shall see, he also saw them as having a serious educational purpose, quite apart from their value as recreation or entertainment.

The constraints of standing orders notwithstanding, Brise was able to report that in the previous year 1,441 lectures and 'addresses' had been given and the voluntary services of 285 lecturers obtained. The chief beneficiaries were juvenile-adults in the gradually emerging borstal system.[45] In prisons for women, 257 lectures were given by lady visitors or friends introduced by them. He reported that on the religious side there were yearly 'missions' to all prisons conducted by the Church Army and other groups, and chaplains were encouraged to invite 'outside' clergy and suitable laymen into their pulpits both on weekdays and Sundays. Nor was music neglected. Brise explained that carols and oratorios rendered by local choirs were occasionally performed. Famous singers, Clara Butt for one, had also sung, and 'lately at Portland the band of the Somersetshire Light Infantry, quartered at the Verne, volunteered a concert which had a most admirable influence, the convicts being affected greatly both at the time and afterwards, as shown in letters to their friends'.[46] Brise declared himself, indeed, to be 'greatly in favour of music as an influence upon prisoners' and thought it should be encouraged.

He therefore welcomed Churchill's proposals for 'a regular system' of 'entertainment',[47] which he thought should have 'a moral and elevating purpose', albeit 'introduced independently of moral and religious addresses – and especially at the Convict Prisons'. He thought that governors of these institutions should be instructed to arrange such an 'entertainment' once a quarter, with the expenses, 'if any, defrayed by the State'. Preference should be given to music, 'military or other orchestrations, and singing by individuals or choirs'. When this was not possible, lecturers, 'with illustrations, of a high class should be invited, at a guinea fee and expenses'.

However, he emphasized that these developments should be confined to the convict prisons as inmates of local prisons did not have the same need. They were a 'fugitive and ever-changing population', 95 per cent of them were in custody for three months or less and 62 per cent for two weeks or less. Furthermore, the majority were in the first or penal stage of the progressive stage system. He thought it unlikely that the public would approve a 'system ... of entertainments at public expense under these conditions'. On the other hand, he did not like the idea of shutting local prisoners entirely out of the scheme, so suggested that local prison governors should be informed that the Commissioners were in favour of 'entertainments' from time to time, especially if they were musical in character, and of 'illustrated lectures likely to stimulate reflection and to elevate the mind; and a small fee with out-of-pocket expenses would be sanctioned in such cases, if voluntary services were not forthcoming'.

Brise concluded by stating that £500 a year ought to cover the expenses of such a system. Nevertheless, Treasury approval would be required as no specific provision had hitherto been made for the project in the Commission's approved parliamentary estimates. Churchill found Brise's response acceptable, and in a memorandum encouraged him to go further:[48]

> I agree that we should deal especially with Convict prisons. The Local prisons may for the present be left to voluntary effort. Propose me a plan in greater detail for the Convict prisons. Let an imaginary programme be laid out fully. Music especially and magic lanterns. Is there any reason why special classes should not be formed for study of suitable subjects from among the more educated convicts?

By posing this question, Churchill revealed that he was probably the first Home Secretary ever to envisage a system of serious and organized study, certainly beyond basic literacy and numeracy, for adult prisoners. At the time, the Commissioners were looking into the suitability of such study for young offenders detained in borstals and Churchill was aware of their progress.[49] It is reasonable to suggest that Churchill was influenced by their ideas, and combined them with his own, which, as we know, had been forming since his captivity.

Brise responded with a scheme that embraced two separate programmes: one for lectures, the other for music.[50] He suggested that at each of the four convict prisons – Maidstone, Portland, Parkhurst and Dartmoor – two lectures and two concerts could be held each year. He pointed out that the only room in each of these prisons big enough for these events was the Church of England chapel. Because there was no means of darkening its windows, however, lantern lectures would have to take place in the late autumn and in spring at 4 p.m., reserving the concerts for summer and early autumn. At Dartmoor and Parkhurst there was a further problem. Their chapels were not large enough to accommodate Protestant and Roman Catholic convicts simultaneously, so at each of these prisons two lectures or concerts would have to be given on the same day.

Brise obtained a tender from Messrs. Newton and Company of London for lectures. For an inclusive fee of eighty guineas they would supply twelve lectures annually, delivered by 'competent popular lecturers'. The necessary lanterns and appliances, however, would have to be purchased from them at a cost of £12 9s. 6d. each. At each prison an officer would be trained to operate them, saving travelling expenses and operators' fees. The lectures would deal with popular scientific subjects, 'foreign countries and native races, Pompeii and Herculaneum, the eruption of Mont Pelée. Experience at the Convict Prisons has shown that for an audience of such mixed education as the convicts this sort of lecture is generally the most popular. The men like the lectures to be instructive as well as amusing'.

The summer afternoon concerts would complement the existing Christmas musical services, Brise thought. Whenever a band could be obtained, a concert could easily be arranged. Some of the pieces could be solo, and vocal solos could be introduced, too. Moreover, in August there were generally vocal quartets or choirs performing at Plymouth and Weymouth, so the governors of Dartmoor and Portland should have the opportunity to secure their services quite easily. Brise thought that concerts could be arranged at an inclusive fee of £10 (or £15 at Dartmoor and Parkhurst, with their requirement of double concerts). The annual cost would therefore be £100.

Brise concluded his minute with a comment on Churchill's proposed 'special classes ... for study of suitable subjects from among the more educated convicts'. He informed Churchill that he would like to defer his opinion until a later date, when he would have had an opportunity to judge the worth of an experiment the Commissioners were running at Lincoln Borstal involving the International Correspondence Schools. He reminded Churchill that he had already drawn his attention to this in discussions over 'a higher educational system in the Borstal Institutions'.[51] Meanwhile, he was collecting opinions from the convict prisons 'as to the institution of some practical scheme for teaching such subjects as modern languages, shorthand, book-keeping, mechanics, etc.' and would report further on the matter.

The correspondence courses to which Brise referred turned out to be a success. In the Commissioners' Annual Report to Parliament for the year ended 31 March 1911 the chaplain of Feltham Borstal recorded that nine of its inmates were following correspondence courses. The chaplain of Maidstone Prison mentioned that three of its convicts were doing likewise, concentrating on marine engineering, mechanical engineering, and building instruction.[52] The courses were publicly funded and gradually became a feature for suitable prisoners undergoing long-term imprisonment. While credit is due to the Commissioners for the introduction of post-basic education in the borstals, Churchill achieved even more by prompting the Commissioners to extend its application to the adult prison population.[53]

Although Churchill generally favoured Brise's model, it was in his view too modest for his requirements. In his next memorandum to Brise he stated he would 'like to aim at six lectures and concerts – one every two months for both Catholics and Protestants,' adding that 'the financial arrangements should be formed on this basis'. He asked that a letter should be addressed to the Treasury forthwith and that a statement should be prepared for publication 'when the time comes with other prison changes currently in contemplation'.[54]

Brise challenged this directive, largely for prison operational reasons. He pointed out that in convict prisons nothing should be left to chance, and it would be leaving a great deal to chance to congregate masses of convicts in darkened rooms. Nevertheless, the Commissioners were willing to run the risk on two conditions. The first was that entertainments should be so rare and so interesting that the attention of convicts would be riveted. They would therefore appreciate the great privilege and indulgence being offered to them and so would not make mischief or use the occasion for purposes of disorder. The second condition was that no convict would be admitted to the entertainments if he had been on report in the past six months. In this way, the entertainments could be a useful instrument of discipline and good conduct. The Commissioners viewed lectures and concerts as a concession. To raise their number from four to six, additional cost aside, 'would only lead to indifference and would be a good thing spoilt'.[55]

Brise advised that the scheme should be incorporated in the forthcoming Annual Report of the Prison Commissioners to Parliament, currently in preparation, which was the usual procedure followed in cases of this kind. 'I am not aware', he primly declared, 'of any precedent for publication in any other form of matters relating to the interior economy of Prisons.' Troup supported Brise's view, and Churchill decided that the four annual events a year would 'be sufficient to begin with', and that he would 'consider further the question of publication'. In the event, Churchill announced the introduction of the scheme in his Commons speech on 20 July. The Commissioners published it in paragraph 31 of their Annual Report to Parliament for the year ended 31 March 1911.[56]

All that now remained was to secure Treasury approval of funding for the scheme. A letter prepared by Brise was accordingly dispatched there under cover of a Home Office letter dated 21 June.[57] The total funding sought was £164 per annum for lectures and concerts in convict prisons, a one-off purchase price (£42 11s.) for magic lanterns, and £50 per annum (maximum) for lectures at local prisons and borstals. The Treasury reply was down to its usual level of generosity: 'Their Lordships request you to inform the Secretary of State that with the exception of the cost of lantern apparatus, to which They would not feel justified in agreeing, They sanction an expenditure within the above limits, i.e. not exceeding £214 a year.'[58] Churchill minuted the file on 20 September: 'I should like to be kept informed of the working of this scheme.'

Although he'd been twitted in the House of Commons when announcing the lectures and concerts, and attacked in the press for the same reason, it's fair to say that Churchill had changed the face of imprisonment in England and Wales.[59] The lectures and concerts gradually became normal parts of convict regimes, and it was not long before local prisons obtained their own funds to mount similar events. They have flourished ever since.

Prison libraries

Library facilities comprised the last of Churchill's initiatives to strengthen the humanitarian ethos of prison regimes. The Prison Rules in force at the time required a library to be made available for the exclusive use of prisoners in every convict and local prison. However, they were stocked with only such books as the Prison Commissioners chose to sanction. The Rules described the kinds of books and the circumstances under which the prisoners could have access to them. Thus a prisoner in his first month of detention was allowed to have in his possession 'books of instruction in addition to the usual religious books', and in succeeding months also to have 'library books', with the opportunity to exchange them frequently, 'according to his conduct and industry'. Prisoners adjudged not to have done their best to profit from these facilities were penalized under the Rules 'in the same way as if they had been idle or negligent at labour', which usually meant deprivation of their privileges.[60]

In every convict and local prison the Prison Rules further provided for a chaplain to be appointed and specified his duties in considerable detail.[61] In addition to conducting chapel services and offering moral and spiritual guidance to individual prisoners, he was required 'to give daily his personal superintendence' to 'the instruction of prisoners in reading, writing, and arithmetic'. This meant he oversaw the teaching staff and the prison library. He had an important role in the selection of books for stocking the library and, within the terms of the Rules, in the suitability of particular books which individual prisoners were allowed to read. The prisoners' reading had to conform with such moral and religious guidance as the chaplain was offering them. In short, prisoners' reading was subject to the censorship of their chaplains. This was especially true in relation to what were described in the Rules as 'library' books, because the Rules did not precisely specify the meaning of this term. In the absence of any definition, chaplains seem to have interpreted it as any non-religious or non-educational book. This power to assess the suitability of reading matter inevitably led to disputes between the chaplains and the prisoners.[62]

These difficulties and inconsistencies had come to the attention of Gladstone towards the end of his Home Secretaryship and caused him to enquire into them, but he left office before he could arrive at a solution. Churchill set his mind to the task as part of his campaign to increase humanity in the treatment of prisoners.[63] A prisoner's petition afforded him valuable ammunition for his purpose.

On 6 December 1909 a suffragette, Violet Bryant, had been convicted by Haslingden Petty Sessional Court of 'wilful damage to windows and a lamp' and sentenced to one month's imprisonment in lieu of a fine at Preston Gaol. On the following day she petitioned the Home Secretary concerning the treatment division in which she had been placed.[64] On 15 December, when Gladstone's reply had been received, the governor passed it on to her, but only after she had been dealt with over another incident. The governor reported to the Home Secretary on the same day that Bryant persistently refused food and was both insolent and violent. Furthermore,

> I visited her about 9 a.m. to-day [15 December], and she asked for a library book. I told her the Rules did not permit her of having one, as her sentence was only a month, but she might have a set of devotional books, if she would tell me what her religion was, to which she replied 'my religion is votes for women,' and she turned to one of the female Officers and said 'it is a damnable shame she could not have a library book.' Shortly afterwards the Matron reported to my office that the prisoner had smashed four frames of glass in her cell window and was violent.

The line in this report concerning the refusal to grant Bryant a library book was subsequently underscored at the Home Office, and on 16 December the report was submitted to Gladstone. He commented on the underscoring to the effect that he could not understand what justification there was for refusing prisoners 'all books excepting religious or "educational" books ... during the first month'. He wanted to know if the Commissioners had 'definite reason for maintaining this first-month Rule'.

The papers were then submitted to the Commissioners on 18 December for their observations. They replied by minute on 24 February 1910, by which time, of course, Churchill had assumed the Home Secretaryship and responsibility for dealing further with the matter.[65]

Brise explained that prisoners' reading material was regulated by the progressive stage system of prison discipline.[66] Books of 'secular and religious instruction' were available to prisoners in the first stage of the system which coincided with the first month of imprisonment. Books of 'secular instruction' were not merely educational in the scholastic sense, such as primers of arithmetic and grammar, but included 'histories, essays, etc. and generally speaking such literature which is not of a light, amusing, or sensational character, for example, novels and magazines which would fall technically under the head of "library" books, which are a special privilege of the Second and later stages of the system'. He then went on to argue that the prohibition of such light literature in the first month was to give effect to the accepted value of a progressive system of punishment, in which prisoners earned by industry and good conduct a gradual amelioration of their lot. He believed that complaints made about these arrangements in the past were not due to a defect in the regulations as such, but rather to a narrow definition by the authorities at the prisons of 'secular instruction'. He concluded that, to avoid a further confusion of this kind, instructions had been issued that in future the term should be defined in the wider sense he had indicated.

On 2 March the Home Office's senior officials responded to Brise's explanation. They said that while the distinction between books primarily concerned with recreation and those primarily concerned with education was real, it was not well expressed by calling the former 'library books' and the latter 'religious and educational'. However, 'it seems impossible to devise any better nomenclature'. They queried where the dividing line should be drawn between recreational and educational magazines, quipping, 'the prospect of the *Strand Magazine* as a substitute for Hallam [presumably the constitutional historian] must be a powerful incentive to good conduct!'

On 4 March Churchill responded to this advice, agreeing that the distinction was unsatisfactory, and continuing: 'Some people would prefer

Hallam to the *Strand*. It would be better to draw up two catalogues – a limited and a more extensive one. Would it be worth while having a small committee to consider the subject?' The outcome of this exchange was that the Prison Commissioners agreed on 17 March to the formation of this 'small committee'.[67]

As drafted by Churchill himself, the committee's terms of reference were 'to consider what are the principles which should govern the supply of books to the prisoners in HM Prisons and to the inmates of Borstal Institutions, regard being had to the reformative purposes of prison treatment and to the maintenance of the progressive stage system. And to report what, if any, amendment of the existing rules and practice on the subject is desirable.'[68]

The membership of the committee as determined by Churchill was much wider than Brise's original suggestion of a small committee of officials (a Commissioner, the chaplain-inspector, and a prison inspector). The chairman was Maurice Waller, a recently appointed Commissioner who had been promoted from the post of private secretary to Gladstone when Churchill had taken over at the Home Office. The members were the Revd C. B. Simpson, the Chaplain-Inspector; Mrs Olive Birrell, Lady Visitor at Holloway Prison; the Honourable A. L. Stanley;[69] Professor Walter Raleigh, first occupant of the Chair of English Literature at Oxford University and fellow of Magdalen College; and Basil Thomson, secretary of the Prison Commission.

Churchill's unusual contribution to the make-up of the committee was his invitation to Raleigh. He asked his principal private secretary, Eddie Marsh, to write to Raleigh and to clear the letter with him before its dispatch.[70] Unfortunately, this letter has not survived, although Raleigh's reply does.[71] He asked Marsh to give Churchill his warm regards and to tell him that he would be most willing to serve on the committee, although he was somewhat distrustful of his power to help, because he lacked 'intimate acquaintance with prisoners'. Nevertheless, he would like to talk to some of them and find out what they liked to read. He went on to say that some years previously he had visited Liverpool Prison and been shown round by Basil Thomson, who was then the prison's deputy governor. Raleigh clearly held Thomson in the highest regard. This may have convinced Churchill to appoint Thomson to the committee, although the fact that he was an experienced and enlightened prison governor and secretary to the Prison Commissioners was probably sufficient in itself.

The secretary of the committee was A. J. Wall, a member of the Commission's office staff, and destined to rise in its service. Altogether, it was a remarkably different committee from the one Brise had envisaged, and reflects Churchill's desire for new thinking in the corridors of the Prison Commission.[72]

Between 26 April 1910, when Churchill signed the warrant appointing the committee, and 27 October 1910, when the committee presented its Report,[73] the members examined twenty witnesses and held seven sittings, four of them in Prison Service institutions – Holloway, Wormwood Scrubs, Borstal and Dartmoor. At each of these places, besides taking formal evidence, the members interviewed inmates in their cells and examined their books. While they concentrated on the principal issues drawn to their attention in their terms of reference, they also looked into and made recommendations on a number of detailed matters, since, as their report rightly explains, 'the regular supply of suitable literature depends to a considerable extent upon good organization of the libraries and proper methods of distributing the books'.

The committee ultimately found nothing seriously amiss with the prison library system, but concluded there were ways in which its operating processes could be improved in order to enhance the value of libraries in the treatment of prisoners.[74] These devices constituted the substance of the forty-eight recommendations with which the committee concluded its report and earned Churchill's approval. Provided they were regularly, intelligently and diligently applied, they enabled libraries more effectively and efficiently to widen the horizons of the inmates' minds and allowed them to occupy themselves usefully, overcoming to some extent the boredom and frustrations of imprisonment, the very issues which had exercised Churchill in the first place.

The committee recommended the abolition of the term 'books of secular instruction' and its replacement by 'books of education', and clarified what was meant by 'library' books, thus solving the main problem.[75] 'Books of education' were henceforward to comprise not only what would be described nowadays as books of primary, secondary and technical education, but books of *all kinds*, except works of fiction. These were to be made readily available to prisoners in local prisons undergoing first-stage sentence treatment. Works of fiction, on the other hand, were formally classified as 'library books' and were to be made available only to prisoners in the second and later stages of their sentences. This restriction (inevitable because of the progressive stage system of discipline) was, however, subject to a caveat. The committee inserted a recommendation that 'in special cases the Chaplain, when satisfied that such a course is proper and desirable, should have discretion to allow an imaginative book of *standard* rank (officially classified as a library book) to a prisoner in the "first stage".'[76]

Library books, though, were not exclusively works of fiction. This category was to include, for example, 'good histories, biographies, books of travel, and philosophical and political writings'.[77] These were found to be in particular demand in convict prisons, where the committee noted the better-educated prisoners were held and where the prisoners had more time for reading because, unlike local prisoners, they did not have evening tasks to perform. Even so, in the larger-populated local prisons, there was, too, some scope for books of serious academic study. Arrangements to meet the needs of the better-educated local-prison inmates were therefore required, albeit on a smaller scale than in the convict prisons.[78]

The committee considered in this respect the suitability of the book stock for prisoners' reading: 'The reformative object of modern prison discipline must be kept in view. Books are an instrument of the first importance in the attainment of that object ... Moreover many prisoners never read at any other time than during their terms of imprisonment. Such favourable conditions should be used to the best advantage by those who direct prisoners' reading.' Morality, however, should not be overdone: 'Example is better than precept, in literature as in life ... We approve, therefore, of the present practice of admitting to prison libraries a liberal choice of novels, both standard and new.'[79] But 'Novels of an unhealthy moral tone, novels of a morbidly introspective kind, novels of the "trashy" order' all had to be excluded. The same went for novels such as *Robbery under Arms* and *Raffles*, because they encouraged the commission of crime, even though the villains came to a sticky end. Among novels of 'lesser' writers, 'stories of a healthy, bracing, outdoor nature' were to be preferred, especially for young prisoners.[80] Chaplains were specifically adjured to enforce these principles when stocking libraries and advising prisoners on their choice of reading.[81]

The committee also gave some thought to bound magazines. Standing orders to governors, they noted, required 'about one-third' of such books should be bound volumes of periodicals and provided an official list of the periodicals which could be ordered. The list included such reputable publications as *Chambers's Journal* and the *Cornhill*, of which the committee approved, but most of the publications were ordinary popular magazines. Bound volumes of a magazine, because of their size, were considered equivalent to two library books. They were popular with prisoners on account of their illustrations (many prisoners had reading difficulties) and the variety of their reading matter. Female prisoners liked them for their articles on home-making and domestic matters more generally. The committee also saw value in bound magazines for 'a few prisoners, especially among women, whose mental depression is so profound and whose intelligence is of so poor an order, that the kindest, and indeed the only possible course for the authorities is to attempt to divert their minds a little from their position by giving them the lightest of reading matter'.[82]

It further recommended that certain magazines on the approved list which had indulged in purveying articles offensive to prison discipline should be removed, as should the standing order requirement that a third of library stock should consist of bound magazines. Needs and circumstances differed widely from one prison to another and it would be sufficient to allow the proportion of this type of literature to be decided by the chaplains concerned under the supervision of the Chaplain-Inspector and the Commissioners.[83]

Weekly or monthly reviews 'of a superior class', containing articles on current events, politics, literature and science – for example, the *Nineteenth Century*, the *Saturday Review*, the *Spectator* and *T. P. O'Connor's Weekly* – were, the committee recognized, essentially 'the periodical of the educated man', and there was a market for them in convict prisons. Their influence was healthy, and the committee recommended that their availability should be continued. The members considered that 'A man's mind cannot be entirely divorced from the world outside the prison walls.' They recognized that, in prisons, letters and visits from relatives and friends, the arrival of new prisoners, and the library books themselves all provided contacts with the outside world. What a prisoner learned about it only stimulated a desire to learn more, and 'To satisfy it, so far as prison conditions admit,' they argued, 'is right in itself, while the widening of a man's mental outlook which follows when his attention is directed to public affairs cannot fail to improve his general tone of thought.'[84]

They took a very different line, however, where newspapers were concerned. The committee considered their distribution to the mass of prisoners was not 'possible or desirable'. This was partly on account of the cost involved, but one suspects the committee may also have been influenced by their content, some of which could be at variance with the morality it was the duty of the chaplains to preach. Not, however, that the committee explained its reason in these terms. Nor could it do so, because in the borstals inmates of the special grade were permitted to associate for an hour in the evenings three times a week for recreational purposes; at this hour, they were supplied with current issues of some of the daily and weekly illustrated papers. However, 'Borstal', declared the committee, 'partakes of the character of a Reformatory, rather than of a prison, and this is one of the special indulgences granted to the Borstal boys who wear the "blue dress", which have no counterpart in ordinary prisons.'[85]

An increased supply of technical trade manuals and magazines related to the construction industry, tailoring, commerce (shorthand and bookkeeping), farming and so on was recommended. These were popular among prisoners and in some instances had a bearing on employment *in* prison as well as outside, thus widening prisoners' employment opportunities on release.[86] Spiritual needs were also addressed, with recommendations made for additional alternative literature for moral instruction and devotional purposes, books more appropriate for prisoners of the Wesleyan and nonconformist persuasions, books for use by the chaplains themselves and certain prisoners approved by them, and books concerned with ethical and philosophical issues.[87]

The committee thought that all books should continue to be bought through HM Stationery Office.[88] In this manner, such money as was available for book purchases could be made to go a long way, because the Prison Commission benefited from the discounts which accrued from the Stationery Office's bulk purchases of books and other literature required by all government departments. Greater use of cheap editions of standard works was recommended.[89] Nevertheless, the members also suggested that the capitation allowance for the purchase of books per inmate of 1s. 3d. should be raised to 1s. 6d. for convicts and borstal inmates (while remaining at the lower level for local prisoners). The committee justified the lower-rate in local prisons because of the prevalence there of very short sentences, within which, moreover, so few prisoners proceeded beyond the first stage of the progressive stage system, and because they had evening tasks to carry out which further limited their time for reading.[90] Convicts, however, on their long sentences, and for whom there were no evening tasks, were intensive readers, many were well educated, and consequently their need for books was greater. In borstals, the higher capitation allowance was required to enable them to fulfil their avowed education and training regimes.

Evidence of the importance the committee attached to the funding of prison libraries can be found in the well-argued letter, signed by all the members, which it sent to Churchill on 27 October 1910, the day it presented him with its report, seeking his particular support for its recommended increase in library funding. The file does not disclose Churchill's response, but it must have been favourable, because the Treasury on 5 July 1911 agreed that the discount allowed by the Stationery Office to the Prison Commission should be increased from 20 to 25 per cent on all books supplied; and that the capitation allowance should be raised as requested.[91] It further agreed that books of moral instruction, regarded as part of cell furniture, should not be a charge on the capitation grant.

Yet further recommendations in the report related to the simplification and standardization of the mechanics of library administration, in place of the somewhat haphazard arrangements the committee found prevailing at the time.[92] The most important of these in relation to the development of prison library administration concerned each prison's library catalogue: 'the catalogue of a good free library or some similar institution should be taken as a basis, say the catalogue of a well managed public library of recent foundation in a popular centre'. There should be sufficient copies for each prison and the prisoners should be properly informed of the reading facilities available to them. Other suggestions concerned the use of suitable prisoners to undertake librarian duties, the procedure for applying for books, increased frequency of book exchanges, a more generous allowance of books which prisoners might have at anyone time and so on.

* * *

It is clear from the committee's report that winds of change were going to sweep through what had long been a rather musty corner of prison regimes. Certainly Churchill, who was looking for a strong, positive role for libraries as agents for the supply of prisoners' 'brain-food', was pleased with the findings of the committee: 'It is', he minuted, 'a good and thoughtful Report. Thank the committee.'[93] Or, with the benefit of hindsight, the report was 'a signpost towards present-day arrangements for library service in prisons'.[94]

CHAPTER 5

Young Offenders

On 21 December 1908, Parliament enacted a Bill Part I of which provided the courts with a new sentence, borstal detention, to help curb the criminality of a designated class of young offenders. The Bill as enacted, the Prevention of Crime Act, came into operation on 1 August 1909.[1]

It concerned persons who were convicted by the courts, on indictment, of offences for which they were liable to be sentenced to penal servitude or imprisonment. In cases, however, where it appeared to the courts that such persons were aged not less than sixteen and not more than twenty-one, that by reason of their habits they had settled into criminal careers, and that it was expedient they should be detained under instruction and discipline conducive to their reformation, it would be lawful for them to pass on such persons the new sentence of 'borstal detention' in lieu of penal servitude or imprisonment. The sentences were fixed at not less than one and not more than three years. Before passing such a sentence, though, the courts were obliged to consider any report or representations made to them by or on behalf of the Prison Commissioners as to the suitability of the persons concerned for detention in a borstal institution, and to be satisfied that their character, state of health, mental condition and other circumstances of their cases would enable them to profit by the instruction and discipline provided. The Home Secretary was empowered to make regulations for the rule and management of borstal institutions, which the Act defined as places for 'industrial training and other instruction', and for the exercise upon their inmates of such 'disciplinary and moral influences as will conduce to their reformation and the prevention of crime.'[2]

Another provision in the Act was of particular interest to Churchill when he took over at the Home Office, because it conferred on the Prison

Commissioners, subject to the Home Secretary's regulations, discretion to permit the release on licence of persons under borstal training

> at any time after the expiration of six months, or, in the case of a female, three months, from the commencement of the term of detention, if satisfied there is a reasonable probability that the offender will abstain from crime and lead a useful and industrious life, on condition that he be placed under the supervision or authority of any society or person named in the licence who may be willing to take charge of the case.[3]

In 1910 borstal detention was still novel, of course, so it is hardly surprising that Churchill wanted to have a hand in shaping its development. By June of that year, prompted by Gladstone's hand-over notes, he had settled into an investigation of the court calendars to ascertain how the sentence was being applied. What he found troubled him greatly and in a memorandum to Troup and Brise he set out the grounds of his disquiet.[4] He said he had detected an 'increasing tendency' by the courts to inflict 'sentences of three years' imprisonment at Borstal for offences which would not in the ordinary course of events receive more than six months' imprisonment'. Some check on this practice was required. He added: 'I should certainly not consent to be responsible for any system that can be shown to aggravate the severity of the Penal Codes.'

Here, as he did so often, Churchill was expressing the view that offences and the sentences applicable to them should demonstrate the exercise of fair and logical proportionality. This seemed to him to be lacking in borstal sentencing. 'Certain minimum conditions by which to regulate and limit the class of persons liable to Borstal imprisonment' were required. He added he would not object to the period of borstal imprisonment being uniformly three years, but if this were to be so, then

> the class of offences and of offenders requiring such severe punishment and drastic treatment must be clearly defined. I entirely demur to the idea that such treatment is good in itself, or a useful educational experience for young men. It is bad in itself and only becomes good in relation to the other forms of prison discipline. I should be glad, therefore, if the Prison Commissioners will communicate to me their idea of the minimum conditions of vice and crime which, in their opinion justify the imposition of a three years' Borstal sentence and should submit them to me at an early date.

Churchill then floated ideas of his own for 'some new method of punishment, restraint or training for young people whose offences did not justify the infliction of such a tremendous sentence'. For very slight offences 'arising from the rowdy moods of youth', he put forward the idea of a non-custodial penalty – a system of reporting at designated police stations or one of Swedish drill (physical education with or without the use of dumb-bells) – backed up with imprisonment for offenders who did not comply.[5] For cases of dishonesty which were not sufficiently numerous or serious to justify a borstal sentence but which were difficult to cover under the Probation of Offenders Act, he wondered if conditions of imprisonment could be devised between periods of a month and a year which – even though the results would not be as complete as those claimed for full borstal sentences – would check ill-doing without being 'positively injurious' to the young offenders concerned.

He stated he was prepared to concede that the borstal system opened the door to new possibilities, but this meant that it could not possibly be allowed to remain in its present state. Here he voiced his misgivings about the character of the training he discerned associated with it:

> The moment Borstal training comes to be regarded not as a mitigation for young convicts, but as a beneficial discipline for poor lads, similar to the old system of apprenticeship, it becomes utterly inadequate to the complexities of the problem. There ought to be, in fact, a complete chain of disciplinary institutions for youth of bad propensities, ranging from the reformatories to the full Borstal sentence, and we should not then be forced to occupy the strange position of holding that no punishment other than the longest and the most severe can be inflicted upon youths of the working classes with any hopes of beneficial result.[6]

A week after submitting his first memorandum, Churchill circulated another.[7] This elaborated his ideas into a ladder of alternative penalties for convicted offenders in the sixteen to twenty-one age group, rising by stages from the least to the most severe:

- The first stage involved twenty-eight daily sessions, each of an hour and a half, of Swedish drill in lieu of fines with or without imprisonment, to curb 'rowdyism, gambling, stone-throwing, etc.' Unless other arrangements were made, it should take place at a police station. If the offenders were slack or inattentive,

this part of their drill would not be counted towards the completion of the penalty. 'Contumacy', he wrote, 'must involve, first, detention in police cells, and in extreme cases, prison.' The offenders' suitability on medical grounds would have to be considered.
- The second stage concerned young people sentenced to imprisonment. They would serve a term of not less than one month, to be made 'extremely unpleasant' for them, based on a special course of modified borstal training, 'disciplinary and instructive, without, however, being degrading'. He envisaged it being a period of 'constant effort, but essentially educational and reformative in its character as well as deterrent'.
- The third stage was the Commissioners' own existing system of modified borstal training, confined, however to a period of six months.
- This left the commissioners' existing maximum borstal sentence of three years available as the fourth stage, reserved for young offenders found guilty of grave offences, such as violence, arson, burglary and so on, but 'subject to proper safeguards and warning'. It was reserved for offenders regarded as 'incorrigible', who, if they were adults, would be sentenced to penal servitude. 'No young person under twenty-one should, except for murder, receive a heavier sentence.'

Churchill believed this system would allow the courts to choose a more appropriate sentence in each individual case. He stressed he did not see his stages as 'progressive' in their incidence. Rather, he thought any of the stages could be repeated, but each was 'a distinct, perfectly recognizable thing in itself; and side by side with each of them should run, in all cases, the option of probation'.

The memorandum concluded with Churchill's views on probation itself. He thought of it as a double-edged sword: 'admonition' and 'discipline'. Each was to be regarded as distinct and yet working in tandem with the other. 'Admonition in all its forms', he declared, 'will be under the Probation Officers, as at present. Discipline will be dealt with by the police. The defaulters' drill system will fall entirely within the disciplinary section of probation.'

By this time, the borstal system was coming to be regarded in both the Home Office and the Prison Commission as the jewel in the crown of the prison system of England and Wales. Consequently, Churchill's criticisms were viewed with dismay by the Home Office's senior officials and the Prison Commissioners, who felt obliged to rally strongly in its support.

Nor was it difficult for them to do so, because, unfortunately for Churchill, he was mistaken in thinking that borstal sentences were fixed prison sentences of three years' duration.[8] Brise responded in a memorandum to Troup for transmission to Churchill.[9] Enclosed with it – according to him, at Churchill's request – was a further memorandum on the subject addressed to Brise by Waller, who had the day-to-day oversight of the developing borstal system, which supplied Brise with supporting evidence for his own response.

Brise first took Churchill step by step through Part 1 of the 1908 Act. Thus he was able to show that a borstal institution was an extension of the reformatory school system suitable for the age group concerned, *not* a prison. Moreover, the borstal sentence was not fixed at three years' duration: sentences could be passed for terms of one year and not *more* than three. Release for the offender concerned could occur at any time after six months (or three months in the case of girls) between these two terms, subject to a favourable response on the inmate's part to the treatment and training regime of the borstal. The sentence was therefore a combination of a judicial 'tariff' and the authorities' assessments of behaviours and prospects. The sentence carried two safeguards. The first was that the courts could not pass it without first taking into consideration a report prepared for them by the Prison Commissioners or their representatives as to the suitability of the offender for the sentence within the criteria clearly specified in the Act. The second was that on discharge from the borstal the offender was at liberty under a properly supervised licence until such time as the term for which he or she was sentenced expired, unless sooner revoked or forfeited. He was also able to show that the available statistics for borstal sentences, contrary to Churchill's allegation, disclosed no evidence of an increasing tendency on the part of the courts to inflict the maximum borstal sentence. Most of the sentences were for eighteen months or less.[10] Nor could it be argued that even these last-mentioned sentences were for offences which would not in the ordinary course receive more than six months' imprisonment. It was precisely to guard against the courts passing unsuitable sentences that the Act specifically required them to consider reports from the Prison Commissioners or their representatives (usually the governors of the prisons where the offenders were held before trial) on the offenders' suitability or otherwise for borstal sentences.

Brise then challenged Churchill's criticisms that borstal training was 'bad in itself and only becomes good in relation to ... prison discipline'; and that it could be interpreted not as a 'beneficial discipline for poor lads, similar to the old system of apprenticeship'. He could find no basis for the first criticism in terms of his own lengthy observation of the custodial system. In fact, the contrary was the case (he hoped Churchill would pardon him for frankness). Furthermore, he regarded the purpose of borstal treatment as being to arrest the criminal habit by firm treatment and strenuous labour, and to prevent young persons while still impressionable 'from graduating inevitably to penal servitude'. The question of apprenticeship did not arise. Continued hard labour and physical exertion were the aim:

> to inspire the habit of industry which will enable a lad to settle down to a day's work on discharge ... We are not ambitious enough to pretend to teach these lads skilled trades,[11] but we are ambitious enough to believe in the formation of habit under stress of exact, but humane discipline, and under the influence of a daily task of labour carefully supervised, which, if well executed, will carry its own reward in the shape of earlier release and other priviliges [sic].

Brise next attacked Churchill's ladder of graduated sentences by claiming that this ladder already existed, rising from probation, through short and sharp local imprisonment, to the modified borstal system which was currently operating in all prisons. In certain of those (collecting centres) for young offenders serving prison sentences of less than four months, work was available under trade instructors, as was the opportunity to learn manual and even skilled labour. If all these initial stages failed, the full borstal system was available. He agreed that probation, still in its infancy, was a weak rung in the ladder, and that consequently there was too ready a resort to imprisonment in the first instance or to the 'ordinary mechanical alternative' of a fine, but these were matters which could be remedied in time. He also thought that reporting to a police station could form part of the probation service and went so far as to say that he was strongly in favour of it.

Waller supported Brise's presentation, although from a rather different angle.[12] In his days as Gladstone's private secretary, as he reminded Brise, he had sat through all the debates on the Prevention of Crime Bill as Gladstone had piloted it through the House. He was therefore able to confirm that it was not Parliament's intention when enacting the Bill that the length of the offender's borstal custody should be weighted according to the crime:

> Parliament, like the framers of the Bill, regarded Borstal Detention as a measure not merely as a punishment to deter, but of training and education to improve the offender who had embarked on a downward course; and recognized quite clearly that the month or so of ordinary imprisonment which might in former times have been regarded as adequate for the former purpose was quite insufficient for the latter.

On this particular point, Waller expressed himself more strongly than Brise:

> You do not play cricket and football in a prison. You do not associate in a common room with newspaper and weekly illustrated magazines in a prison. I gather that the Secretary of State has not yet seen Borstal and I venture to suggest that it might be desirable that he should acquaint himself with the System before issuing any general directions to alter the principles of commitment.

Waller went on to underline the point made by Brise as to the type of offender suitable for borstal training and drew attention to the stress the Commissioners had laid on this in their circular of 10 July 1909, which he suggested Churchill should consult.[13] Courts, in his view, understood perfectly well as a rule the conditions laid down by Parliament and impressed on them by the Commissioners. He was not in favour of laying down further instructions to them, but, if there was a case for doing so, he thought it would be sufficient to draw attention yet again to the Commissioners' 1909 circular. Nor did he think Parliament's own guidance about offenders suitable for borstal training set out in the 1908 Act could be improved upon.

On Churchill's erroneous point about borstal imprisonment being uniformly three years, his view was that if Churchill could succeed in persuading courts not always to give sentences of twelve months, he would have done a considerable public service. On the other hand, he did not think a uniform period of three years was necessary or desirable because some courts would be unwilling to commit for three years if that were fixed as a minimum. The fact was that 'large numbers of lads are licensed and placed out with perfect success at the end of twenty-one months or two years; a certain number at the end of eighteen months or so'. He favoured the retention of the three-year sentence as a maximum and fixing the minimum at two years for training purposes, while reminding the courts of the possibilities of early release on licence and the safeguard of a longer period of supervision and after-care. As for Churchill's view that borstal training was 'bad in itself', this was disproved, in Waller's view, by the 'sheaves' of letters written by discharged borstal inmates to the borstal chaplain.

Waller shared Brise's views on the ladder of graduated sentences, and, like him, noted the current weakness of the probation rung. It was a particularly useful one for dealing with Churchill's 'rowdy' youths, but the courts were not making sufficient use of it. He thought a circular from the Home Secretary would no doubt 'have a good effect' on bringing about an improvement.[14]

On 14 July Troup forwarded Brise's and Waller's memoranda to Churchill under cover of a short memorandum of his own,[15] wherein he recorded his agreement with 'the substance [his underlining]' of what they had said about borstal and borstal sentences. He also pointed out that Brise's graduated ladder of young offender sentences corresponded closely with Churchill's, apart from the latter's second stage – Swedish drill. What concerned him more, however, was that Churchill was due to address the Commons in six days' time: 'Sir Evelyn Ruggles-Brise is very anxious that you should read his memorandum and also Mr Waller's before you say anything about Borstal.'

Despite the clarity with which Brise and Waller had outlined Churchill's misunderstanding of the system as it currently operated, the Home Secretary did not formally accept defeat. In the course of his speech to the Commons on 20 July he aired his views on these matters at considerable length, informing Members that if he were in office during the following year he hoped 'to make more detailed proposals' for dealing with offenders under twenty-one.[16]

The very next day, indeed, he addressed a minute to Troup which included a demand for action on Swedish drill, the borstal regime and the conditions needed 'to justify a sentence of a month, six months, or three years' Borstal correction'.[17] Just over a month later, on 27 August, in a handwritten note on Troup's memorandum of 14 July, he commented:

> Read. We have got on rather beyond this now: some of the difficulties I felt at the outset have been removed by further study and reflection. But I contemplate prescribing an elaborate scale of minimum conditions of criminality before any lengthy sentences can be imposed.[18]

CHAPTER 6

Preventive Detention

The 1908 Prevention of Crime Act provided the courts with another new sentence, in addition to borstal detention: preventive detention. This was designed to curb crime committed by a designated class of habitual offenders.[1]

The preventive detention sentence had its origins in a recommendation of the 1895 Report, which identified 'a large class of habitual criminals' that the existing system of repeated short sentences had failed to combat satisfactorily. The report concluded that a new and cumulative sentence was required

> by which these offenders might be segregated for long periods of detention during which they should not be treated with the severity of first class hard labour or penal servitude, but would be forced to work under less onerous conditions. As loss of liberty would to them prove eventually the chief deterrent, so by their being removed from the opportunity of doing wrong the community would gain.[2]

The translation of this recommendation into legislative form, however, proved difficult, raising as it did such issues as the precise definition of 'habitual', the relationship between the proposed new sentence and penal servitude, and the length of the sentence, whether it should be fixed or indeterminate. A Bill of 1904, indeed, intended to provide the courts with the new sentence proved so controversial that it had to be withdrawn.[3] Nevertheless, this did not deter Gladstone, the author of the 1895 Report, from returning to the matter when he succeeded to the Home Secretaryship in 1905.

Section 10 of the 1908 Act concerned itself with persons convicted on indictment who subsequently admitted that they were, or were found by a jury to be, habitual criminals and on whom the courts had imposed a penal servitude sentence. If, then, the courts considered that by reason of their criminal habits and modes of life it was expedient for the protection of the public that the offender should be detained for a lengthened period, the courts might pass a further sentence. This would order that at the termination of the sentence of penal servitude the offender be detained for between five and ten extra years. This further custody constituted preventive detention.

Thus the Act did not seek to define habitual criminals. This was one of its weaknesses. Its authors were conscious of the omission and sought to bypass it by laying down two conditions which had to be fulfilled before criminals could be found to be habitual. The first was that the jury was obliged to find on evidence that, since attaining the age of sixteen, the offender had been convicted of at least three previous crimes, and was therefore leading a persistently dishonest or criminal life; or that he had previously been sentenced to preventive detention based on this criterion. The second condition was that a charge of being a habitual criminal should not be inserted in an indictment without the consent of the Director of Public Prosecutions and only then in accordance with certain requirements specified in the Act.[4]

There were two other important features of preventive detention. The first permitted the Home Secretary to act in the case of an offender sentenced to penal servitude for five years or more. He could commute the whole or any part of the residue after the first three years to a sentence of preventive detention. He must be satisfied that the offender had been a habitual criminal within the meaning of the Act, and the prisoner's combined term in penal servitude and preventive detention could not exceed his original sentence.[5] The second feature concerned the treatment of offenders under preventive detention. It provided for 'such modifications in the direction of a less rigorous treatment as the Home Secretary may prescribe by Prison Rules within the meaning of the Prison Act of 1898'. The treatment was required to reflect 'disciplinary and reformative influences', involving employment on 'such work as may be best fitted to make them able and willing to earn an honest livelihood on discharge'.[6]

On 20 July 1910 Churchill informed the Commons that, as a result of his examination of the court calendars, he had concluded that the working of the 1908 Act with respect to preventive detention needed careful scrutiny, particularly because of the disparity he had observed between different sentences.[7] He had discerned 'scores of cases which could just as properly be characterised as habitual as those which have been made the subject of special prosecution and of this extremely severe treatment'. He attributed this to the fact that, although the charge of being a habitual criminal could not be inserted into an indictment without the consent of the Director of Public Prosecutions, the latter nevertheless depended on the police authority in the prosecution case concerned for the information he required to carry out his statutory duties. Churchill was concerned about this because in his view police authorities lacked sufficient guidance on the compilation of their reports to the Director. He informed the House he was therefore considering how best to guide the police in their reporting functions in order 'to secure a much more general and a much more even application of these very special powers and sentences of such great severity which the House has thought fit in its wisdom to authorise in the past'.

Churchill concluded this part of his speech with a cautionary comment.

> There is a great danger of using smooth words for ugly things. Preventive detention is penal servitude in all its aspects. There may be modifications, but in the main it is a form of confinement and of surveillance which must necessarily be of a severe and rigorous character. I only hope those who are charged with the administration of this Act in its very early days will very carefully bear in mind the very severe character which all forms of penal detention must necessarily take in the present state of our prison system.

Churchill's definition of preventive detention as 'penal servitude in all its aspects' set alarm bells ringing in the Home Office and Prison Commission. Waller's private letter to Gladstone of 18 August 1910 explains why:

> I'm sorry to say that W.C. does not regard Preventive Detention with favour ... W.C. most unhappily said in the H. of C. Vote that 'P.D. was only Penal Servitude under another name'. Wallace [Sir Robert Wallace, at the time chairman of the County of London Sessions] has been foolish enough to take that up and make a pronouncement from the Bench saying if that is so he will beware of it – he thought it would be something quite different. W.C. is also trying to lessen the number of committals

to it. His point of view quite ignores the fact that P.D. will be no more and no less than he chooses to make it.[8]

Wallace's statement, in short, was being interpreted in the Home Office and Prison Commission as indicating the unravelling of the preventive detention provision in the 1908 Act.

Shortly after these proceedings, however, the whole matter moved out of the corridors of power and into the public arena as a result of the activities of a specific habitual offender, David Davies, the 'Dartmoor Shepherd'. He was detained in Dartmoor Prison under a preventive detention sentence, and Churchill chose to cite his case inside and outside Parliament as a good example of all that was wrong with the sentence and its modus operandi.[9]

Churchill first raised Davies's case publicly on 26 January 1911, and *The Times* published his account the following day. He explained that shortly after arriving at the Home Office he had begun to investigate the working of the Prevention of Crime Act, 'to find out whether or not it was increasing the severity and disparity of sentences'. A memorandum on this subject was laid before him listing everyone who up to then had been convicted as a habitual criminal, together with their punishments. Davies, then aged sixty-seven, had appeared before Shrewsbury Quarter Sessions on 19 October 1909, where he pleaded guilty to stealing two shillings from Whitchurch Parish Church in Shropshire and to being a habitual criminal. He was sentenced to three years' penal servitude, to be followed by ten years' preventive detention. Churchill was outraged by these sentences. Of the 120 prisoners named in the list before him, convicted up to then as 'habituals', there was, he declared, 'no crime so petty, and since the passing of the 1908 Act there have been only two sentences so long'. What struck him particularly was the 'grotesque contrast' between thirteen years of prison on the one hand and the theft of a mere two shillings on the other. 'It seemed', he said, 'impossible to balance the offence and the penalty against each other, or even to bring them into any possible relation.' This prompted him to call for a report on the circumstances of this particular case.

The report revealed that Davies had first been imprisoned in June 1870. His current sentence was his tenth. Of the previous nine, four had been under penal servitude, the rest under ordinary imprisonment. The penal servitude sentences were for seven, ten, fifteen and five years. The ordinary imprisonment terms were one month, eight months, one month, three months, and three months. Churchill described this litany of sentences as 'certainly not less terrible for its punishments than for its crimes'. He also observed that Davies 'enjoyed a melancholy celebrity for the prodigious sentences he had endured, for his docility and good behaviour in prison, and for his unusual gift of calling individual sheep by name'.

Nevertheless, Churchill declared that what struck him most was that there was nothing criminally daring or 'professional' about Davies. He did not go about his activities armed, the amounts stolen were always very small, the property was in most instances recovered, and Davies had never engaged in cruelty or violence. Churchill therefore asked whether the sentences Davies had received fitted his crimes:

> When we turn from the character and offences of the convict to the punishments he has received, a far more striking and unusual array is presented. David Davies has been sentenced to no less than fifty-one years' imprisonment, penal servitude, and preventive detention [Churchill is here including the 1909 sentences] and has actually served thirty-eight years in prison. The sentence of fifteen years' penal servitude which he received in 1887 for a burglary without any aggravating circumstances [a theft from a country house of clothing and other articles belonging to a butler and an usher] was one of extraordinary severity. Such sentences are usually reserved for the most dangerous and brutal crimes, short of actual murder. His last sentence of thirteen years [the 1909 sentence] was, for a man of sixty-seven years of age, to all intents and purposes a life sentence. He would in his [Davies's] own words, 'never see liberty again'.[10]

Churchill reinforced his arguments about proportionality by comparing Davies's criminal career with those of five other similarly circumstanced offenders, chosen at random from the court calendars of the various criminal sessions throughout the country. This indicated that the sentences of any two of these five men, 'all worse and more dangerous criminals than David Davies', when combined, were less than Davies singly had received. Aware as he was that wholly exact comparisons were not possible on the basis of the information available, he nevertheless took the view that Davies had been treated 'both in previous sentences and in his present sentence with a severity which, if not unparalleled, is certainly exceptional and excessive'.

At this point, Churchill rebutted arguments advanced in *The Times* on 16 January 1911 by a retired and distinguished High Court Judge, Sir Alfred Wills, whose attention had been drawn to the case by Lloyd George's reference to it at a hustings on 21 November 1910, reported in the *Daily News* the following day.[11] Churchill then went on to say that in July 1910, having studied Davies's case for some three months, he believed the prisoner should be given 'another chance', and that as soon as employment could be found for him he should be released on conditional licence. This meant that the sentence that had been passed upon him would not have to be set aside.

On 24 October 1910, when Churchill visited Dartmoor Prison, he used the opportunity to see Davies and to discuss his case with the prison authorities. 'Everything I heard and learned confirmed me in my intention,' he declared, 'and on my return to London I directed that he should be informed officially that he would presently be released on licence.' Preventive detention, Churchill concluded, 'may be applied without hesitation to dangerous and brutal criminals whose passions for predatory violence or ferocious lust render them a peril and affront to civilised society. Among such characters there are no grounds for including the pilfering shepherd of Dartmoor.'

The circumstances of individual prisoners in custody were not usually made public, but, thanks to Lloyd George's citation of the Davies case, parliamentary and public interest had been aroused and the 'Dartmoor Shepherd' became a *cause célèbre*. Nevertheless, released from prison under a licence obliging him to take up employment found for him by the Royal Society for the Assistance of Discharged Prisoners, he managed to disappear. His employment was located on a farm near Wrexham, where it was thought his shepherding talents could be put to good use. His licence required him to remain there for not less than six months unless he obtained the society's permission to leave earlier or was dismissed by his employer. Yet, within a few days of arriving at the farm, he absconded, and, despite all attempts to find him, including the use of a Welsh-speaking Scotland

Yard detective whom Churchill himself had specially assigned to the task, he eluded capture.[12]

Needless to say, all this was very embarrassing for Churchill. His critics, inside and outside Parliament, attacked him for releasing a man of Davies's character before the time set by his sentence, and there was a spate of parliamentary questions and newspaper articles about the case until Davies was eventually apprehended. The Conservative Party in particular revelled in the Home Secretary's discomfort.[13]

Apprehended on 1 April 1911, when he had forcibly entered from outside the cellar of Moreton Hall, a Shropshire country house, and stolen four bottles of whisky valued at £1, Davies was committed for trial at the Shrewsbury Assizes on 4 July. He received a sentence of nine months' imprisonment with hard labour and a requirement to serve in addition the unexpired one year and 187 days of his last penal servitude sentence. His life of petty crime continued until his death, well into his eighties, in 1929.[14]

If Churchill's speech to the Commons on 20 July 1910 made public his dissatisfaction with preventive detention and his championing of the Davies case illustrated the difficulties which would arise if measures to rework it were not put in hand, neither fully reflected the energy the Home Secretary had exerted on the issue. Discussions with the Director Public of Prosecutions (Sir Charles Matthews), Troup and Brise had been taking place in the privacy of the Home Office since June 1910 in an attempt to find a way of reworking the sentence to meet Churchill's objections to the current procedure. By 30 October 1910 these discussions had reached conclusions that would shortly be put into effect.

Churchill and Matthews had already been in discussion about preventive detention before the latter wrote to the former formally about the issue on 13 June.[15] Matthews stated he was guided by a Home Office circular of 6 September 1909 on the application of the 1908 Act, a document of considerable authority submitted to and approved by the judges prior to its issue.[16] He added it was his desire to conform to its widest, most lenient and most humane interpretation, but if it could be shown that he was wrong to do so, he was afraid he could not depart from his action without 'the sanction of the Attorney-General', the official head of his department. 'Of course,' he added, 'if it will please you to supersede Mr Gladstone's circular by one of your own upon somewhat different lines, you will need no reassurance that I shall be as anxious to carry out your views as I have been in endeavouring to fulfil those of your predecessor.'

Gladstone's circular, in Churchill's view, lacked the necessary rigour in its definition of habituality (and the nature of the offence precipitating the possibility of a habituality charge) to ensure fair proportionality between the offence and the sentence.[17] He concluded a new and clearer-worded circular was needed, and immediately dictated a memorandum to the Home Office's senior officials, asking them to draw one up. He offered them guidance in this in the form of conditions which should govern applications by the police to the Director of Public Prosecutions for authority to prosecute accused persons as 'habituals'. These conditions were: (a) that the accused's record should disclose three previous sentences of penal servitude, or of imprisonment of eighteen months and over; and (b) that the accused's immediate conviction should be for a serious crime, such as burglary, house-breaking, coining, blackmail, robbery with violence, and the like, excluding all forms of larceny unaccompanied by violence. To these conditions, Churchill added that all persons who were included in them should, in the absence of mitigating circumstances, be reported to the Director of Public Prosecutions as liable to prosecution as 'habituals'. 'None who do not fulfil them shall be so liable,' he wrote. 'The Police will make a special Report to the Director of Public Prosecutions upon each case sent forward. The Director of Public Prosecutions shall decide each case upon its individual merits guided by the general principles in the circular of 6 September 1909.'

On the same day that Churchill dictated this memorandum, the Prison Commissioners embarked on an exercise to determine the effect on the number of persons liable to face prosecution under 'habituality' if Churchill's proposed restrictions were applied to the selection process. They deemed that, out of 113 persons sentenced to preventive detention between 1 August 1909 and 31 March 1910 who were still under sentence, no less than 88.5 per cent would have escaped prosecution as habitual criminals (an alternative figure of 76 per cent was documented by Blackwell, who interpreted Churchill's criteria less generously).[18] Brise forwarded these figures to Troup and Churchill, making the point that they took insufficient account of offenders' early convictions and did not attach sufficient importance to larceny, which in some cases could be a very serious crime indeed.[19] The implication was that Churchill's proposed conditions created opportunities for too many accused persons to escape prosecution as habitual offenders. A new circular would have to be submitted to the judges before it could be issued, and it was certain they would not approve what amounted, as the figures indicated, to a wholesale repeal of Part II of the 1908 Prevention of Crime Act.

Brise suggested that Churchill's views might be accommodated if the Director of Public Prosecutions were asked to withhold permission to proceed in cases where, notwithstanding the prisoner's record, a sentence of penal servitude would not, in the Director's opinion, have been called for if the 1908 Act had not been passed. 'That would mean', he wrote, 'a slight modification of the Director's practice which would not entail the issue of a fresh circular to the Police.'

Troup forwarded a lengthy note to Churchill setting out his own views on the proposals in the light of Brise's letter.[20] He rightly pointed out that the very purpose of preventive detention was to increase the length of custody for habitual criminals. This, he stressed, was made clear in the 1895 Report; it was stated again in the speeches on the Bill; and it appeared in the Act itself. The sentence had been introduced because the old system – which led to constant alternation between short spells in prison and misused liberty – was useless and discredited. Prolonged detention under milder conditions should, therefore, break the cycle of frequent crimes and short sentences. 'It is', he added, 'in fact a part of the modern system which abandons the idea that the punishment should always be made to fit the crime and aims at making the punishment fit the criminal.'[21] Troup left Churchill in no doubt that it was 'useless to attempt to work Preventive Detention in such a way as not to prolong sentences'. Its essence was 'the prolongation of detention under easier conditions', and he concluded this part of his argument by saying that if it were held that such prolongation was wrong, then Part II of the Act 'ought to be repealed.'

Troup next turned his attention to Churchill's proposed conditions to limit the discretion of the police when preparing cases for scrutiny by the Director of Public Prosecutions. Here, too, he was just as hard-headed.

After pointing out what the effect of them would be, he commented that Churchill's condition (a) appeared to be *ultra vires*. The Act stated in express and definite terms how many and which previous conditions were necessary to qualify for indictment as a habitual criminal.[22] From this he adduced it was not 'properly speaking in the power of the Secretary of State or anyone else to impose a new condition to the effect that no previous conviction is to count unless a sentence was imposed of at least eighteen months'. Moreover, for the same reason, it seemed to be doubtful that Churchill's condition (b) was *intra vires*, for its effect was to exclude from his definition of 'crime' certain classes of offence that were expressly *included* in it by the Act. Indeed, some of the most serious crimes against property coming before the courts would be excluded from the operation of the Act.

Churchill reacted sharply to Brise's and Troup's comments. He set out his views fully in two memoranda.[23] In the first he pointed out that his note of 14 June was intended as a guide to a new circular, not as the new circular itself. He accepted that where larceny was serious there was no reason why it should not serve as the ultimate cause of the prosecution. He saw a simple solution as being the addition of 'petty' before 'larceny' in his earlier, (b), proposal: 'what would the effect be? Pray consider this,' he asked. He added that he would be willing to consider some small and reasonable modification of his other proposed condition, 'if it is desired to spread the net a little wider'.

Here, however, he came to the gravamen of his disagreement with Troup and Brise. 'The proposal put forward "that the Director of Public Prosecutions should be asked to withhold permission in cases where, notwithstanding the prisoner's record, a sentence of Penal Servitude would not in the Director's opinion have been called for if the Act had not been passed," is wholly inadequate, and does not begin to meet my views on this serious matter.' He was concerned by the lack of a uniform principle to regulate whether an application should be made to the Director of Public Prosecutions for authority to prosecute as 'habitual'. The matter was largely left to the personal judgement of numerous police forces up and down the country, 'not equally competent to settle grave questions of this character and with no common principle of action'. It was therefore a matter of chance whether application was made. Churchill maintained that his examinations of court calendars (and here one detects the influence of the Davies case upon his reasoning) showed a great many cases identical to or worse than those in which convictions of 'habituals' had been obtained and heavy sentences imposed where no prosecution had been instituted, and no application had ever been made to the Director of Public Prosecutions. He saw no attempt in the memoranda from Brise and Troup to resolve this. The real authority who decided effectively whether a prisoner should have a few months' imprisonment or up to thirteen years' penal servitude and preventive detention was, in his view, not the jury, nor the judge, 'but an obscure and irresponsible Police Officer deciding according to his lights, or his deficiencies, whether the fateful application shall be made or not'.

At this point in his analysis Churchill threatened his advisers with dire consequences if they did not come up with proposals more supportive of his view:

> It is to these aspects of the law that it will be my duty to draw the attention of Parliament, and unless I can see my way to regularise and mitigate its operation I shall be forced to subject the whole system to drastic legislative amendment. I rely, however, upon the Department to aid me in endeavouring to avoid legislative action.
>
> Let a case be stated for the Law Officers upon the question of whether such a circular as I have in mind would be *intra vires* or not. If not, in what form could it be cast to bring it within the existing law? To what extent can I compel the Police Authorities to make applications in all cases where certain conditions are fulfilled and forbidding them to make applications in cases where they are not? Of course, if the Act is hopeless, the sooner that is realised and steps are taken against it the better, but I defer coming to this conclusion until all other solutions have been exhausted.[24]

In his second memorandum Churchill asked Troup promptly to set in motion further enquiries of a statistical nature related to the detailed working of the preventive detention sentence, and apologized for the considerable additional burden these would impose on the department. He especially requested information on, first, 'the least six bad' of the existing cases already sentenced to preventive detention as 'habituals', considering together their records of previous convictions and the gravity of their final offences; and, second, from an examination of all the calendars of sentences imposed since the preventive detention legislation came into force, how many cases on these lines could have been made, according to paper record, the subject of similar 'habitual' prosecutions. This information was forwarded to him on 16 July.

Furthermore, Churchill demanded a great deal of information about the actions of the Director of Public Prosecutions. This included the number of applications made to him, together with the police forces making them; the number competent to make them; the number who had used their powers, and to what extent they had done so; the number of applications refused and approved by the Director; the number acquitted and convicted on the specific charges; the number not dealt with as 'habituals'; and any other figures bearing on this subject which might incidentally occur. This information did not reach Churchill until 27 July.[25] Nevertheless, he must have been given an indication of it beforehand, because he mentioned in his speech to the Commons on 20 July that 439 applications from police forces had been lodged with the Director between 1 August 1909 and that very day, with 305 being allowed by him. At the time of his speech, 174 people had been convicted as 'habituals' and sentenced to terms of penal servitude and preventive detention.

Churchill's solution arose out of the statistical information Brise presented to him. Brise himself recommended that no person who had not previously served a sentence of penal servitude should be indicted. He also suggested that the standard adopted by the Director with regard to past and present offences should be raised. He revealed that, in the course of discussions with the Director, Matthews had stated his willingness to raise the standard. Brise argued from this that Churchill's wishes in the matter could be realized by having further consultations with the Director and by the use of persuasive approaches on police applications. This would be more effective than imposing on the police, via a Home Office circular, a rigid sentence vis-à-vis past and present offences and forbidding the presentation of any person who fell below it. That could be done only by excluding certain offences (such as simple larceny) from the definition of 'criminal' contained in the Act.

Brise considered any attempt to standardize the punishment of criminals by reference to the *name* of the crime would lead to the most unequal results. It overlooked far more important considerations that needed to be taken into account, such as the age, character and antecedents of the criminal, and the circumstances in which the crime was committed. He pointed out that, of the 193 men already sentenced to preventive detention,[26] 45 were thirty or under, and, of these, 10 had not previously been sentenced to penal servitude; of those over thirty, 16 had not previously been so sentenced. This brought him to the crux of his argument about offenders' ages, and reflected his sound professional knowledge, derived from observing their behaviour in custody. He believed that some offenders aged under thirty, especially if they had already served a sentence of penal servitude, might well be fit subjects for preventive detention. As a general rule, however, a person under thirty who deserved to be indicted as a habitual criminal would stand a better chance of being saved from a life of crime by having a term of supervision by the new Central Aid Society after his penal servitude, rather than a period of preventive detention. Reformatory influences could be brought to bear on him in a convict prison as well as in a preventive detention establishment, where association with inmates much older than himself under less stringent disciplinary conditions was not likely to diminish his criminal persuasion. It would also be difficult to prescribe Rules for a less rigorous treatment under Section 13 (2) of the Act which would be suitable for both men under 30 and older 'habituals', who would constitute the majority of inmates at Camp Hill.

Brise concluded this part of his advice by explaining that the Director of Public Prosecutions was in full possession of Churchill's views on the subject of persons fit for indictment. His refusal of individual police applications and his reasons would soon lead to the adoption by the police of his standard. Meanwhile, no person would be indicted who did not come up to that standard. Nevertheless, he thought it would be advisable to direct the police, as far as was possible, not to present any person to the Director who was under thirty and had not previously served a sentence of penal servitude. He calculated that, allowing for exceptional circumstances, 50 of the 193 men already sentenced would have been excluded under this direction.

Churchill accepted Brise's advice, and on 30 October 1910 sent the proposed new arrangements to Matthews.[27] This letter explained that the police would be instructed in future not to submit any cases to him for prosecution as 'habituals' unless, apart from the statutory qualifications, they were over thirty and had been already sentenced to a term of penal servitude. They would be enjoined to consider very carefully with a view to submission to him the cases of every person thus qualified. Churchill expressed the hope that this might mitigate the inequalities which had arisen in the implementation of the Prevention of Crime Act, and might also go some way 'to restrict its scope'. Pending a trial of these arrangements, it was not intended 'to prescribe any other rigid rules to govern the actions of the police'.

Churchill then outlined his views on the standard by which applications for 'habitual' prosecutions should be judged. First, the criminal record of the accused should show, except in unusual cases, that he was not merely a nuisance but a danger to society. Violence conjoined with other crimes would in this connection appear to be an important factor. Second, the accused's general mode of life should be considered, and not only the period since his last discharge and new arrest. Any spell of honest work should count in his favour as showing that he was not a hopeless case. 'Hopelessness', declared Churchill, 'is a very important element in justifying Preventive Detention.' Third, the new crime ought, *in itself*, to be a substantial and serious offence. In saying this, Churchill clearly had in mind the case of the Dartmoor Shepherd, for he went on to add:

> Mere pilfering, unless accompanied by special circumstances of aggravation, should not in itself be made the occasion for a prosecution of such grave consequences, although the scale of a larceny is no certain measure of its guilt. The public conscience is shocked by the appalling disparity so often exhibited between the amount stolen and the sentence inflicted. Even if otherwise in all respects qualified, a man ought not to be sent to prison for so many years for a trifling offence.

Matthews's reply assured Churchill that no effort would be wanting, and indeed that very little effort would be required on his part to carry out Churchill's wishes.[28] This alluded to Churchill's Commons speech, when he had said that preventive detention was 'Penal Servitude in all its aspects.' Until then, Matthews stated, he had been under the impression that reform, not punishment, was to be the essence of preventive detention, or at least that it would equally combine reform and punishment. However, when Churchill had gone on to explain that the Home Secretary would have authority to make Rules for a less rigorous treatment of convicts, and that authority was not likely to be exercised to convert a prison into a reformatory, Matthews had concluded that criminals under thirty were not proper subjects for preventive detention. Since that time, he had, on his own initiative, ceased to present them.

In the light of the purpose of preventive detention as he now understood it, Matthews added that he was already working on the basis that presentation should not turn merely on 'persistently leading a dishonest life' but should be evidenced by violence or some other aggravating fact. He was, however, currently guided in determining such cases by the fact that punishment by the ordinary law including at least one term of penal servitude had proved ineffectual before he held the Act to apply.

He then asked Churchill to bear in mind that he still had problems when considering the question of presentation. Even so, he concluded, and Churchill must have found this very reassuring, 'whether my task be difficult or easy, I beg to assure you that in this, the third of the important subjects dealt with in your lucid and weighty letter, my best efforts will be made towards the fulfilment of your wishes'.

The police, at this stage, were informed very much on the lines of the correspondence already exchanged between Churchill and Matthews, that, in future, and in the interests of greater uniformity and the enforcement of the law against habitual criminals, a new methodology should be followed.[29] The letter notified the police that the Director of Public Prosecutions concurred with this, and expressed the Home Secretary's hope that the police would be careful, on the one hand, 'to bear in mind the conditions which should be satisfied before an offender could properly be indicted as an habitual criminal and would on the other hand use their best endeavours to submit with a view to proceedings under the Act the cases of all criminals who might appear to satisfy those conditions'. The opportunity was taken to remind them of the conditions: 'There must be three convictions of crime since the offender was 16 years of age; he must be 30 or more; he must have been sentenced at least once to penal servitude, and there must be evidence that he was leading persistently a dishonest or criminal life at the time he was arrested.' In conclusion, it was suggested that the police should also take the opportunity seriously to warn a criminal of the effect of the Act when it appeared probable that by continuing in his existing way of life he would soon bring himself within its provisions.

Having dealt with this, it was now necessary to prepare statutory Rules for the operation of the preventive detention regime and Standing Orders to guide the governors concerned with their application at Camp Hill on the Isle of Wight for men and Aylesbury for women.[30] Churchill took a keen interest in their drafting.[31] The Rules, however, had to be tabled for parliamentary approval before they could be brought into force and had to include an explanatory memorandum. As provisionally sanctioned by Churchill on 4 January 1911, the Rules were tabled in their final form on 17 February 1911 and came into operation on 1 May.[32] Camp Hill was opened on 5 March 1912.[33]

The explanatory memorandum informed Parliament of the Home Secretary's views on preventive detention and its application to individual cases.[34] The draftsman was in all probability Troup, in his capacity as permanent under-secretary of state, but the words and phraseology in which it is couched are clearly Churchill's. The memorandum neatly encapsulates his penal thought at this time and so deserves careful consideration.

It explains that the Rules being laid before Parliament give effect to the requirements of the 1908 Prevention of Crime Act, which requires persons undergoing preventive detention to be generally subject to the convict prison Rules, albeit tempered by new Rules which oblige the Home Secretary to modify the conditions of custody 'in the direction of a less rigorous treatment'. It goes on to say that the Rules had been drawn up by the Prison Commissioners to make the conditions of preventive detention custody 'as easy as circumstances would allow'. Such modification of the convict prison Rules, however, did not alter the fact that preventive detention remained imprisonment. Several hundred criminals 'of the most skilful and determined class' had to be confined within prison walls for a considerable time and by a staff which could not be too numerous without undue expense. This meant that during their custody prisoners always had to be held in locked cells or under close supervision. Discipline had to be maintained and hard work enforced if escape, mutiny or vice were to be avoided. It was therefore important to understand (and here Churchill was clearly referring to the closing sentences of the peroration to his speech to the Commons on 20 July 1910) that, while it was possible to maintain the sufficiency of food, adequacy of clothing, warmth and shelter which were available to all convicts, *and* to allow further relaxations by way of conversation, association, minor luxuries and recreation, nevertheless the convict remained completely deprived of his liberty and was subject to constant control and supervision in everything he did. The idea should not be allowed to grow that preventive detention was 'a pleasant and easy asylum for persons whose moral weakness or defective education had rendered them merely a nuisance to society'.

The memorandum then reminded Parliament that an important reason for the mitigations of convict life was to allow for the longer detention of persons who were 'professional criminals engaged in the most serious forms of crime'. Attention was here drawn to the repeated statements of Churchill's predecessor, when the preventive detention sentence was under consideration in Parliament: the measure was devised:

> for 'the advanced dangerous criminal', for 'the persistent dangerous criminal', for 'the most hardened criminals': its object was 'to give the State effective control over dangerous offenders'; it was not to be applied to persons who were 'a nuisance rather than a danger to society', or to the 'much larger class of those who were partly vagrants, partly criminals, and who were to a large extent mentally deficient'.

Thus, the sentence was not concerned with all habitual criminals. Rather, it was 'an exceptional means of protecting society from the worst class of professional criminals'. This explained why the legislation not only restricted 'the use of Preventive Detention to people already found deserving of three years' Penal Servitude', but provided 'many safeguards against the too easy use of the new form of punishment'.

Experience of the implementation of the legislation so far indicated the need for uniformity of procedure within the country's 180 police forces. Here the memorandum rehearsed the arrangements already agreed upon by the Home Office and the Director of Public Prosecutions and communicated to the police.

With that, the memorandum closed with an expression of hope for the future, holding out the possibility of further treatment mitigations once a better idea of the amount of punishment involved in a preventive detention sentence had been gauged.

* * *

Churchill left the Home Office almost five months before the first batch of preventive detention prisoners arrived at Camp Hill, and therefore had no responsibility for overseeing the operation of the prison and its regime. Nevertheless, he must have been aware that his intervention had effected a dramatic impact on the number of men sent there. Between 1 August and 31 December 1909, 45 men had been sentenced to preventive detention, a number which rose to 177 in 1910, the first full year of the sentence's operation, the year in which Churchill was reworking it. However, following Churchill's new guidelines of January 1911 this figure (177) was drastically cut: to just 55 in 1911, and 88 in 1912, a figure it would never attain again.[35] Churchill had achieved his objective: he had reduced the prison population, while keeping people who were a danger to society safely under lock and key.

CHAPTER 7

Abatement of Imprisonment: Draft Administration of Justice Bill, 8 April 1911

On 20 July 1910, in the Commons, Churchill declared, 'The first real principle which should guide anyone trying to establish a good system of prisons should be to prevent as many people as possible getting there at all.'[1] With these words he signalled his legislative intentions to abate prison sentences.

Less than a month later, in an eight-page document which he circulated to Masterman (his parliamentary under-secretary of state), his senior Home Office officials and Brise, Churchill referred to statistics he had for 1909.[2] In that year, 61 per cent of all sentences passed had been of less than a fortnight: 'nearly 125,000 perfectly purposeless short sentences imposed every year, and of these more than a half imposed upon first offenders ... I want you to consider and advise me how this gigantic number of useless and often pernicious committals can be abolished, or, at least, vastly abated.' He had two principles in mind: petty criminals should *never* be sent to prison for one specific offence and they should *never* be sent to prison for less than a month. Whether they were juvenile adults, prostitutes, inebriates or vagrants, 'there should be a considerable period of statutory warning, and then a disciplinary sentence of adequate length and suitable character'. Based on these principles, he offered some suggestions.

The main one was that in the event of a court opting for a sentence of less than one month's duration, it should, or the Secretary of State might, declare that the sentence was 'suspensory'.[3] Measures would have to be taken to ensure the identification of the offender, who, on subsequent conviction, might be compelled to serve his old sentence or sentences in addition to any new one. All this, however, should be conditional on such sentence or sentences added to the new one amounting to no more than one month in the aggregate; also that no person should be called upon to serve outstanding suspended sentences if not convicted afresh within, say, two years. Churchill further floated the idea of adding a provision enabling the courts to impose a sentence of one year on an offender convicted more than three times in twelve months, and of two years on one convicted more than six times in twenty-four months.

He was positive that nothing should be allowed to prejudice the existing operation of the Probation of Offenders Act. The courts would still have the option not to pass even a suspended sentence of imprisonment on first or infrequent offenders; the power of the courts to award a fine in lieu of suspended imprisonment should not be impaired; and, as time to pay the fine would not be necessary with a suspended sentence, the special legislation contemplated on this point would be superseded. Moreover, defaulter's drill for juvenile–adult offenders should be regarded as a way of increasing the range and flexibility of treatment meted out to younger petty offenders, and as a substitute in petty cases for short suspended sentences of imprisonment.

The Prison Commissioners had long lobbied senior Home Office officials and successive Home Secretaries to persuade the courts to make more use of second-division sentences in local prisons and to abolish the 'hard labour' option, as, over the years, it had lost its significance. Churchill took the opportunity to respond to their plea, while also insisting he did not envisage any alteration to the current power and discretion of the courts with respect to the length and character of the sentences they imposed, except as required by the foregoing statutory provisions he had suggested. All the same, he thought that, rather than 'circularising them extensively on the difference between first and second division sentences and sentences with and without hard labour', power should be taken by the Home Secretary (if, indeed, it did not already exist) 'to make any administrative modifications, not in excess of the original sentence, which he may think convenient and desirable'. With this end in view, he envisaged the establishment of a board, or a system of coordinated boards, of classification. Immediately an offender left the court, under whatever sentence had been imposed on him, his case should be reviewed administratively by the board to determine the treatment 'most suitable to his circumstances and character'. He regarded this procedure as 'a mere extension, possibly not needing any legislation, of the Parliamentary Rule recently made in regard to privileged prisoners'.[4]

To ensure that prisoner classification was effective, Churchill considered that some twenty principal categories would be required. Each should be distinguished by the particular treatment in which it specialized. Churchill envisaged these various treatments as falling under three main headings: penal, corrective and detentive. Penal treatment would be the lot of convicts, recidivists and persons sentenced to long terms of imprisonment with hard labour. Corrective treatment would be reserved for all forms of borstal training and all sentences for petty offences. Detentive treatment would be for 'persons sentenced as habituals, the weak-minded offender, and inebriates'.

However, for Churchill it was not enough that sentenced offenders should be categorized: the categories themselves had to be conveniently distributed throughout the prisons of the country. He attached a great deal of importance to this: it stood for a rationalization of the prison system and the more effective use of its resources:

> If the prisons were cleared of all the enormous burdens of purposeless congestion for petty offences, a far greater specialization in the treatment offered by each prison would become possible. Instead of having a lot of prisons of substantially the same type and reproducing the same features, scattered about all over the country, we should have a regular series of scientifically graded institutions which would gradually and increasingly become adapted to the treatment of every variety of human weakness.

Churchill thought the effect of a substantial reduction in the number of persons committed annually to prison and the abolition of *all* sentences of under a month, 'even if to some extent discounted by the increase in the length of sentences, in certain classes of cases, should afford a most valuable relief and easement to the whole administration of the prisons'. It would also enable classification 'to proceed with far greater refinement than at present'. He conceded that some new institutions would have to be built, but, if a reduction of 'even 10% in the average number of the daily prison population were secured, there would be a great deal of elbow room in the existing buildings and many changes would be possible, which are now impossible without heavy expenditure.' He thought, too, that relief of this kind would also benefit prison staff, freeing them from 'the heavy special duties connected with the reception and discharge of vast numbers of prisoners on petty sentences', giving them 'more time and strength to deal with the increasingly specialized duties which will gradually devolve upon them'.

Churchill concluded this lengthy memorandum by asking his senior Home Office officials and the Prison Commissioners to supply him with the statistics essential for the compilation of a detailed plan whereby his ends could be realized. He displayed all his usual thoroughness, including a request for information on the easement to prison accommodation and staff which would follow from a 33 per cent reduction in annual committals to prison, and from a reduction of up to 15 per cent in the annual average prison population. He also wanted a report 'in as full a detail as possible' upon the circumstances and conditions of the offences and offenders 'in the 61% dealt with last year by sentences of under a fortnight or less'.

His suggestions were forward-looking, good examples of the new thinking he was trying to introduce into the criminal justice branch of the Home Office and the Prison Commission. They recall his earlier remark to Blunt: 'I am dead against the present system and if ever I am at the Home Office I will make a clean sweep of it.'[5] He was now making a bid to do just that. Perhaps, too, he may have considered that, if his ideas were consolidated in an Act of Parliament, his reputation as a social reformer would be enhanced and his opportunity for yet more political advancement furthered.

Both Brise and Blackwell delivered early 'off-the-cuff' comments on Churchill's suggestions. Their ideas were sensible, practical and helpful.[6] Brise then came forward with a more considered opinion in a fifteen-page letter to Troup.[7] He asked that this should also not be treated as his final view because he was due to sail to America the following day and he was not therefore able to give Churchill's 'vast projects' the attention they merited.[8] It was, indeed, only at Churchill's special request that he was committing his thoughts to paper.

At the outset, he stressed he was 'strongly in favour of prison reform' along Churchill's indicated lines, and he reminded Troup of the views he had often repeated to him on the 'great evil both social and political of short sentences and unnecessary commitments and of the failure of the Courts to use such powers of classification as they possess'. Thereafter, he dealt with each of Churchill's suggestions.

He believed that, broadly speaking, these were already operating, on the understanding that penal servitude corresponded with the penal, the local prison and borstal systems with the correctional, and inebriate and debtor confinement with the detentive principle.[9] All the same, he realized the existing arrangement did not precisely meet Churchill's specifications, which he interpreted as reserving the penal principle for the worst offences, the correctional for offences which were less so, and the detentive for persons whom time limits had little effect. Nevertheless, he thought the existing arrangement could be translated into Churchill's plan on condition that it was recognized there was 'no real distinction in essence between the class of man who receives a sentence of penal servitude or of imprisonment for a grave indictable offence'. The first step required in a logical penal system, he averred, would be to abolish the term 'penal servitude' and to use penal servitude prisons, along with a selected number of local prisons, 'as places for the punishment of grave indictable crime'.

As far as correctional prisons were concerned, he envisaged them being populated by offenders convicted of indictable offences and tried summarily, together with those similarly tried whose offences involved moral turpitude. He added, 'the treatment to those above a certain age would be on the lines of the present local prison treatment, which contains a strong deterrent element'. The term 'hard labour' would disappear, 'and with it much confusion and mischief'. The prisons selected for 'correctional' treatment would be those affording the best opportunity for dealing with longer sentences. He did not think the cost of transfer would be prohibitive if the prisoners sentenced to the shorter terms were not transferred for the special treatment, 'which, of course, would be useless unless there was time for it to take effect'.

Turning to detentive treatment – 'the great and pressing need of the hour' – he considered that Churchill's wish to reduce the prison population by dispensing with useless and mischievous commitments could be met along the legislative lines he had suggested: by recourse to labour colonies for vagrants and habitual petty offenders, and special institutions for weak-minded prisoners, inebriates and prostitutes. Based on the most recent judicial statistics, he suggested that if detentive provision were created for all these offenders, the average prison population could be reduced by a third. The economies resulting from a development of this kind 'might largely compensate the initial cost of special institutions for the classes named'.

As far as classification by special board and treatment in separate institutions were concerned, Brise displayed many misgivings. If Churchill's suggestions were to be implemented, he considered the existing and distinctive sentence of penal servitude would have to be abolished altogether, and all grave offences classified under one heading. Only long sentences would then come up for classification, and only to them could classification be applied with any real chance of success. In this context, he saw the Prison Commissioners, in their legal capacity as Directors of Convict Prisons, continuing to be the natural authority for all cases falling within the proposed new category of 'penal sentences'. In so doing, he assumed that no sentence for grave indictable crime would be less than six months, and that, subject to this limitation, the Commissioners would be 'quite able to order the classification'. He feared that any other system or multiplication of boards and classifying authorities would collapse, 'to say nothing of the grave impingement on the authority of courts of law which would be strongly resisted'.

Implicit in Churchill's suggestions, it seemed to Brise, was a requirement for the executive to play a larger role in the judicial process. Brise's conclusion was that there were serious obstacles, especially with the judiciary, to classifying prisoners by a special board and treating them in separate institutions. If, on the other hand, these obstacles, with the consent of the judiciary, could be overcome, he saw great advantage in indeterminate sentences (to which, it will be remembered, Churchill was opposed) for the 'individualization' of penal practice, subject only to the provision

> that the Commissioners, in cooperation with the Secretary of State's Office, should be the determining authority as to the date of release in the case of every man sentenced under the indeterminate system. The establishment of classification boards to interfere with all sentences, long and short, would, in my opinion, be a fatal mistake.

He took his stand on the principle that there were only three bodies which could give 'a sound or wise opinion as to the treatment of an individual prisoner'. These were:

1. The court which tries the prisoner.
2. The prison authorities who have the man in their custody and under their observation.
3. The Home Secretary, who, with a view to public policy, can judge each case on general principles.

Brise believed that, if probation were to be an effective alternative to imprisonment, it would have to be operated by the country's police forces. This was certainly true for all offenders whose cases demanded an assertion of the power, dignity and deterrence of the law, he argued. However, he conceded that authorities of a charitable nature could supervise the probation of offenders if their cases were suitable for benevolence and kindliness. 'The Probation Officer, though a good and earnest man,' he wrote, 'often connected with religious or other societies, is obviously not competent to assert the dignity and force of the law.' For all trivial offences, especially where committed by young offenders, he favoured a suspended sentence of not less than one month, formally entrusting them meanwhile to the police of the localities concerned, who would be responsible for their behaviour for such length of time as the court prescribed.[10] Brise further thought that if the court saw fit, it should also be able to supplement the suspending order by an additional one obliging the defender to undergo defaulter's drill at the relevant police station. Police manpower ceilings would have to be raised to bear the additional responsibility, and this, of course, would need funds, but, in his view, not a 'considerable amount'.

His verdict on all these matters was thus very agreeable to Churchill: 'I regard the views of the Secretary of State as to the cooperation of the system of suspension with that of police probation, as a most effective alternative for imprisonment, and, in that way, a cure for the great evil of unnecessary commitments and short sentences.'

On the issue of cumulative penalties, Brise cautioned that, if Churchill's views were to be adopted, offenders would graduate quickly into longer sentences. They would pass through the correctional filter and into the penal one, although the offence might be trivial and not necessarily identical with previous ones. In all likelihood, such offenders would be vagrants, drunkards or habitual recidivists; and, if they did not qualify for detentive custody, there would have to be power to subject them to penal treatment under a longer sentence, where they would be classified by the prison authorities.

Brise saw identification as being the most serious problem here. Certainly this was already the case with 'vagrants, loafers, and idlers', because they were continually on the move. This could be countered only by an enormous extension of the finger-printing system, which currently applied solely to those engaged in serious crimes who had been sentenced to at least one month in prison. Increased police manpower ceilings and costs would be unavoidable. Nevertheless, this was a fact that had to be faced, for, as Brise remarked, 'it lay at the root of any system which aims, not only at finding alternatives for imprisonment, but also at the consequential following up of petty offenders who relapse into crime after a warning given'.

Brise concluded his memorandum by supplying Churchill with all the statistical data he had requested, apart from one item. This concerned the circumstances and conditions of the 61 per cent of offenders from 1909 who had received sentences of under a fortnight. Instead, Brise submitted a return giving particulars of those in this category who were in custody on 31 August 1910.[11] However, in the case of the note Churchill had requested concerning the easement to prison accommodation and staff which would accrue from a reduction of one-third in the annual committals to prison, and from a reduction of up to 15 per cent in the average annual prison population, Brise was obliged to draw attention to the unavoidable administrative fact that no appreciable reduction of staff would follow from a reduction of even 10 per cent of the population, owing to the large number of small and scattered prisons, all of which would still require a minimum number of staff. Troup forwarded Brise's memorandum to Churchill, along with his own observations on short sentence suspension and imprisonment for debt,[12] the two points on which Brise had not commented, because they were already being dealt with in the Home Office. Troup stated that, if Churchill's suggested suspended sentences were to have 'fair chance' of success, it would be necessary to exclude two classes of offences from their operation. The first embraced offences so bad that it was unlikely public opinion would allow even short first sentences in respect of them to operate under suspension – aggravated assaults on women and girls, cruelty to children and animals. Also excluded should be offences such as street-betting and brothel-keeping, where the return of the offender to his or her former way of life would be so certain that to make the offence suspended 'would be a farce'. Churchill subsequently annotated his agreement to the exclusion of these offences.

The second class included a large number of offences ordinarily punished by fines, for which the penalty of imprisonment was the ultimate sanction, even though it was rarely invoked. These offences had been created in the first instance 'to give compulsory force to the new branches of modern "social" legislation'. These 'branches' included: food and drugs; diseases of animals; explosives; fisheries; mines; factories; employment of children; public health; weights and measures; and revenue. Troup calculated that in 1908 16,216 fines had been levied in respect of all these offences, of which only 368 had led to imprisonment in default of payment. He pointed out that if the offender could count on practical immunity for his first offence, law enforcement would be greatly weakened. Churchill annotated his agreement to exclude these offences too, but this time added, 'subject to "grace to pay"'.

Troup next drew attention to the sentences involving imprisonment remaining under Churchill's scheme. They amounted in all to some 130,000, once allowance had been made for the aforementioned exclusions. They covered: drunkenness; prostitution; vagrancy; Poor Law offences; larceny, embezzlement and so on, tried summarily. This figure accounted for two-thirds of the total of 184,000 cases of imprisonment for criminal offences. In addition there were 'several thousand cases of street obstruction, trespass, etc.'. He thought that suspended sentences might be applied 'to these cases and to some others, but too much should not be expected of them'.

Troup was troubled that, while sentences of fourteen days or less formed Churchill's 61 per cent of the total number received in prison, a very different figure emerged when consideration was given to the proportion of the prison population which on any one date was under sentence of fourteen days or less. Short sentences bulked largely in the annual returns of prisoners received, 'but as each short sentenced man was only a short time in prison, he affected the prison population in a much less degree, and *only about 15% of the prison population were under sentences of fourteen days or less*.[13] Troup therefore concluded that even if half of them could be eliminated by suspended sentences, in the end the prison population would be reduced by only 8 per cent. He doubted, indeed, that even this could be achieved, because he thought this figure would be outweighed by the increased number of sentences of one month or more. Regard in this respect had to be paid to the large number of short sentences passed on tramps, drunkards and prostitutes who had already been in prison within the last two years. These, under Churchill's suggested scheme, would be increased by one month. Similarly, while, under Churchill's scheme, first offenders would receive a suspended sentence, if they offended again, the courts would be obliged to sentence them to a month, rather than a much shorter term. Troup here gave vent to his 'strong impression' that the scheme 'would not tend to decrease but to increase the prison population ... and would therefore not assist in any way towards the very desirable object of providing accommodation and staff for the further classification and better treatment of prisoners under longer sentences'.

Churchill, however, was not altogether persuaded by this gloomy prognosis, for he annotated Troup's argument thus: 'This depends on the conditions we prescribe as governing the infliction of the more serious punishments.' Troup's statements of the difficulties ahead were well argued, but in Churchill's mind they could be overcome.

In concluding what he had to say about suspended sentences, Troup drew attention to the point made in Brise's memorandum about the need for an accurate record of offenders' identities. He thought this would require 'elaborate and costly machinery'. The legal effect of the sentence would depend on the prisoner's identity, which would have to be judicially proved, something rarely required at the time. This would lead to many remands, which would fill the prisons and cause as many problems 'as the short sentences now do'. Once again, Troup had made a valid point.

Once again, however, Churchill was not to be thwarted: 'Finger prints,' ran his annotation: 'this is being examined.' And, on Troup's point about an increase in the prisons' remand population and its attendant problems, he noted, 'this difficulty must be encountered and conquered'. He was determined to have suspended sentences, whatever the obstacles.

Churchill's suggestions for abating the scale of imprisonment, as set out at the beginning of this chapter, had not mentioned action of any kind for diminishing the number of persons imprisoned for failure to pay their debts. Nevertheless, the matter was being dealt with in the Home Office at the time in connection with other business, which probably explains why Troup saw fit to refer to it in connection with Churchill's abatement memorandum. Clearly, if debtors could be dealt with other than by imprisonment, the number of people in prison would fall. Moreover, Troup would be aware of Churchill's minute of 23 August to senior Home Office officials about this matter.[14] Troup's view was that the credit system could not be passed over lightly. If, however, the penal context was the only consideration, he could think of ways of reducing the number of cases of imprisonment for debt without resorting to its abolition. Thus he alluded to a belief current at the time that a judge on the Durham Circuit, by his handling of certain cases, had in effect abolished imprisonment as a sentence for debt. (All the judge had done was to restrict imprisonment to cases where it was likely to be effective in enforcing debts; that is to say, where the debtor had the means to pay. The judge, indeed, was opposed to the abolition of imprisonment as the final sanction to secure debt repayment.) 'I have no doubt', declared Troup, 'that if other Judges and Registrars took as much trouble as he has done to enquire into the cases and to commit only where there is real evidence of means, imprisonment throughout the country would be reduced by 90% without affecting the existing system of credit.' He said that Churchill had 'a very strong case' against maintaining the system of credit, and in this context it was right to propose abolition, 'even if it should ultimately be necessary to retrace our steps for part of the way'. Churchill added another of his annotations: 'and without creating new crimes'.

Troup concluded his memorandum by saying he was strongly in favour of a reform of the prison system in the direction of more effective sentences and better classification. He refrained from discussing details but set out the following suggested headings for the reform scheme as he now saw it developing:

- Abolish hard labour: it existed only in name. Churchill annotated: 'then there is little gained in abolishing it. On the other hand it would excite an outcry and much misunderstanding.'
- Abolish the distinction between second- and third-division treatment, the courts having failed to apply it in the way Parliament had intended, and entrust its application entirely to the Prison Commissioners, who currently conducted the only effective classification, that between 'Stars' and 'Non-Stars'. To this, Churchill annotated: 'Yes.'
- Creation of a broad distinction between short sentences, if good for anything, only deterrent in character, 'making the prisoner hate for ever the name of prison'; and long sentences, always reformist in character, 'except in the case of the hopelessly weak-minded', reflecting 'careful classification and grouping, continuous instruction in manual work, graduated remission, and all the other reformatory methods the Prison Commissioners have so successfully introduced for convicts and Borstal lads'. Between these particular sentence lengths there should be no further sentences. Troup here expressed doubt as to whether the complete prohibition of short sentences was possible, but asserted that, if it were attempted, its best chance of success might be in relation to vagrancy offences, such as begging and sleeping out, petty larceny and street offences. Drunkenness and prostitution, on the other hand, were doubtful additions. On this, however, Churchill annotated: 'I am very anxious that drunkenness and prostitution should be treated in the series rather than in the instance.' Extension of the probation system by empowering the courts to make penal drill (to which Churchill added 'including "punishment school"'[15]) a condition of probation, and in such a case to appoint police officers to act as probation officers. Troup thought the Home Secretary might be empowered to define by Rule the cases where, and the conditions under which, this should be done.
- Enable sentences of seven days or less to be served in police stations where there is proper accommodation. To this, Churchill annotated: 'Yes.'
- Abolish imprisonment for debt. Churchill annotated: 'Yes.'
- Imposition of fines for stealing more than forty shillings (added to the foregoing list in Churchill's own handwriting which, however, specified no maximum limit to the fines).

To all these headings of reform, but constituting part of the scheme for the better classification of convicted offenders implicit in them, Troup incorporated three proposals recommended by committees or royal commissions: the control and care of the feebleminded; the amendment of 'the present useless and ineffective law concerning inebriates'; and the creation of institutions for detaining habitual vagrants.

Shortly after Troup had suggested these headings, he produced a more formal version under the title 'Heads of Proposed Abatement of Imprisonment Bill'.[16] Meanwhile, Churchill had laid before the Cabinet his proposals for abating the scale of imprisonment, based largely on his recent correspondence with Asquith. Despite an attack on the proposed introduction of defaulter's drill for certain young offenders by Walter Runciman, President of the Board of Education, the Cabinet accorded its approval.[17]

Troup's formal draft made no reference to probation, none to the imposition of fines for stealing over forty shillings, and none to special institutions for the feeble-minded, inebriates and habitual vagrants, although it added suspended sentences. The drafting was general in character and avoided all mention of the administrative problems that would have to be overcome in practice.

According to a memorandum from Troup to Churchill dated 1 November 1910, the former showed this draft to Brise and asked him for comments on 'any points which he wanted to question'.[18] However, in Troup's words, 'owing to a misunderstanding', Brise treated this request for his input as 'official and sent up the annexed official minute'.[19]

This annexed minute was largely concerned with unmentioned detail in Troup's 'Heads of Proposed Abatement of Imprisonment Bill', which in Brise's view would have to be thoroughly teased out before detention in police stations, courts and night schools could be implemented. The issue of finger-printing needed to be faced because of the large number of people who would be remanded for identification. Measures would also be needed for medical inspection, diet, the right of petition in cases of ill-treatment and so on. All of these issues would have consequences for prison clerical staff and the availability of accommodation. Brise framed his minute very much from a prison administrator's angle. He was primarily conscious of the realities of the daily operational scene and thought it was premature to be discussing the headings for a parliamentary Bill before these issues had been properly resolved. He was also strongly critical of suspended sentences, unless there was a mechanism in place for their supervision. On his recent visit to the United States he had been impressed by these sentences because they were supervised by 'a highly organized system of probation'. Moreover, probation officers collected fines in instalments as well as restitution for damage. He drew attention once again to the need for a proper system of finger-printing to be in place before a system of suspended sentences could operate effectively.

Brise could find no mention in Troup's 'Heads of Proposals' (or 'draft Bill', as he now preferred to call it[20]) of the three general categories of prisoner classification – penal, corrective and detentive – to which Churchill had referred in his memorandum of 13 August, and he assumed that Churchill had therefore abandoned these ideas. In particular, it seemed to him that 'detention' in terms of long periods and for specific categories under specific treatment had given way to detentive treatment under austere conditions for trivial offenders lasting a period of more than one month. Imprisonment, strictly so-called, appeared to commence on sentences of three months, 'with power to the Commissioners to classify offenders'. This classification would take into account character and antecedents, but not, he inferred, capacity to labour. These two classifications would clash. He welcomed classification being entrusted to the Commissioners,[21] but if classification for labour was intended, it should be remembered that over 80 per cent of the committals were for one month and under, and only 5 per cent were for six months and over – 'the period regarded by practical men as the indispensable minimum for trade instruction, with profit to the individual and without loss to the state'.

It might be possible, Brise thought, for the Commissioners to do more for the classification of treatment and labour than was currently being done, if they 'had a free hand and if all sentences under three months were abolished'. He considered classification on an individual character basis impracticable, except in a very general way: for example, by distinction generally between cases showing and those not showing 'moral turpitude'. Troup annotated his disagreement with this particular statement: 'Surely the weak-minded can be separated,' he wrote, 'and there is the distinction between "stars" and old offenders which is now made.'

Brise also cautioned about the movement of convicted prisoners from one prison to another on grounds of cost, and because it was undesirable to move them through public places, unless this was definitely beneficial for both the state and the prisoner. He stressed, too, the extraordinary strength of local sentiment and tradition which attached to local prisons, and the local opposition which was encountered when relatives and friends of prisoners had to travel long distances to see them.[22] All the same, he thought the principle of 'collecting prisons' for the various categories was 'strictly a right one', and would be profitable under a system of longer sentences than obtained in Britain. He remained doubtful, however, even with 'all the goodwill in the world', if these movement and location issues implicit in the abatement headings could be accomplished to justify the expenditure and dislocation involved.

On these headings, however, Brise's overall conclusion was bleak and blunt: they had not been properly thought through from the essential angle of the prison administrator:

> Although the Commissioners see great difficulty in carrying out the changes referred to in the HO memorandum [the abatement headings] and are not in favour of many of the proposals, they wish it to be distinctly understood that they are most strongly in accord with the desire of the Secretary of State to mitigate or remove the great and admitted evil of short sentences of imprisonment under the existing law and practice.

By saying this, Brise placed himself under an obligation to state what the Commissioners would do to ensure 'any real and effective alteration of the Prison System on the principles laid down by the Secretary of State from time to time'. They had five proposals. First, they suggested the abolition of the legal distinction between sentences with and without hard labour. Its existence greatly hampered prison administration, confused the courts and (crucially, in Brise's view) created 'a false conception in all Foreign Countries of the character of the English Prison System, which ought to be an example to the world'. Second, the Commissioners wished to have no sentence of imprisonment for a period of less than four months. They thought that ordinary and trivial offences against the law should be dealt with by 'detention under penal discipline' for a period not exceeding one month, but that this penalty should not be invoked until all the alternatives suggested in Troup's abatement headings had been applied. Third, they considered no sentences should be suspended without probation oversight. They wanted a corpus of probation officers, selected from the police or otherwise, attached to every court, to whose care and supervision every case of suspension should be referred. Fourth, they suggested vagrants, drunkards and 'defectives' should be dealt with in a separate category, under special laws, and interned for long periods. Finally, they proposed the formation of a Probation Commission to ensure the proper working of the probation system. All probation officers would act under its authority and be accountable to the Home Secretary. They viewed probation as 'the alternative to imprisonment in cases where the law has been broken ... real and effective and not, as I [Brise] am afraid it is now in too many cases, a mere shadow of a name'. Troup responded: 'I do not agree that this attack on the probation service is justified, but it is certainly not, and was never intended to be, a system of police supervision and coercion.' Brise concluded his minute by indicating he would be glad if the Home Secretary could be acquainted with the views of the Commissioners in regard to 'these very grave and important matters'.

Troup, as already mentioned, forwarded the memorandum to Churchill on 1 November.[23] He related it to a circular to certain magistrates and others that Churchill himself was in the process of drafting, which outlined his ideas on prison abatement. Brise had not so far seen this circular, so Troup suggested that he should be shown it, and that there should be a discussion of it with Brise and Sir Edward Henry, the Metropolitan Police Commissioner. Troup was concerned about two points in Churchill's circular. The first related to sending offenders to borstal for one month (the Act stipulated the minimum was one year). The second involved difficulties in obtaining and proving pre-convictions in order to label an offender 'habitual'. Churchill annotated his agreement to the meeting. In his formal response of 2 November to Brise's minute, however, Churchill made clear that he had not changed his stance from the one he had set out in his memorandum of 13 August. On the contrary, both his cabinet memorandum of 25 October and now his draft circular were 'expressions' of it. He brushed aside Brise's observations on this point with a curt 'he had better come and see me'.[24]

Troup annotated Churchill's response on 7 November to the effect that he had sent copies of the draft circular to Brise and Henry. In a note to Churchill dated 17 December he explained he had been through the circular with them. In the copy of it which he attached to his note he drew attention to amendments on which all three of them had agreed, and 'a number of other points on which difficulty arises'.[25] The latter related to practical matters which, as far as the circular was concerned, ought to be met by the amendments and omissions indicated in pencil. 'But', counselled Troup, 'they are all points that require serious consideration at some stage.' He suggested that Churchill should perhaps initially discuss them with Brise and Henry. However, having minuted in this way, he seems to have had second thoughts. In a postscript of the same day he stated he believed the circular ought to issue at once with the amendments he had suggested. 'They make some of the statements less definite,' he wrote, 'but do not impair materially the general presentation of your scheme. It is very important to get into touch with the Magistrates as speedily as possible.' Churchill agreed and, on Christmas Day, annotated Troup's note on the draft circular: 'Now print at once and let me see a proof.' As printed, it was signed by Troup as a Home Office circular and dated January 1911. In the event, however, the circular was never dispatched. The file cover reads: 'This circular was not issued. The committee presided over by Mr Blackwell was appointed instead.' It would seem that Troup's statement about 'points that require consideration at some stage' was decisive in this. Churchill had realized that the circular's dispatch would have to be delayed until further consideration had taken place, and that for such consideration an appropriate committee would have to be appointed. Thus came into being the Abatement of Imprisonment Committee on 29 December 1910.[26]

Churchill had requested its formation in a memorandum sent to Troup 'and others' six days earlier. It was needed to deal with 'practical difficulties relating to the new finger-print calendar and of the Identification of Habitual Offenders ... "immediate punishment" [a task imposed on a convicted offender to terminate at the end of the day on which the court sat, a matter on which, according to Churchill, Blackwell was already 'familiar' with Churchill's views.] ... and details of Penal Drill on which a Committee was to have sat some months ago'. Brise and Henry had entertained misgivings on all these matters during their discussion of Churchill's draft circular with Troup. As was usual with Churchill in cases of this nature, he set out in some detail the data which he required, all to be furnished 'without any unnecessary delay'.

The committee's chairman was Blackwell. The members included two officials representing the Home Office and the Prison Commission, two senior officers drawn from the Metropolitan Police (in a memorandum to Blackwell of 9 January 1911 they were excused attendance when matters under discussion were not relevant to them) and a metropolitan magistrate. To this membership, Churchill added on 7 February 1911 the Clerk to the Liverpool Justices. He was brought in because of the expertise he could bring to bear on the consequences for court procedures and administration of the committee's sentencing recommendations.

Having been formed to find solutions to the problems raised by Troup, Brise and Henry, the committee's terms of reference were enlarged by Churchill in memoranda to Blackwell on 9 and 12 January 1911.[27] In the first memorandum, Churchill confessed his realization that

> the provision of Bridewells [institutions for immediate punishments], the treatment of vagrants and inebriates and, to a certain extent, the general treatment of petty offenders, may, like so many other social subjects at the present time, prove incapable of a final or satisfactory solution except in conjunction with the final reform of the poor Law.[28]

He added that if Blackwell's committee came to this same conclusion, it should nevertheless persevere as far as possible in exploring the special subjects remitted to it.

Churchill then asked Blackwell to split the committee's recommendations into two parts and indicated his views on what should be the subjects for each. The first part would form the basis of a Bill to be enacted in 1911; the second part for enactment thereafter. Clearly he was thinking he would be in office long enough to pilot both parts through the new Parliament.

In the second memorandum, Churchill made what was, in some ways, a unique proposal.[29] This entailed taking statutory power to prohibit any person being sentenced to imprisonment for less than three months. For petty offences and what he termed 'ordinary offences of police', he had in mind a new custodial sentence which he described as 'disciplinary detention' lasting not more than six weeks or, better still, not more than a month. Traditional 'ordinary imprisonment' would be held in reserve for persons found guilty of disgraceful offences of violence, cruelty or dishonesty.

Disciplinary detention would be completely separate from imprisonment, being shorter, more rigorous and less shameful. He suggested one or two ideas for the offenders' respective regimes, although the formulation of these would mainly be a matter for the Prison Commissioners.

In the concluding passage of this memorandum he outlined his previously canvassed ideas for a ladder of graduated sentences. In this way, he pointed out, the courts would have before them a choice of sentences. In all cases they would be able to admonish and discharge; fine and accord 'grace for payment'; bind over; sentence to disciplinary detention or imprisonment, allowing for binding over on probation; sentence to immediate disciplinary detention up to six weeks (or a month), or to imprisonment for not less than three months; or, in the case of habitual petty offenders, convict in existing circumstances, as an habitual inebriate, prostitute or vagrant, under procedure similar to the one associated with the Vagrancy Acts. This last alternative, Churchill pointed out, would involve relegating the offender to imprisonment pending a hearing before quarter sessions justices, and then further relegating him or her up to two years in an institution proper to his or her case. Churchill was clearly eyeing the future here. Apart from the existing two state reformatories and comparable non-state institutions for inebriates, and some privately operated refuges for prostitutes, there were only multi-purpose workhouses for dealing with the particular cases he had in mind. More institutions would obviously have to be established.

The Blackwell Committee's Principal Findings as Embodied in the Draft Administration of Justice Bill[30]

The committee recommended and the Bill as eventually drafted provided for fined offenders of fixed abode time to pay their fines in whole or in part (unless for special reasons) and set out the detailed procedure to be followed. The committee's examination of the available data led it to conclude that 'decent working men and women' formed 'a very small proportion of those sentenced to short terms of imprisonment', and that under the proposed system of grace for payment 'that proportion would be reduced to vanishing point'. The committee's view was that the great majority of people committed to short terms of imprisonment either absolutely or in default of payment of fines were more or less habitual drunkards, beggars, workhouse offenders, tramps, vagrants and prostitutes. With regard to all these people, the committee thought it was necessary to rely 'to a great extent upon the punishment in default being of a distinctly arduous and deterrent character'. Its members believed that time for payment would doubtless enable many drunkards who currently went to prison to pay what they owed instead. Beggars, tramps and vagrants, on the other hand, would discover that the workhouse and casual wards were preferable to prison under the new regime. Workhouse offenders would be chary of changing their quarters for a spell of really hard labour on reduced fare.

Following Churchill's speech in the House of Commons on 20 July 1910 Troup, Brise and Henry had met to draw up a detailed scheme relating to penal drill. On 7 September 1910, after it had been cleared by Churchill, a copy was sent to the chief constables of four counties and fifteen boroughs in different parts of England and Wales for their observations.[31] Responses had been mixed. Some unease was expressed about using the police to supervise the offenders while undergoing their tasks and drills, and about the physical fitness of the offenders for this sort of treatment. On the whole, however, the police's response was favourable, and on 25 September Churchill had minuted his satisfaction with their replies. The committee, having studied all the correspondence and other related documents, recommended and provided in the draft Bill that a court, if it so wished, might establish a system of penal drills or task work within the district for which it acted. The Bill laid down the circumstances under which the court could prescribe the sentence, specified the duties of the police authority concerned in setting up and overseeing the operation of the scheme, laid down what was to happen to offenders who did not comply with the sentence, explained the funding arrangements, and prescribed the statutory duties of the Home Secretary in all these regards.

Even so, it is clear from the committee's report that its members had misgivings about the idea. They expressed the view that it would be difficult to design a system of drills and work tasks without preliminary medical clearance of the offenders and that some distinction would have to be made between regimes for 'the strong pit-boy' on the one hand and 'the newsboy of eighteen, ill-fed, over-smoked, and under-developed' on the other. This would seem to explain why the draft Bill sanctioned the Churchill scheme in experimental rather than substantive terms, and made its introduction in the first place permissive rather than mandatory.

The committee made provision in the draft Bill for a court, if it were so minded, to substitute detention for one day within its precincts, or in a police station, of a summarily convicted offender in lieu of imprisonment without the option of a fine. This also applied if default occurred in the payment of a fine imposed in lieu of imprisonment. Detention was to last until such hour as the court required, but was not to terminate beyond 10 p.m. on the day of the offender's conviction. Where provision had been made for carrying out penal drills or task work at or in the vicinity of the place of detention, the offender was required to perform such penal drills or task work as the court specified in its order. The offender, while so detained, was deemed to be in legal custody.

The draft Bill also provided that no one should be sentenced to imprisonment or committed to prison by a court of summary jurisdiction for a period of less than five days; and that no part-payment under the Bill of any sum adjudged to be paid should operate to reduce a period of imprisonment below five days. The Home Secretary, however, on the application of a police authority, was empowered to certify any police cells, bridewells or lock-up houses provided by the authority to be fit places, alternative to prisons, for the custody of persons sentenced to detention in police custody not exceeding five days, and to make regulations for the treatment of offenders thus held.

The committee accorded no support whatsoever to the notion of compulsorily suspending sentences of up to one month for minor offences. Members preferred fines for such offences, energetic efforts to ensure they were paid, and a little as possible resort to imprisonment. There was, however, in their view, a strong case for imprisonment as a reserve power in the case of fines which were not paid. 'Suspended sentences of imprisonment passed in default of payment of a fine after time had been allowed would quickly bring the administration of justice into ridicule,' they argued. Nor did they favour suspension when the sentence was without the option of a fine. If granted in this circumstance, offenders would be allowed to commit offences 'upon credit', until the total of their imprisonments amounted to more than a month.

All that said, the committee had a certain sympathy for the principle of suspension if it could be applied more satisfactorily. To this end, it recommended and provided in the Bill that courts of summary jurisdiction be empowered to record a sentence against any offender for which punishment without the option of a fine could be imposed. Such a sentence would be discharged on condition that, if he should be reconvicted within twelve months of an offence punishable in the same way, he should be obliged to serve the recorded sentence *in addition* to any sentence that might be imposed on him for his fresh offence. If, on the other hand, he remained free of any offence for a year, the recorded sentence would be expunged. The committee recognized that the same outcome could be achieved by binding over to keep the peace, but it took the view that the threat of a particular period of imprisonment would be more efficacious.

According to the committee, it was extremely difficult to devise a set number of previous convictions to justify a court treating any offender as 'habitual'. It thought such a definition should rest with magistrates and the courts of quarter sessions, which customarily dealt with cases of this kind. However, the committee proposed a minimum of three previous convictions in a year or six altogether, where the offences were punishable by imprisonment without the option of a fine or were offences of prostitutes soliciting. Furthermore, it proposed that quarter sessions courts should have the power to discriminate between persons who should be sent for a term of imprisonment not exceeding twelve months and those who would gain more advantage by a longer term of detention in a suitable establishment. Such establishments were borstals in the case of juvenile-adults, inebriate reformatories for those whose offences were caused by drink, and secure homes in the case of prostitutes. All of these facilities were already in existence. For vagrants or tramps, a labour colony would have to be created.[32]

The draft Bill so provided and defined the circumstances in which prostitutes could be found to be habitual offenders and in which those under twenty-one could be sent to a secure home or borstal institution.

The committee agreed that the term 'hard labour' in connection with a sentence of imprisonment should be abolished. Provision for this was made in the draft Bill. Nevertheless, the court was required, having regard to the character and antecedents of the offender, to direct as part of the sentence (and to write into the commitment) that he be treated as an offender of the first, second or third division. Classification, therefore, would depend entirely on the character and antecedents of the offender, not on the nature of the offence, except so far as it afforded evidence of character.[33] The Visiting Committee, for its part, was empowered to transfer prisoners sentenced under summary jurisdiction from a lower to a higher division, but not to the first division (where the regime was pretty free and easy) without the permission of the Home Secretary. The committee proposed that if imprisonment had to be served in the third division, then it had to be made as disagreeable as possible, irrespective of whether the imprisonment was absolute or in default of paying a fine. The committee's particular interest here was to ensure that people who could pay fines but preferred imprisonment to doing so should be made aware that the latter course in the third division would be no rest cure.

The numerous briefings which Blackwell had received from Churchill referred here and there to the imposition of restrictions on the lengths of prison sentences. The members concluded that a ban on prison sentences of less than three months (one of the suggestions put forward) would be impracticable. The members thought it would necessitate a complete remoulding of the Summary Jurisdiction Law, under which, as a rule, a magistrate's powers were limited to imposing sentences of not more than three months.

They also turned down a further suggestion that no sentence of absolute imprisonment (i.e., without the option of a fine) of less than one month should be passed. They believed that such a provision 'would certainly result in increased severity of punishment in certain cases'.

They then rejected Churchill's proposal for disciplinary detention, his sanction that was distinct from ordinary imprisonment, and shorter, more rigorous and more shameful. 'By whatever name it be known and by whatever dress may be worn by those who have to undergo it,' ran the committee's argument, 'the fact that in existing circumstances it would as a rule be served in prison, and under conditions more rigorous and unpleasant than any other form of imprisonment, must of necessity render it shameful. We do not see how this is to be avoided.' Furthermore, the committee did not think in practice that cases dealt with by a pecuniary fine and those punished by direct imprisonment differed sufficiently in character to justify such a distinction. It quoted figures in respect of a variety of offences to substantiate its view. 'If such offenders are sent to prison in default of paying their fines,' the members continued, 'we see no reason why they should be treated as less deserving of obloquy than the prisoners committed without the option of a fine.' Moreover, the whole situation would be anomalous because prisoners under disciplinary detention for not paying their fines 'would be undergoing a severer punishment than the one accorded to persons imprisoned for shorter terms for graver offences'.

The committee reported that the abolition of debt in certain cases had been reserved for action elsewhere, and had not therefore received its attention. However, it drew attention to sections 6 (3) and (4) of the 1898 Prison Act, which treated as debtors all persons imprisoned for arrears under orders enforceable as Affiliation Orders, and all persons in default of sureties. In the Bill, certain minor but useful measures were included which would tend towards the abatement of imprisonment.

Other issues were also covered in the draft Bill which had not featured in the committee's original terms of reference. High among them were the payment and allocations of fines and fees, a uniform scale of court fees in respect of all courts of summary jurisdiction, and the appointment and remuneration of justices' clerks. It would seem, too, that the opportunity was taken to tidy up one or two other issues. These included minor amendments to the 1907 Probation of Offenders Act in respect to conditions of probation and the procedure for varying them, and summary proceedings in cases of malicious damage to property not exceeding £20.

* * *

The committee's report was presented on 6 March 1911. The draft Administration of Justice Bill, suitable for a first reading in Parliament, was published on 8 April, but in the event was never read.[34] It was still in circulation, gathering comments from all the various public interests concerned, when Churchill transferred to the Admiralty in October 1911. His successor as Home Secretary was Reginald McKenna, his predecessor at the Admiralty. McKenna's interests in criminal justice were more orthodox than Churchill's, with the result that the draft Bill proceeded no further. Some of its provisions, however, were influential, as will become clear in the final chapter.

CHAPTER 8

The Royal Prerogative of Mercy: Churchill and the Judiciary

Legislation was not the only means to which Churchill resorted to abate the scale of imprisonment in England and Wales. He was also attracted to the contribution the Royal Prerogative of Mercy could make towards this end. This, as we have already noted,[1] was an authority vested in the sovereign, inherited from the early days of English history, to intervene in the criminal process by the application of Mercy as a corrective in cases where it could be shown that an injustice had occurred. Persons who sought redress submitted petitions to the Home Secretary. His senior officials were responsible for examining them and advising which ones merited prerogative clemency. They also scrutinized the Court Calendars and brought to the notice of the Home Secretary any cases there which they themselves discerned as needing his corrective intervention. The Home Secretary's recommendations to the sovereign were customarily agreed: the monarch might comment on them or query them, but the long-accepted constitutional convention was that the Royal Prerogative of Mercy was to all intents and purposes exercised by the Home Secretary in the sovereign's name.[2]

The prerogative operated through a system of pardons, remissions and respites. Pardons were of two types: a free pardon enabled the person under jurisdiction to be treated as if he or she had not been convicted; a conditional pardon, or commutation as it is perhaps better known, substituted one penalty for another – for example, penal servitude for death, or ordinary imprisonment for penal servitude, in other words a milder penalty for a more severe one. A remission reduced the length of a sentence or the amount of a fine without changing their character as penalties.[3] A reprieve, or respite as it is sometimes known, postponed the implementation of a sentence pending further consideration and the announcement of a final resolution. It was particularly used in cases which involved a decision as to whether execution should be authorized or its place be taken by penal servitude.

Free pardons were rare: four were granted in 1909, two in 1910 and four in 1911. Conditional pardons were somewhat more generous. In 1910, 12 out of 28 prisoners sentenced to death had their sentences commuted to penal servitude for life; in 1911, the sentences of 13 out of 31 death-sentenced prisoners were similarly commuted. Remissions of sentences, on the other hand, were numerous: 248 in 1910 and 201 in 1911. The corresponding figure for 1909 was 420.[4]

The decision over whether to uphold Mercy in an individual case took place in circumstances outside the established format of court proceedings, and was a matter for the personal judgement of the Home Secretary of the day. Gladstone, addressing the House of Commons in 1907, expressed the matter thus:

> It would be neither desirable nor possible to lay down hard and fast rules as to the exercise of the royal prerogative of mercy. Numerous considerations – the motive, the degree of premeditation or deliberation, the amount of provocation, the state of mind of the prisoner, his physical condition, his character and antecedents, the recommendations or absence of recommendations from the jury, and many others – have to be taken into account in every case; and the decision depends on full review of a complex combination of circumstances, and often on the careful balancing of conflicting considerations. As William Harcourt said in the House, 'the exercise of the prerogative of mercy does not depend on principles of strict law or justice, still less does it depend on sentiment in any way. It is a question of policy and judgement in each case, and in my opinion a capital execution which in its circumstances creates horror and compassion for the culprit rather than a sense of indignation at his crime is a great evil.' There are, it is true, important principles that I and my advisers have constantly to bear in mind; but an attempt to reduce these principles to formulae and to exclude all considerations which are incapable of being formulated in precise terms would not, I believe, aid any Home Secretary in consideration of the difficult questions which he has to decide.[5]

Both Gladstone and Harcourt, of course, in expressing themselves in this way, had in mind Mercy in the context of the death penalty, when the decision to grant or withhold it was at its most onerous. Most Home

Secretaries would probably have liked to be relieved of the responsibility, but in the law as it stood they could not escape the call of duty. Churchill felt the burden especially acutely.[6] Remissions, of course, could sometimes generate painful feelings, too; but, on the whole, they laid less stress on the conscience. They were granted for all manner of circumstances, of which a short selection can be quoted here, by way of illustration. Prisoners could benefit from them on medical grounds; to attend a funeral; on grounds of previous good character; to take up employment; if they had been soldiers, to rejoin their regiments which were about to go overseas; if they had assisted prison staff to put down a riot or save a life; and on the recommendation of the judge or the jury. Sentences of imprisonment imposed on women for concealing the birth of their children could be set aside in favour of detention in a refuge for the term of their imprisonment; on alcoholics whose imprisonment could be set aside in favour of their transfer to inebriate reformatories for the duration of their imprisonment. Remittance of fines in whole or in part, especially where the offence was considered to be relatively minor, was sanctioned. Especially good conduct in prison could attract earlier release over and above the normal remission for good behaviour. Remissions of sentence lengths were sanctioned in cases where it was thought they were out of proportion in relation to the offences committed.

Although the statistics are confusing, they nevertheless reinforce the view that Churchill's use of pardons and remissions was nothing out of the ordinary. Here, however, it is necessary to draw attention to the fact that in 1910 the number of remissions recorded in the statistics did not take into account that special remission of sentences under the Royal Prerogative granted to prisoners to commemorate the coronation of King George V. The Criminal Justice Statistics indicate that 11,873 prisoners benefited. This, however, was a one-off event, a practice that has been used now and again to mark the accession to the throne of a new sovereign. The remission was given on a graduated scale, based on the term of imprisonment prisoners still had to serve.[7] Churchill was careful to stress the context of this measure when he addressed the House of Commons on his prison and sentencing policies on 20 July 1910.

If, therefore, there was nothing unusual about Churchill's use of the Royal Prerogative of Mercy, why did his use of it cause dismay among his senior officials and the Prison Commissioners, some Members of Parliament, and the legal profession? The answer may partly be found in some of the cases he thought suitable for the application of the prerogative which he discerned from his personal scrutiny of the Court Calendars (a practice recommended to Churchill in the handing-over notes which Gladstone left to him). Churchill's cases did not always square with the criteria for the prerogative's suitability under which his senior officials were accustomed to make their own recommendations to him. Partly, too, it may be found in the abruptness with which he sometimes authorised remissions, without prior consultation with the parties responsible for the original sentences.

Matters came to a head on 26 June 1911, when in a House of Commons debate on the Home Office Supply Vote Churchill was challenged on three cases where he had used the Royal Prerogative of Mercy to alter sentences without prior consultation with the judicial authorities originally concerned.[8] The first case related to his visit to Pentonville Prison in October 1910, where, in his words, 'on his own personal responsibility' he ordered the release of 'a certain number of youths who were there under sentence for very minor offences'. He explained that he had been struck by the many Members of the House who had brought to his notice that 'evil was done by sending boys to prison for very small offences', and he went on to say that he had a Bill in hand for substituting a stern but non-custodial alternative penalty for dealing with them (a reference to defaulters' drill), for which he required parliamentary time that he was afraid would elude him. He justified his use of the prerogative because he wanted 'to draw public attention in a sharp and effective manner to this evil to which other Members of the House had also drawn attention'. He claimed that his initiative had led to a marked decrease in the number of committals of youths in the period since his visit to Pentonville; and he justified his lack of consultation with the magistrates concerned in the sentencing of the youths because the latter's sentences would have expired before the correspondence could have been completed. He did, however, emphasize that it was the intention of the Government, 'whenever it is possible and whenever it is convenient', to make full use 'of the great experience and knowledge of the magistrates and court in dealing with these particular cases'.

Churchill's second case concerned a man who could not afford a dog licence for his pet. The dog had belonged to his daughter, who had died some time previously. The case came to Churchill's notice as one for which a small fine, twenty shillings, might be required. The fine was remitted to avoid sending the man to prison. Churchill did not tell the House at the time he remitted the fine, or before coming to a decision, that he had consulted with the London County Council. It was thought to be a 'hard application of a heavy penalty for a minor fault'. He added that in further communication with the Council there was more to be said for their view than had at first been apparent. Nevertheless, he thought the case was problematic and justified the use of the Royal Prerogative. He had no quarrel with how the London County Council had administered the legislation which led to the fine in the first place: 'I am afraid', he said, 'the form of my first letter might have been taken as implying dissatisfaction at their action, an impression I desire to remove.'[9]

The third case enabled Churchill to twist his critics' tail. The Gainsborough magistrates had sentenced a man on first conviction to fourteen days' imprisonment with hard labour for begging. This was a harsh sentence, far more severe than was usually imposed for this sort of activity elsewhere in the country. In this particular case, the Home Secretary explained, he was not involved in the decision to remit the sentence:

> My Noble Friend, Lord Crewe, was administered the Home Office during my absence from this country and he decided the case in the ordinary and regular way. But I am quite sure that if the Gainsborough bench had only known that the decision was not the decision of the wicked Home Secretary, but was the decision of the good Lord Crewe, we should not have heard a word of controversy raised upon the point. However, 'all's well that ends well'.[10]

All three of these cases found their way into the public domain, but many others were dealt with behind the closed doors of the Home Office. These formed part of Churchill's quest for standardizing sentencing policy, achieving a better proportionality between the offence and the sentence. They reveal the distance which separated his views from those of his senior officials; the oscillations which occurred in his thinking as he tried to find a less discretionary basis on which to base proportionality; his ensuing frustration; and the officials' alarm at the consequences for the relationship between the Home Office and the judiciary, which they believed was jeopardized by Churchill's attitude. The Home Office files are revealing on these matters.

There was, for example, the case of Annie Connolly, whom the Salford Hundred Quarter Sessions ordered to keep the peace and to be of good behaviour for six months, meanwhile being released on her own recognizance after paying a fine of £5. Her offence was that, while drunk, she had thrown pepper into the eyes of a six-month-old child in its mother's arms, a consequence of bad feeling between the two families. Churchill was outraged at the lenience of the punishment and wanted the magistrate concerned to be rebuked:

> He is unfit to hold his position ... It is, in my opinion, one of the most brutal and unnatural crimes a woman could commit, and certainly six months' hard labour was richly deserved ... The most awful disparity between the punishments inflicted for the most trivial offences against property and the gravest offences against the person was never more strikingly illustrated.[11]

Troup tried to dissuade Churchill from taking further action on the grounds that such action could be construed as interfering with the independence of the judiciary. Nevertheless, Churchill required an official letter to be written to the Chairman of the Quarter Sessions, obliging him to explain the decision. The Chairman's answer was simple: 'If you had seen and heard the witnesses you would have approved the sentence.'[12] On this occasion, Churchill's officials successfully dissuaded him from sending the magistrates a formal rebuke which he had drafted.

Another case concerned a certain Bessie Carter, whose release was pending from Reading Gaol, where she was serving a sentence for false pretences. There was a warrant out for her arrest on a similar charge which was due to be served on her as soon as she left prison. Churchill informed the Chief Constable of the Warwickshire Constabulary charged with serving the warrant that in his 'strong opinion' the Chief Constable should not proceed, on the grounds that Carter was mentally unstable and came from a 'respectable family'. The Chief Constable protested, prompting Churchill to comment, 'What does he mean by using such expressions as "at a loss to understand" and "before taking further action?" His tone appears disrespectful and I am doubtful whether he shd be answered.' The outcome was that Troup sent a letter to the Chief Constable for daring to write in such a manner.[13]

Churchill's senior officials were right to be worried by the way he went about these and other cases. The Home Office shared with the magistrates and judges responsibly for the administration of the country's criminal justice system, and in its overseeing role needed to exercise tact when dealing with them, especially where formal advice was concerned. Churchill was not easy to restrain when he got the bit between his teeth.

The attitude of the legal profession more generally may be discerned in its journals. The *Law Journal* of March 1911, for example, picked up on some remarks which Churchill made in the course of addressing a delegation from the Trades Union Congress Parliamentary Committee. These comments related to what a Member of Parliament, a certain Mr Wardle, had said when addressing a recent meeting of the Amalgamated Society of Railway Servants. He had appealed to the meeting not to stop subscribing to the parliamentary funds of the society 'because some old fossil of a judge declared it to be illegal to pay working-men for Parliament out of their own money'. The *Law Journal* thought it was high time the House of Commons took measures 'to protect the Bench from studied insults of its ignorant critics'. The need to do this was all the more necessary, in its opinion, because of what Churchill had told the TUC delegation: 'On several occasions', Churchill had said, 'statements had been made from the Bench reflecting on Trade Unions in language which was extremely ignorant and out of touch with the general development of modern thought.' The *Law Journal* considered this attack was calculated to damage the Bench as a whole, and felt that the Home Secretary should have been more specific in his allegations. 'It is astonishing', it continued, 'that a Cabinet Minister, especially one occupying an office closely allied to the administration of justice as does the Home Secretary, should encourage these ill-mannered attacks by adding unjustifiable observations of his own calculated to reflect on the judicial character of a Bench which, happily, stands above all politics.'[14]

The situation exploded in the House of Commons on 30 May 1911, when Churchill fiercely singled out for attack judges whom he considered had acted unfairly in trade union cases which had come before them. It was, he said, his intention 'to relieve Trade Unions from the harassing litigation to which they have been exposed and set them free to develop and do their work without the perpetual check and uncertainty of frequent trials and without being brought constantly in contact with the courts.' He added that trade unions in recent years had been 'enmeshed, harassed, worried, and checked at every step and at every turn by all kinds of legal decisions, which came with the utmost surprise to the greatest lawyers in the country'. Had he left the matter at that, there might have been no furore, but he could not resist the temptation to draw class and party issues into the debate. 'It is', he continued, 'impossible to pretend that the courts command the same degree of general confidence' as they do in criminal cases. 'On the contrary, they do not, and a very large number of our population have been led to the opinion that they are, unconsciously, no doubt, biased.'[15]

This statement was greeted with cries of 'No! No!' and 'Withdraw!' from the Conservative side of the House. Churchill, however, was unmoved. In no way was he deflected from advice on how he should deal with the judiciary, following his appointment as Home Secretary, offered by Sir Francis Hopwood, Parliamentary Under-Secretary of State at the Colonial Office: 'Keep an eye on the sentences passed by fat-headed people and reduce them fearlessly whether they emanate from the Ermine or "the great unpaid".'[16]

But out of these exchanges was born unforgiving hostility to Churchill in the ranks of his political opponents and the legal profession. In particular an old argument was given new life: that the Home Secretary must be a lawyer. This was suggested at the time of Churchill's appointment by both the *Law Journal* and the *Law Times*.[17] Hardly surprisingly, the legal profession was delighted when Asquith eased Churchill out of the Home Office and into the Admiralty, with McKenna making the opposite journey, in October 1911. McKenna was its heart's desire, a lawyer, and the *Law Journal* expressed its satisfaction:

In view of this intimate connection with the administration of the law – his exercise of the royal prerogative of mercy and the large amount of legal patronage at his disposal – there are obvious advantages in the Home Secretary being an experienced lawyer. Mr McKenna, though he has ceased to be an active member of the profession, may be relied upon to avoid the mistakes which, both in regard to his attitude towards the judges and the character of his appointments, have marred Mr Churchill's career at the Home Office.[18]

CHAPTER 9

Churchill's Penal Thought and Practice: An Assessment

In attempting to assess Churchill's penal thought and practice during his time at the Home Office, one must, of course, take into account the context in which he operated. It was one of constraint, and it applied to all the responsibilities of his office. This was generated by the brevity of his Home Secretaryship and by the conservative nature of the Home Office and the Prison Commission. He held the office of Home Secretary for just over twenty months, little enough time to put into practice the penal thinking he had in mind when he was first appointed, let alone that which he devised when dealing with prisons on a day-to-day basis.[1] During his tenure, moreover, his attention was needed for other matters, in addition to criminal justice, to say nothing of the time he had to set aside for cabinet discussions, attending the House of Commons (where, from time to time, he wound up debates for the Government), speaking engagements up and down the country, and the needs of his constituency. A related constraint was that, when he became the Home Secretary, he had no idea how long he would remain in the post, although he suspected his tenure might be short because of the likelihood of an early general election to resolve the continuing constitutional crisis which was polarizing the two Houses of Parliament. Even if he were to hold his seat and the Liberal Government were to return to office, he could not be certain he would continue to serve as Home Secretary. This uncertainty clouded his first ten months in office.[2]

Once the December 1910 general election was won and he was back at the Home Office, it is possible Churchill may have thought he had a full parliamentary term ahead of him in which to introduce all the changes he had in mind for the criminal justice system. What he could not foresee was that, in October 1911, Asquith would transfer him to the Admiralty. His replacement in the Home Office, McKenna, did not share to the same degree Churchill's interest in penal reform, so there was no continuation of the business Churchill had set in train. As a result, Churchill's impact on the criminal justice system fell short of what it might have been.[3]

Nevertheless, there were issues on which he was able to leave his mark. His policies reflected new thinking and challenged received opinion, and were destined to influence prison treatment and sentencing in the future, especially after the First World War, when tendencies towards mildness in these matters developed at a pace.[4] However, it is difficult to assess the full extent of his impact, for, within three years of his leaving the Home Office, the First World War broke out and the country's prison system was thrown into disarray. Post-war however, the humanization of the system was accelerated, and we can safely say that Churchill approved of that, perhaps also that he had helped to prepare the way for it.[5]

At the heart of Home Office business lies managing the delicate balance between the claims of liberty and authority. In a sense, therefore, the Home Office is more or less forced into conservatism which, on occasions, can be interpreted as negativism. When problems arise, precedent becomes all important, and Home Office personnel are especially its guardians. Understandably, they view change in inherited policies and practices with considerable caution. This is not necessarily a fault but it may be seen as such by a Home Secretary like Churchill, a man determined to make a name for himself as a reformist and to rise even higher in the ministerial ranks. He had a desire to make considerable changes to the criminal justice system, the 'ark of the Home Office covenant', and he felt he had to make those changes fast. Consequently, the established 'slow-and-bide-a-while' methodologies to which his senior Home Office officials were accustomed were not welcome to him.

Conversely, the furious pace at which Churchill conducted Home Office business was often unwelcome to the officials. One set of new proposals after another would cascade upon them. They were given little or no time for contemplation. There were almost continuous demands for detailed factual and statistical information. Their advice was frequently challenged and their responses to these challenges had to be instant. Especially alarming to them were Churchill's interventions in court cases, against all protocol, usually to mitigate sentences. Hardly surprisingly, tension between the Home Secretary and his senior officials was never far below the surface.[6]

Churchill's methods aside, what lay behind the friction was the senior officials' fear that his proposed changes would weaken the deterrence of the criminal justice system and thereby lead to an increase in crime and possibly to social disorder. They were fully aware of the changes in prison sentencing and treatment which had gradually evolved in the nineteenth and early twentieth centuries, and they were reconciled to them, but they felt the tendency towards mildness had gone far enough. It was time to apply the brakes. However, both Gladstone and Churchill were convinced that further forward movement was possible *and* realistic. And, moreover, Churchill was a man in a hurry.

If the senior Home Office officials were cautious and a brake on Churchill, the same could largely be said of the Prison Commissioners, but with one important difference. The latter oversaw the prison system, and at the heart of that was the relationship between prisoners and prison staff. The management of people in custody, face-to-face, day-today, demanded flexibility.[7] For prison staff, the carrot was just as important as the stick. Thus they were sympathetic to several of Churchill's proposals, provided their requirements for safe-guarding the daily operations of the prisons were recognized, the status quo was not modified too suddenly, and such adjustments as were necessary caused as little disruption as was possible. Churchill, aided probably by his military background, understood this situation, and generally showed himself willing to take the Commissioners' views into account.

Where Churchill's proposals impinged on sentences, however (their lengths and proportionality to offences), the Prison Commissioners and the senior Home Office officials were usually on the same side. Churchill consequently had to apply the full weight of his ministerial authority to overcome them. From the officials' and Commissioners' points of view, Churchill's proposals were simply too far ahead of their time to be acceptable. They raised constitutional issues with the judiciary which seemed insurmountable. Churchill wanted to establish codifications of both offences and the sentences appropriate to them, with proportionality duly observed.

His successful reworking of the preventive detention sentence is a good illustration of what he had in mind, and, as he made clear on a number of occasions, especially in dealing with young offender sentences and the abatement of imprisonment, he would undoubtedly have pursued this line further if he had remained longer at the Home Office. Suffice it to say that codification has not yet been achieved to this day.[8]

* * *

Churchill's primary concern was to effect a reduction in the size of the prison population generally and, more particularly, the size of the recidivist element within its ranks. As far as the whole prison population was concerned, he favoured an extension of the existing non-custodial penalties. Chief among these was probation, which he wished to see more uniformly adopted. To this end, he dispatched a circular to every magistrate in England and Wales explaining the provisions of the Probation Act, urging them to take advantage of it on every occasion. Allowing for the fact that the Act was only partially adopted at the time, Churchill was able to report to the House of Commons that there had been 'a most sensible improvement'.[9] With the passage of time, however, he advocated a tightening of the Act, dividing it into two branches – one for counselling and the other for discipline – but, with Churchill's transfer to the Admiralty, no development of this kind ensued, and nor has it ever done so.

Churchill wished to empower the courts to give fined offenders time to pay, instead of sending them immediately to prison if they were unable to pay at the time of their sentence. He also championed suspended sentences and penal drill. All of these non-custodial sentences were to be utilized to reduce the prison population. However, as his Administration of Justice Bill got no further than first-draft stage, no legislation was introduced on these matters during Churchill's Secretaryship. Nevertheless, time to pay fines was eventually included in the 1914 Administration of Justice Act. As Churchill had anticipated three years earlier, this had a remarkable effect on reducing the flow of people into prison, and it remains to this day a memorial to his Home Secretaryship. As for suspended sentences and penal drill, the memory of their first appearance on the criminal justice agenda lingered long in the Home Office and they surfaced much later in the century. Suspended sentences finally found their way into the criminal justice system under the 1967 Criminal Justice Act. The Criminal Justice Act of 1948 had already made provision for young offenders to give up some of their free time on Saturdays to attend centres, where they would be required to participate in a variety of activities, some physical, not necessarily of the offenders' choosing. The centres were never widely available, little use was made of them and they gradually fell into disuse. These provisions nevertheless are good examples of the new thinking Churchill brought to bear on the criminal justice system.

For offenders for whom there were no alternatives to imprisonment, Churchill's main area of interest lay in securing proportionality between offence and sentence. In the case of the preventive detention sentence, he was able to ameliorate the situation he had inherited, with the result that fewer people fell within its ambit than had originally been estimated. This contributed to the gradual withering of the sentence after he left the Home Office.[10] Churchill had had similar plans for borstal, but was not given the time to implement them.[11]

The proportionality issue led to another of Churchill's sentencing projects. Sentences and terms of imprisonment had evolved ad hoc over the centuries to the point where, in his opinion, there was little logic in them. He wanted to tidy up the whole system and for this purpose he advanced the idea of a codification of offences locked into a codification of sentences suitable for them. Alongside changes of this nature, he envisaged a great expansion of the classification system for prisoners. Moreover, he proposed the earmarking of particular prisons for specific forms of prison treatment and training, presided over by a board which would determine the particular treatment each prisoner should receive. All of these ideas had much to recommend them logically, including an end to the multi-purpose character of individual prisons (which continues largely to this day). It may have been possible, for example, to practise the individualization of prison treatment more effectually.

In the circumstances of the time, one suspects that Churchill's scheme could not have been put into practice, certainly on the scale he envisaged, given the independence of the judiciary and magistracy, and it is significant that from his time to the present his proposals have never been followed up.[12] They were not reflected in the terms of the Blackwell Committee's report or in the draft Administration of Justice Bill and at the time Churchill would seem to have acquiesced in this. Nevertheless, they are yet another example of the new thinking he brought to the country's criminal justice system.

Churchill possessed genuine compassion, was sensitive to the economic and social conditions of those less privileged than himself, wanted to improve their lives, even when they were imprisoned. Up to a point, this was a humanitarian question, and to this extent Churchill had the backing of the 1895 Prison Department Committee, whose report (paragraph 33) had stressed the need 'to humanize the prisoners, to prevent them from feeling that the State merely chains them for a certain period and cares nothing about them beyond keeping them in safe custody and under iron discipline'. Gladstone, the author of that report, was acting upon this proposition when, shortly before he handed over the Home Office to Churchill, he indicated to its senior officials and the Prison Commissioners that he wished to mitigate the harsh conditions under which the suffragettes and other passive resisters laboured in the local prisons. He also wanted to do the same for convict prisoners, who were required in the initial stages of their penal servitude sentences to live in conditions of separate confinement. Churchill shared Gladstone's views and put his predecessor's plans into action on a more generous scale.

His humanity, however, should not be confused with sentimentality, as he made clear that forcible feeding should continue for the suffragettes and others who went on hunger strike to gain what they wanted, usually first division treatment which was refused them. Moreover, in the case of convicts, Churchill stressed that while the length of separate confinement should be reduced, it should not be abolished altogether. He was a firm believer in making the first period of prison life unpleasant.[13] Similarly, there was nothing sentimental about his attitude towards flogging. On a 1911 Bill to abolish it altogether, he marked, simply, 'Block.' Nor did he support the total abolition of the death penalty.[14] Churchill, for all his humanity, was a realist in that he recognized the limitations inherent in even the most liberally managed prison system. As he put the matter to John Galsworthy:

> The whole process of punishment is an ugly business at the best. The prisoners are unhappy, and are meant to be much less happy than others outside in this not too happy world. The conditions in gaol must necessarily be squalid, the cost of maintenance narrowly scrutinized, since it is raised from the taxation drawn, in part, from the poorest of the poor; and the process of meting out measure for measure according to human standards must be crude, imperfect, and full of discordances.[15]

Similar thoughts infused Churchill's famous and long-remembered peroration to his speech to the House of Commons on 20 July 1910. He set out the balance of considerations to be observed in drawing up the penal system for an enlightened country, and reminded the House that, even when every material improvement has been effected in prisons, 'the convict stands deprived of everything that a free man calls life'.[16]

Once these changes had been put into practice, however, there could be no going back. The scene was set for further extensions. The special arrangements for the treatment of the suffragettes and passive resisters, in the event, tended to fall into desuetude as the former disappeared from the scene at the outbreak of the First World War and as alternative arrangements were made during the inter-war years for dealing with other offenders eligible to be treated under mitigation. As for separate confinement for convicts in the initial stages of their sentences, the first steps towards its abolition were taken in 1922, a year after Brise's retirement, when the feature was experimentally suspended on the authority of the Home Secretary, on the ground that 'a man brooding alone in his cell became morose and vindictive'.[17] Following reports from governors and medical officers six months later that discipline had been maintained and physical and mental health improved, the Home Secretary authorized the continuation of the suspension pending the introduction of new Statutory Rules. On their appearance in 1931, preliminary separate confinement for convicts officially ended. The new Rules also brought to an end the month's local prison preliminary confinement.[18]

Humanity also underlay Churchill's introduction of a mitigated regime for aged convicts, regular lectures and concerts, and opportunities for serious study, especially among prisoners serving long sentences, together with improvements in library facilities for the generality of prisoners. Aged convicts aside, however, humanity was not the whole explanation of these developments. Both Gladstone and Churchill were influenced by the concept of imprisonment as outlined in the 1895 Report: an opportunity for prisoners to engage in useful employment, including skills training, and generally to remake their lives in such a way that on their release they would be able to reintegrate effectively into society. For this purpose, mental stimulation was just as important as effectiveness in manual labour. Churchill in particular did not regard imprisonment as a sort of a dead-end siding to freedom's main line, but as a branch line that led back to it. This lay behind his proposal for a special party to be formed in each convict prison, to be trained and employed on appropriate but strenuous labour, and to which generous sentence remission would be attached as an incentive to participate. Furthermore, these prisoners would be helped into employment on their release with the aid of suitable certificates of reliability and competence. This particular proposal did not take off at the time, but it led immediately to the establishment of a scheme of state aid and civilian supervision (replacing police supervision) for convicts on release, where before there had been none. In particular, the scheme gave help towards securing employment for ex-convicts. The Central Association, for the after-care of convicts and preventive detention offenders, incorporating the Borstal Association, marked the true start of the state's role in this particular field. Credit for the detailed planning should go to Brise and his fellow Commissioners, but it was Churchill's backing which got it off the ground, and it endured until its role was taken over under the Criminal Justice Act 1967, which gave formal recognition to the enlargement of the probation into a Probation and After-Care Service. It is another example of Churchill's forward thinking.

In today's climate it is easy to deride the moralizing and philanthropic bases of these release arrangements, their lack of 'incisiveness and realism', especially in relation to the characteristics of recidivist offenders. However, in the context of pre-First World War Britain, the verdict of Radzinowicz and Hood[19] is just: 'It cannot be denied that the movement to forge a system of after-care worthy of a modern, prosperous state, and in tune with its developing social conscience, had at last begun to take root.'

* * *

If Churchill accepted the Home Secretaryship with alacrity in February 1910, he abandoned it just as cheerfully twenty months later. It was as if a cornucopia had turned into a poisoned chalice. An indication of this is afforded by his valedictory message to the Home Office staff. He described the department as being 'charged by a great variety of serious duties, ranging from the most disagreeable to the most stately functions in public affairs'.[20] In his memoirs of 1930 he clarified what he had meant by 'disagreeable duties': 'Although I loathed the business of one human being inflicting frightful and even capital punishment upon others, I comforted myself on some occasions of responsibility by the reflection that a death sentence was far more merciful than a life sentence.'[21] He spelled out this view of his Home Office duties more clearly still some nine years later: 'All I can say is that there is no post under the Crown in which the holder has more need of the kindness and goodwill of his fellow men.' He conceded, however, that there was a 'bright side' to being Home Secretary, concerned with great ceremonial occasions, but even so, the post was 'certainly not one which, having held it, I would in any circumstances wish to occupy again'.[22]

The usual reason given for Churchill's departure from the Home Office is that Prime Minister Asquith wanted to strengthen the administration of the Admiralty at a time of looming international conflict. He astutely considered Churchill to be the best man for that job.[23] But there may have been a less positive reason. It is often said that an essential qualification for the office of Home Secretary is 'a safe pair of hands'. As has been shown, however, the rumbustious Churchill pressurized his senior officials and the Prison Commission, and rode rough-shod over protocol in the pursuit of his prison and sentencing reforms. In short, he caused friction. Furthermore, public furore accompanied his handling of some of his other Home Office responsibilities, notably the 'siege of Sydney Street' and the maintenance of law and order (or lack thereof) in a time of demonstrations and riots associated with the suffragettes and industrial action.[24]

Asquith was well acquainted with the Home Office, having himself served as Home Secretary in Gladstone's administration of 1892–4 and Rosebery's of 1894. He was personally known to the Prison Commissioners, and had been responsible for setting up the Prison Department Inquiry of 1894–5, and appointing Brise as Chairman of the Prison Commission. He knew, too, the very civil servants who had since risen to be Churchill's senior officials. In these circumstances, he might well have asked himself if the Home Office were in 'a safe pair of hands'. It could be that Asquith thought by swapping Churchill at the Home Office with McKenna at the Admiralty, raising the temperature in the latter while lowering it in the former, he would succeed in killing two birds with one stone. McKenna, of course, unlike Churchill, was a lawyer. As such, he was unlikely to trample legal niceties in the pursuit of his Home Office objectives as Churchill had sometimes done.

It suited Churchill to make the move, too.[25] He was essentially a man of action, hands on, from a military background, and accustomed to having an immediate and direct impact where it was needed. He was frustrated by having to work in a tradition-ridden government department where everything was subject to argument, negotiation, delay and compromise. This and the strain on his conscience associated with the Home Secretary's role in relation to the death penalty were all part of the 'disagreeable' aspect of his Home Office tenure. So long as he remained at the Home Office, however, he certainly had no intention of abandoning what he considered it was necessary for him to do to realize the objectives of his penal policy. He was no quitter.

That said, he could still boast of remarkable achievements, all the circumstances considered, which he managed to make in prison treatment and sentencing during his time at the Home Office. Once he had moved on and the hiatus of the First World War had been overcome, the impetus he had given to these changes would resume, sustaining the enlightenment for which he had striven in his Home Office days.

Notes

Notes to Preface

1   Hansard, Fifth Series, vol. 19, col. 1354. Radzinowicz and Hood 1986, p. 774.

Notes to Chapter 1

1   Conservative MP, Oldham, 1900; Liberal MP, Manchester North, 1906; Liberal MP, Dundee, 1908, January 1910, and December 1910; Parliamentary Under-Secretary of State at the Colonial Office, 1905–8, and President of the Board of Trade, 1908–10.
2   'Your speeches from first to last', wrote Asquith, congratulating Churchill on his electioneering, 'have reached a high-water mark and will live in history' (Gilbert 1991, p. 211).
3   When Churchill was serving at the Colonial Office, he visited Britain's recently acquired East African territories. The Governor of Uganda, Sir Hesketh Bell, records that Churchill asked him his age. He replied he was forty-three, to which Churchill exclaimed, 'Do you know I am ten years younger than you are? I wonder where I shall be when I am your age?' Bell then asked Churchill where he thought he would be. 'PM,' replied Churchill. Bell recalls that this answer was given 'in a tone of acute determination' (Bell 1946, pp. 167–71).
4   Churchill 1989 [1900], Chapters 7 to 12. In 1930 Churchill, in reflective mood, retold the story in *My Early Life*.
5   Churchill 1989 [1900], pp. 45, 69, 70 and 80.
6   Carter 1965, p. 187.
7   Elgin Papers, Churchill to Elgin, 1 September 1907, reprinted in R. S. Churchill 1969, 1, pp. 666–7. See also PRO CO/247/168/26220, minutes 24 and 25, July 1907. Also CO/247/168/30435, minute of Elgin, 16 September 1907; Elgin to Governor (private), 17 September 1907 (copy). The Secretary of State (Lord Elgin) favoured political status for the prisoners and was influenced by Churchill's views on their treatment. He wrote privately to the Governor and stressed the need for liberal treatment. See Hyam 1968, pp. 247–53. Churchill's ideas for the treatment of Zulu prisoners on St

Helena were reflected in the Rules he would later make for the treatment of offenders sentenced to preventive detention, as recorded at Chapter 6 of this book, n. 31.
8   R. S. Churchill 1969, 1, pp. 575–8, at p. 576. See also Hyam 1968, pp. 225–9. Elgin's view of this case was that the right of summary dismissal was a necessary one, but it should be used in 'a less bungling fashion'. The guard was eventually re-employed.
9   R. S. Churchill 1969, 2, pp. 1137–8.
10 Churchill rehearsed his thinking for these Acts and measures in a series of speeches, articles and letters. In a speech of 11 October 1906, reprinted in his *Liberalism And The Social Problem* (1909), cited by Gilbert (1981), he expressed the need to 'draw a line below which we will not allow persons to live and yet above which they may compete with all the strength of their manhood' (Churchill 1909, p. xx). In an article he wrote for *The Nation* (7 March 1908), entitled 'The Untrodden Field in Politics', he stressed the need for the sort of measures associated with his presidency of the Board of Trade to boost 'the demand of the ordinary market for unskilled labour so as to counterbalance the oscillations of world trade'. And in a letter to Asquith of 14 March 1908, he declared, 'Dimly across gulfs of ignorance I see the outline of a policy which I call the Minimum Standard. It is national rather than departmental. I am doubtful of my power to give it concrete expression' (R. S. Churchill 1969, 2, p. 755). Churchill, however, was determined that something should be done.
11 Of his mother, he was to write in later life, 'She shone for me like the Evening Star. I loved her dearly – but at a distance' (Churchill 1989 [1930], p. 19). His father was very heavy-handed. When Churchill eventually gained admission to Sandhurst, at the third attempt, he was naturally delighted. Not so his father, who wrote him one of the most withering rebukes a father ever addressed to a son (1991 [1966], pp. 196–8). Yet Churchill revered his father (*ibid.*, pp. 46 and 52–3).
12 Blunt 1919, p. 287, diary entry for 2 October 1909.
13 On this point, consider his speech in the House of Commons on 6 July 1908 (Hansard, Fourth Series, vol. 191, col. 1330): 'They [working people] demand time to look about them, time to see their homes by daylight, to see their children, time to think and read and cultivate their gardens – time in short to live' (Churchill 1909, pp. 181–2, cited Gilbert 1981, p. 45). Now compare this with his vision of what would befall the country if none of these visions were realized, as set out in a speech he delivered in Leicester on 5 September 1909: 'The greatest danger to the British Empire and the British people ... is here in our midst, close at home, close at hand, in the vast growing cities of England and Scotland and in the dwindling and cramped villages of our denuded countryside ... the unnatural gap between rich and poor; the divorce of the people from the land; the want of proper discipline and training among our youth; the exploitation of boy labour; the "awful jumbles" of an obsolete Poor Law; the "horror havoc" of the liquor traffic; the constant insecurity in the means of subsistence and employment which breaks the heart of many a sober hard-working man; the absence of any minimum standard of life and comfort among the workers, and,

Notes to Chapter 1

at the other end, the swift increase of the vulgar, joyless luxury – here are the enemies of Britain. Beware lest they shatter the foundations of her power' (*ibid.*, cited Gilbert 1981, p. 47).

14 Soames 1999, pp. 3–4. Consult also Egremont 1977 for Blunt and his Leconfield relations.
15 Blunt 1919, p. 281.
16 Marrot 1935, p. 675.
17 Gladstone Papers, add. mss, British Library, 45986, vol. II, ff. 152–3, Gladstone to Churchill, 19 February 1910.
18 Some ten days before he submitted his hand-over notes to Churchill, Gladstone had minuted elsewhere on the 'very severe' burden being borne in the Home Office more generally by a 'continuous and self-sacrificing effort.' He continued: 'with a rather guilty conscience I must record my opinion that it has been too great. There has been a constant risk of breakdown. Unless there is a marked decrease in the volume and intensity of the work some relief must be sought' (T1/11272 (HO B/ 27590)).
19 The Home Secretary received official advice from two sources: the senior Home Office officials responsible for criminal justice policy, usually transmitted through the Permanent Under-Secretary of State (Sir Edward Troup); and the Commissioners responsible for the administration of the prison system, usually, but not always, submitted through Sir Edward, who customarily added his own comments. The *Prison Commissioners* were appointed under the Prison Act, 1877 (40 and 41 Vict. C. 21), to supervise the local prisons in England transferred from the ownership of the local authorities to that of the central government. The Directors of Convict Prisons were appointed under the Convict Prisons Act, 1850 (13 and 14 Vict. C. 39), to supervise as one entity the then convict prisons of England, each of which had previously been separately supervised by its own controlling committee, and to subsume the traditional duties of the Home Office superintendent of convicts. Limited vestigial duties as magistrates descended to the Directors, but not to the Commissioners. The Commissioners and Directors were each constituted separately as bodies corporate; each had its own seal and each administrated its own separate and different code of prison discipline. Although the Commissioners and Directors were *unified into one superintending authority in 1898* (61 and 62 Vict. C. 41), they were obliged in law, by virtue of their respective histories, to subscribe themselves in law as Commissioners when conducting local prison business and as Directors when dealing with convict prison business. In popular parlance, however, they were together known as 'The Commissioners'. See also p. 18 of this book for further information.

Notes to Chapter 2

1 Gladstone was born in 1854 and Churchill in 1874.
2 In particular the likelihood of another general election in 1910, which did take place at the end of the year, arising out of disputes between the two Houses of Parliament about their constitutional arrangements; Home Rule for Ireland; and conflicts over the Government's financial estimates.
3 See pp. 173–4 of this book.
4 Troup 1925; Newsam 1954; Nelson 1969, Pellew 1982; Home Office 1982.
5 Evans 1923; Thompson 1932. See also Nelson 1969, pp. 3–4, for a summary of the medieval office of King's Secretary, forerunner of the Secretary of State.
6 The Secretaryship of State is and always has been a single office. Any Secretary of State may perform the duties of another. Sir Edward Grey, as Foreign Secretary, on one occasion in 1910, for example, stood in for Churchill as Home Secretary (Nelson 1969, p. 4, and R. S. Churchill 1969, 2, pp. 1195–6). The Home Office Registers of Pardons and Remissions reveal that on occasions the Lords Crewe and Morley also stood in for Churchill when he was away from the Home Office. Nowadays the Home Secretary's place in the order of ministerial seniority is determined by the Prime Minister when he forms his administration.
7 Instances of this kind arose during Churchill's Home Secretaryship. See R. S. Churchill 1969, 2, pp. 1164–78, 1205–15, 1240–4 and 1268–93. For an instance illustrative of the sort of criminal case to which Mercy might have been applied but was not, see *ibid.*, pp. 1191–6. The death penalty was carried out under the signature of Sir Edward Grey in the absence of Churchill, who, however, had exhaustively researched the case beforehand and concluded that the death penalty should apply. He was a compassionate man and found the duties of the Home Secretary in matters of the death sentence to be deeply conscience-troubling. See also Chapter 8 of this book, n. 6.
8 Gardiner 1923, vol. 1, pp. 389–90.
9 Quoted in Elton 1982, p. 124. 'Twas ever thus,' old Home Office hands still say.
10 James Callaghan, who served as Home Secretary from 1967 to 1970, said much the same thing. Of each Home Office responsibility, he remarked: 'A remote-controlled bomb is concealed in nearly every one with the Home Secretary rarely realizing he will be blown up until it happens' (Royal Institute of Public Affairs Bicentenary Lectures (1982) *The Home Office – Perspectives on Policy and Administration*).
11 *News of the World*, 7 May 1939, p. 12. See also Chapter 8 of this book, n. 6.
12 Pellew 1982, pp. 61, 65 and 135–6, and Appendix E. Incorporated in these departments were the Home Office's ten inspectorates and two sub-departments. The largest inspectorates were those for factories (223 inspectors) and mines (92 inspectors). The remaining inspectorates were very small, ranging from one to nine inspectors. The Prison Inspectorate was incorporated into the Prison Commission, which, like

the Metropolitan Police Department, was a sub-department of the Home Office, but statutorily self-managed and financed separately from the main Home Office budget. Nevertheless, both subdepartments were accountable to the Home Office through the Criminal Department for the conduct of their responsibilities. Police forces outside Metropolitan London were the responsibility of their respective local authorities, although overseen in respect of their effectiveness and efficiency by HM Inspectorate of Constabulary, which in its turn was accountable for its operations to the Criminal Department of the Home Office.

13   Gladstone Papers, add. mss, British Library, 46096, f. 81, 'Notes on Home Office Business', March 1907. Pellew 1982, p. 64 and Table 5.
14   *Ibid.*, f. 269, 'Notes on Home Office Legislation and Other Work 1906–1909'.
15   PRO HO T1 File 11272/4765 (HO B 27590). Pellew 1982, p. 77, Gladstone minute, 9 February 1910.
16   Pellew 1982, pp. 79–80.
17   Except in the Special Department, which on account of its small size was not thought to need one. See *ibid.*, p. 65.
18   *Ibid.*, pp. 33–5 and 95–6.
19   Blackwell came on the scene when sentencing rather than prison treatment was the topic under discussion.
20   See Masterman 1939 and her article for the *Manchester Guardian*, 29 November 1954, p. 4.
21   40 and 41 Vict. C. 21.
22   13 and 14 Vict. C. 39.
23   61 and 62 Vict. C. 41, and Parliamentary Papers, Report of the Departmental Committee on Prisons Cmnd. 7702, recommendations 23, p. 46. For the amelioration of prison treatment, see Section 23, p. 7, paragraph 2; Section 72, p. 25; and p. 8, paragraph 25 of the Committee's Report. See also pp. 17–18 of this book.
24   11 and 12 Geo. 6 C. 58. See also the Annual Report of the Commissioners and Directors of Convict Prisons for 1934, *Review of the Past Twenty-five Years*, pp. 5–15, especially pp. 8–11. Note, too, Fox 1952, p. 4. See also Chapter 1 of this book, n. 19.
25   Parliamentary Estimates 1909–1910, 1910–1911, 1911–1912, Class III, 8, England and the Colonies, in Parliamentary Papers, vols LV 1909, LXII 1910, and XLIX 1911. See also Imperial Calendar 1910 and 1911, p. 333.
26   Thomson was the third of four sons of William Thomson, Archbishop of York and formerly Provost of Queen's College, Oxford. Educated at Eton and New College, Oxford, Basil withdrew from the college because of ill health before taking his degree. He spent his early career in the Colonial Service, stationed in Fiji, Tonga (of which he was Prime Minister) and British New Guinea. He qualified as a barrister of the Inner Temple in 1896, after which he joined the Prison Service in the rank of deputy governor at Liverpool Prison. This was the rank for newly appointed staff to the governor grade and remained so until assistant governors were appointed after the First

World War. Following his first appointment he served as governor of Northampton, Cardiff, Dartmoor and Wormwood Scrubs prisons. His administrative and operative skills were recognized as being of a very high order, and in his last two prisons in particular he was noted for his imaginative approach to regimes for young offenders, equipping them with educational and trade skills. He served as secretary to the Commission from 1908 to 1913, after which he transferred to the Metropolitan Police as an assistant commissioner in charge of the Criminal Investigation Department, from which he resigned in 1921 following a disagreement over the reorganization of the force. During his lifetime he wrote a number of books dealing with fiction, Oceania and historical subjects, of which his history of Dartmoor Prison and his autobiography are especially valuable to prison historians. He died in 1939.

27 Originally appointed from civilian medical practice in 1898 as a Director of Convict Prisons. On his retirement in 1910, Donkin was reappointed to the Commission as medical adviser, free from the usual duties of a Director/Commissioner, for a period of five years, unpaid but with an honorarium for his services. He was knighted in 1911.

28 See Chapter 2 of this book, n. 25.

29 These figures compare, respectively, with 186,396 and 20,904 for 1910–11, and 200,265 and 21,926 to 1909–10. In each year the number of female detainees in the average daily population amounted approximately to one-eighth of the total (Annual Reports of the Commissioners and Directors of Convict Prisons 1909–10, 1910–11 and 1911–12).

30 Thomas 1972, Chapters 1–8.

31 *Ibid.*, p. 41.

32 *Ibid.*, p. 42. It should be noted that the convict prisons which came into being during the middle years of the nineteenth century had a Civil Guard which carried guns and that these were used when the need arose. The Guard was disbanded in 1919.

33 *Ibid.*, especially Chapter 1, pp. 42–50.

34 Churchill's view was that prison officers were akin to police officers, soldiers and sailors. It was therefore not appropriate for them to form trade unions. This remained the official view until 1918, when the prison officers were afforded a representative board, the nearest approximation to a trade union they could secure. Union status came about in 1938 (*ibid.*, pp. 143–8). Not that prison officers were necessarily disadvantaged. A case involving the dismissal of prison officers for indiscipline may be consulted in R. S. Churchill 1969, 2, pp. 1179–82. Churchill disapproved of their dismissal and the Prison Commissioners had to reinstate them. He was particularly sensitive to fair play between employer and employee. It is interesting to cross-reference this particular case with the one highlighted in Chapter 1 of this book, n. 8.

35 Thomas 1972, pp. 131–4 and 136.

36 Born at Boathouse, Blantyre, in 1874. A product of Polmont Public School, Falkirk High School and Glasgow University (graduated in 1887). Private Secretary to

Notes to Chapter 2

Lord Pentland, Secretary for Scotland, 1904–10. Barrister, Middle Temple, 1908. MP for Glasgow, 1910–22. Parliamentary Private Secretary to Churchill, Minister of Munitions, 1917–19, and Secretary of War, 1922. Joined the Labour Party in 1924. Author of *Winston Leonard Spencer-Churchill* (1905) and *Winston Churchill in Peace and War* (1916). Churchill destabilized the Conservative Party, 1900–5, but Chamberlain in his turn destabilized first the Liberal Party over Home Rule for Ireland and the then Conservative Party over tariff reform, hence his unpopularity in political circles.

37 Scott 1905, pp. 261–2.
38 As the Permanent Under-Secretary of State at the Colonial Office later reminded the Secretary of State for the Colonies in a memorandum dated 27 December 1907: 'He [Churchill, at that time Parliamentary Under-Secretary of State at the Colonial Office] is most tiresome to deal with and will I fear give you trouble – as his father did – in any position to which he may be called. The restless energy, uncontrollable desire for notoriety and the lack of moral perception make him an anxiety indeed!' (R. S. Churchill 1969, 2, p. 730).
39 Quoted in Cannadine 1995, p. 132. Chapter 6 of Cannadine should be read for Churchill's family background and the scandals that surrounded him throughout his life.
40 Lucy Masterman, writing in the *Manchester Guardian*, 29 November 1954, p. 4, reported that when her husband, C. F. G. Masterman, Churchill's Parliamentary Under-Secretary of State, tackled him returning from his unnecessary intervention in the Siege of Sydney Street, which provoked attacks on his conduct in Parliament, Churchill's rejoinder was: 'Now Charlie! Don't be croth. It was such fun.'
41 See David, for interesting information on Churchill's conduct in the Cabinet. See also Williamson 1988, pp. 233–4, for further enlightenment. 42 PRO HO P/Com. 7/739. Also *The Times* obituary, 20 August 1935, Pellew 1982 and Leslie 1938.
43 McConville 1995, Chapters 13–17, for the membership, business procedure, recommendations and aftermath of this committee's activities.
44 Leslie 1938, pp. 87–9.
45 *Ibid.*, p. 87.
46 *Ibid.*, p. 88, and p. 92, where Asquith's letter is quoted in full: 'I am as you are aware, very anxious that, as far as practicable, the recommendations of the recent Committee should be carried into effect, and I believe that you have the disposition, as I know that you have the ability, to bring about the object.' Shane Leslie quotes Asquith on leaving office as saying to the committee: 'I have appointed the best Committee ever seen, who will go on with my work. Ruggles-Brise, who is the head, is a splendid little fellow' (see an article, 'Prison Reform', contributed by Leslie to the periodical *The Nineteenth Century*, January 1938, p. 71).
47 As witness the minutes of the Commissioners' meetings and the way he expressed his written views to the Home Office and the Home Secretary, his arguments cogently

presented, frequently at great length. He sought the opinions of his governors on his visits to their prisons and in his written communications with them. Having served in the Home Office for fourteen years, eleven of them in a private secretarial capacity to Home Secretaries, he knew what motivated them and their senior officials and how they went about their business. Indeed, it could be argued that this was one of the characteristics that appealed to Asquith when selecting him for appointment as Chairman of the Prison Commission. From a Home Office point of view, his appointment may be seen as putting an end once and for all to the independence of the Commission, as exercised by Du Cane, who treated it more or less as his private fiefdom. Henceforward, it was under sharper Home Office surveillance. This, in the event, was helpful to the Commission because it placed the Home Office between itself and Parliament, and general public, whereas under Du Cane it had been directly in the firing line. If there was one respect, however, in which Brise replicated his predecessor, it was in his refusal as Chairman of the Commission to function as a *primus inter pares*. The dominance of the Chairman's control of the Commission was as strong as Du Cane's. Once consultation had taken place and decisions reached, there was no going back. As one of his governors described him in his memoirs: 'an absolute sahib ... clever and an autocrat, accustomed to make up his mind and sweep all obstacles out of the way of his will' (Rich 1932, p. 19). The dominance of the Chairman's control set by Du Cane and Brise was maintained throughout the history of the Prison Commission.

48 At Spains Hall are several of Brise's annotated books. Some of his remarks in the Annual Reports to Parliament of the Prison Commissioners and Directors of Convict Prisons can be traced to them and to his own more personal writings. Jowett was a strong supporter of the Northcote-Trevelyan civil service reforms which produced the competitive examination entry system. He regarded the system as providing an excellent device for enabling the output of public schools and universities, especially if trained in the classics, to seek professional and gentlemanly employment in the service of the State. Under Jowett's aegis, Balliol acquired a reputation as 'a nursery of public men' (Faber 1957, p. 404).

49 See Brise 1924. It is a fascinating account of the congresses whose president he was of the executive body charged with their oversight from 1910 to 1926.

50 PRO HO 45/10563/172511, H. B. Simpson (Principal Clerk of the Home Office Criminal Department), in particular, 5 November 1913 and 27 July 1915. Gladstone commended him to Churchill in his handing-over notes as 'a man of brilliancy and it is always well on difficult questions to have his opinion. But his good judgement is occasionally flighty' (Gladstone Papers, add. mss, British Library, 45986, vol. II, f. 151). In his capacity as the author of the introduction to the 1909 criminal part of Judicial Statistics, published in 1911, Simpson fell foul of Churchill largely because he attributed one of the causes of rising crime at this time to 'the marked growth since 1898 of a strong sentiment of compassion for the criminal', citing as

examples 'mitigation of prison discipline, the 1907 Probation of Offenders Act, and the establishment of the Borstal System for young delinquents' (Introduction to the Criminal Statistics, 1909, Part 1, Crime in 1909, pp. 10 and 11). Churchill considered these statements, which he had not seen because the 1909 statistics were not made public until 1911 and as Home Secretary he should have had the opportunity to scrutinize them before they were made public, to be at variance from the criminal justice policies he was endeavouring to implement and in a Home Office internal memorandum he described the publication of the statistics as 'exceedingly ill-timed and will not improbably cause me embarrassment and trouble. I regret that none of those privy to my confidential plans of Prison Reform thought fit to consult me before making this inopportune and injudicious publication.' Simpson's statements certainly embarrassed Churchill, for in a debate in the House of Commons on 26 June 1911 they were quoted by Churchill's critics (Hansard, Fifth Series, vol. 27, cols 245–6) to suggest that he was at fault in the way he used the Royal Prerogative of Mercy to remit prisoners' sentences. The consequence of Churchill's intervention in the Home Office internal memorandum was that in future all Home Office publications had to be finally approved by the Parliamentary Under-Secretary of State to whom they had to be sent after they had been placed before Churchill and who would then settle the date of publication and 'take a final view of the substance' (R. S. Churchill 1969, 2, 3 February 1911, p. 1245). Sir Harold Scott, who knew Simpson, reports that it became 'difficult to work with him, for he was quite capable in his capriciousness of deciding a matter in contrary senses on successive days'. He adds that when he, Scott, and Simpson's successor went through the papers in Simpson's room at the Home Office after his retirement, 'they found tucked away in the drawers of his desk many long-lost files which he had found inconvenient, and had put quietly to sleep' (Scott 1969, pp. 61–2).

51 Forsythe 1991, p. 37.
52 *Ibid.*
53 See Chapters 5 and 7 of this book.
54 A point, incidentally, made by Arthur Paterson (1911, p. 9) in a collection of articles he wrote for *The Times* in June 1910: 'They [the Commissioners] also think, and not without justice, that, having spent many years studying and working at prison administration from every point of view, they are rather better judges of what can be done and should be done than enthusiastic idealists who have not had any administrative experience at all.'
55 Gladstone Papers, add. mss, British Library, 46070, ff. 215–16, Brise to Gladstone, 20 February 1911. Brise was certainly wrong in believing that Churchill had no future in English politics, but, like everyone else at that time, he could not possibly foresee the 1939–45 situation. Yet in 1935, when Brise died and Churchill was in his wilderness years, his 1911 verdict must have seemed to him, as it did to so many others at the time, to have been realized. It was not only on matters of criminal justice, of course,

that the Home Office senior officials were belaboured by Churchill for information and opinions on this and that. They had similar barrages from him in all aspects of Home Office business. Waller referred to this in a private letter he had written to Gladstone on 11 August 1910: '[Churchill] is exercising the minds of other branches of the Home Office greatly! He had a row with John Pedder [in charge of the Special Subjects Department] because J.P. would not alter the introduction of the licensing statistics to suit W.C.'s political views; so W.C. altered it and J.P. refused to sign it – quite right too! It was published unsigned. I hear an occasional hearty "cuss" from other parts of the H.O. too; but maybe we shall settle down. All this for your private ear' (Gladstone Papers, add. mss, British Library, 45994, f. 260, Waller to Gladstone, 11 August 1910).

56 Hansard, Fifth Series, vol. 19, col. 1348, 20 July 1910.
57 R. S. Churchill 1969, 2, p. 1153.
58 For Camp Hill and its importance, see Chapter 9 of this book, n. 15.
59 I am grateful to the Secretary of the Glenalmond Old Students' Association for information about Blackwell's school career and to the librarian of the Inner Temple for information concerning his legal training.
60 Pellew 1982, p. 67. On pp. 67–70 Pellew offers a succinct account of the Beck case, its origin, course and consequences. See also Radzinowicz and Hood 1986, p. 765, for the pardons and compensation.
61 Gladstone Papers, add. mss, British Library, 45986, vol. II, f. 151, Gladstone to Churchill, 19 February 1910.
62 See *The Times*, 23 September 1941, p. 7. The Glenalmond *Chronicle* of September 1941, p. 18, spelled out this verdict in more detail: 'He was one of the greatest authorities in the country on the criminal mind and criminal methods, and one of his duties was to advise the Home Secretary on points of law arising out of convictions. Every petition from convicted persons for many years went through his hands, and in a great many murder cases the Home Secretary relied on his guidance before advising the King as to whether the capital sentence should be carried out or not.'
63 Criminal Appeal Act 7 Edw. 7 C. 23. See also Pellew 1982, p. 70, for the creation of the Court of Appeal. It reflected a long-standing dissatisfaction with the operation of the Royal Prerogative of Mercy, arising largely from the secrecy of its application, but, in itself, it had little to contribute to the nature and volume of work which still had to be done in the Home Office.
64 Pellew 1982, p. 70, and Radzinowicz and Hood 1986, p. 770. See also Troup 1925, pp. 55–72, and for an account of the Royal Prerogative of Mercy as it operated at this time in criminal justice cases, and of the coming into being of the court of Criminal Appeal.
65 He remained active in retirement, being chairman of the statutory committee of the Pharmaceutical Society. The Glenalmond College Old Students' Society's records are replete with accounts of his sporting prowess at the college and in later life, particularly

Notes to Chapter 2

in golf, and his association with the game at the Royal and Ancient Golf Club, St Andrews, where he was awarded its gold medal at the time of his qualification as a barrister and was captain in the year of his retirement.

66   Pellew 1982, p. 23.
67   Strutt 1961, p. 146 cited by Pellew 1982, p. 73. Looking back on my own service in the Home Office between 1967 and 1985, I would say that Strutt's statement continued to ring true until the early 1970s, when one change after another began to be made, a situation which continues to this day, as the Home Office adapts to a rapidly developing society.
68   He did, however, contribute to the *Whitehall Series* (1925), a valuable history of the Home Office and its responsibilities as he knew them when he worked there. He was also responsible for two other publications, one dealing with free trade, in respect of which Balliol College awarded him the Cobden Prize when he was a student there, and the other with *Place-names of Western Aberdeenshire*. In a London *Evening Standard* article of 22 April 1925 (p. 7), however, he permitted himself to outline some thoughts on the making of criminal legislation. These included: the need to oppose legislation which unnecessarily curtailed the freedom of the subject; avoid, unless forced to do so, making crimes out of things which are not crimes already; avoid introducing prohibitive legislation beyond the standard of conduct which will be accepted by the general feeling of the country; and avoid foisting on the police a burden greater than they can carry. Much of the article discusses the problems involved in the application of these principles to particular issues, which enables Troup to reflect on them in his lifetime of work at the Home Office. There is much food for thought in them in relation to today's criminal justice scene.
69   The entry in *Who Was Who* which indicates that he entered the Home Office in 1880, cited by Pellew (1982, pp. 32 and 208, op. cit.) is therefore incorrect. I am indebted to the Registrar of Oxford University, the librarian of Balliol College, and the 25th Annual Report of the Civil Service Commission, 1880 (PRO/CSC4) for helping me to sort out the foregoing details of Troup's early career.
70   Gladstone Papers, add. mss, British Library, 45993, f. 113, Troup to Gladstone, 18 December 1907. See Pellew 1982, p. 71, for a summary of his career.
71   Evidence given in 1888 as recorded in the Second Report of the Royal Commission on Civil Establishments. See Pellew 1982, p. 99.
72   These committees are mentioned against Troup's name in the Balliol College Register, where mention is also made of his service as a private secretary.
73   Gladstone Papers, add. mss, British Library, 45986, vol. II, f. 151, Gladstone to Churchill, 19 February 1910.
74   Scott 1969, p. 28. Scott was later chairman of the Prison Commission and subsequently Commissioner of the Metropolitan Police. During the Second World War, he was the Permanent Under-Secretary of State, Department of Home Security.
75   Guillemard 1937, p. 14. In later life he was governor of the Straits Settlements.

76 Butler 1950, p. 69. In later life he was director of the International Labour Office. The Home Office, of course, was sufficiently small scale before the First World War to enable the Permanent Under-Secretary of State to know its staff and to be able to give them close attention. This, however, had become impossible by the time Butler wrote his memoirs due to the expansion of Home Office operations and the number of staff needed to cope with them. Nowadays it is larger than ever.
77 *The Times* obituary, 9 July 1941, p. 7.
78 Scott 1969, p. 28.
79 *Manchester Guardian*, 29 November 1954, p. 4.
80 London *Evening Standard*, 22 April 1925, p. 7.
81 Masterman 1939, pp. 168 (for Troup) and 165 (for the officials).
82 *Manchester Guardian*, 29 November 1954, p. 4.
83 *Ibid.*
84 London *Evening Standard*, 22 April 1925, p. 7.

Notes to Chapter 3

1 This expression was coined by the Prison Commissioners in their Annual Report to Parliament, 1909–10, paragraphs 42 and 43. It describes Churchill's attempt, highlighted by the suffragette disturbances, to deal with problems caused by the courts' reluctance to use their option of second-division local imprisonment. The quotations that follow, unless otherwise stated, are extracted from the Commissioners' aforementioned paragraphs.
2 PRO HO 144/1042/183256.
3 For a full account of the Commissioners' views, see paragraphs 42 and 43 of their Annual Report to Parliament, 1909–10. There is useful information on the Home Office interpretation of the second division as provided in the 1898 Prison Act in PRO HO 45/12905/116578. The 'star' system is described in PRO HO 45/9747/A57530. These references are mentioned in Forsythe 1991, pp. 98 and 99. There is an excellent description of the trials and tribulations of the suffragettes, the Prison Commissioners and the Home Office in Forsythe 1991, pp. 105–8, and, from a more technical standpoint, in Radzinowicz and Hood 1986, pp. 439–61.
4 Blunt's memorandum, his covering letter, and Churchill's minute to Troup are all published in R. S. Churchill 1969, 2, pp. 1144–8 and 1153–4. For Churchill's minute to Troup, see also PRO HO 144/1042/183256/21. Blunt's memorandum as published in R. S. Churchill 1967, however, omits certain passages that appear in the original memorandum, which is lodged in the Churchill Archive in Churchill College, Cambridge University, reference CHAR 12/4/3–12a.

Notes to Chapter 3

5 Blunt 1919, p. 309, diary entry for 2 April 1910, records a conversation in which Blunt says of Churchill that 'he is obstinate about forcible feeding in spite of all [Granville] Barker and I could say about torture and the Spanish Inquisition, which it closely ressembles [sic]'. But in a case before the courts in 1909, when a certain Mrs Marie Leigh, who had been forcibly fed in Winson Green Prison, Birmingham, sued the Home Secretary and prison officials for assault and sought an injunction to restrain repetition of their acts, Lord Chief Justice Alverstone ruled 'as a matter of Law it was the duty of the prison officials to preserve the health of the prisoners, and a fortiori to preserve their lives' (cited in Radzinowicz and Hood 1986, p. 452, n. 81).

6 Dated 4 March 1910 (R. S. Churchill 1969, 2, pp. 1154–5). Gladstone, in his hand-over notes, commended Troup to Churchill as 'an admirable official. The closeness and the accuracy of his work can always be relied upon, and there is no greater authority in the country on all matters relating to criminal administration.' He was a restraining influence on Churchill's prison sentencing and treatment policies, fearing they would undermine the deterrent features of the inherited, established policies for dealing with these matters, on which he firmly believed the country's social stability depended. He made it his business to ensure that any changes were channelled through the Home Office's traditional formalisms and legalisms. He retired in 1922. For more detailed information about him, see pp. 35–40 of this book.

7 Ruggles-Brise (1857–1935) had served in the Home Office since 1887 and as a Prison Commissioner since 1891. He was the most philosophically inclined of all Chairmen of the Prison Commission, a proponent of the emerging science of criminology. He shared Troup's caution, but was more flexible in his attitudes, largely because he had to face the practical consequences of the Commission's daily face-to-face contact with prisoners (Radzinowicz and Hood 1986, pp. 596–9). See also pp. 27–32 of this book.

8 R. S. Churchill 1969, 2, pp. 1155–6.

9 'Rule 243A', PRO HO 144 /1042/ 183256.

10 Hansard, Fifth Series, vol. 15, cols 177–9, 15 March 1910. See also cols 1457–8, 31 March 1910.

11 R. S. Churchill 1969, 2, pp. 1156–7. Gladstone, in fact, was dissatisfied with Churchill's reference to the work that he, Gladstone, had put in to devising an ameliorated regime in the second division of local imprisonment. Churchill's recognition of Gladstone's contribution, however, was genuine and he was perfectly happy to soothe Gladstone's irritation by arranging for a parliamentary question to be put to him to allow him to offer Gladstone generous recognition (Hansard, 31 March 1910).

12 PRO HO 144/1042/183256/30a.

13 PRO HO 144/1042/183256/30a.

14 PRIO HO 144 / 1107 / 200655, '1910 Suffragette Disturbances'. Forcible feeding, backed by the 1909 Alverstone judgement, continued in all cases where the prison authorities, on medical advice, considered the practice necessary to save life. The

practice as it related to the suffragettes came to an end at the outbreak of the First World War in 1914 when, as a gesture of goodwill, they abandoned their campaign; however, it continued to be employed against prisoners on hunger strike until the 1970s. Between times, more humane and safer methods of keeping hunger-strikers alive were gradually introduced.

15 Blunt 1919, p. 307, diary entry of 18 March 1910.
16 28 and 29 Vict. C. 126, clause 67.
17 This position persists to the present day.
18 R. S. Churchill 1969, 2, pp. 1152–3.
19 McConville 1981, pp. 383–92 and 396–430, for the policy and regime of the convict prisons. I have also followed Ruggles-Brise 1921, Chapters 3 and 4. Likewise, Fox 1934, on the birth of the Penal Servitude Acts and on 'the progressive stage' and 'the marks system', pp. 12–14 and 155–6. I am also indebted to Forsythe 1991, Chapter 5, a good general account of penal servitude, 1835–1939.
20 16 and 17 Vict. C. 99, 1853: penal servitude may be ordered by courts in place of sentences of transportation of less than fourteen years. Also 20 and 21 Vict. C. 3, 1857: sentences of transportation abolished; sentences of penal servitude to be passed for all offences previously punishable by transportation.
21 Prison Rule dated 21 January 1905 made by the Home Secretary under the 1898 Prison Act. Published as Appendix 17c in the Annual Report of the Prison Commissioners to Parliament, 1904–5. Female convicts spent three months in initial separate confinement. For a more general account of penal servitude, see Ruggles-Brise 1921, Chapter 4, especially pp. 40–1. By 1905 the availability of public works as a source of convict employment had sharply declined and its place had been taken by various types of employment in workshops of a kind found in local prisons.
22 PRO HO 45/13658/185668/3.
23 *Ibid.*
24 See PRO HO 45/13658/185668/1. The 185668 series and PRI Com. 7/308 and 309 cover Galsworthy's dealings with Gladstone and the Prison Commissioners during 1909.
25 C-7702 HMSO, April 1895 (the 1895 Report).
26 Marrot 1935, p. 675, Churchill to Galsworthy, 14 May 1909. On the same page there is a letter to Galsworthy, written in much the same vein as Churchill's, from Lord Crewe, the Colonial Secretary. This dropped a hint that the Prison Commissioners were experimenting with the possibility of modifying the system of separate confinement. Marrot's biography reveals elsewhere that Galsworthy had ease of access to government ministers, including Gladstone.
27 The Prison Commissioners, and especially the Home Office senior officials, were resistant all along to the abandonment of separate confinement for convicts in the initial stage of their custody because they believed it gave the necessary penal character to the sentence of penal servitude, on a par with a month's separate confinement

in local prisons as the penal element of the sentence of hard labour. Without it, the sentence would wither on the vine. Gladstone, in his authorization of the new scheme, considered that separate confinement ought really to be used for no more than observation and classification purposes at the start of convicts' sentences, and for disciplinary purposes when they were under sentence. 'The sooner these men can be sent to healthy, hard, industrial work in the convict prisons, the better,' he stated. He agreed to three months' separate confinement for all convicts at the beginning of their penal servitude sentences simply because of the difficulty at the time of providing quarters for an increased number of convicts. He would have liked to press his views beyond Brise's proposals, but, because of this accommodation situation, he indicated he was obliged to take account of Brise's and Troup's cautions (PRO HO 45/13658/185668/3).

28 See Chapter 3 of this book, n. 26.
29 This correspondence is in R. S. Churchill 1969, 2, pp. 1148–50. See also Marrot 1935, pp. 676–8.
30 PRO HO 45/13658/185668/4. Also PRI Com. 7/309.
31 Marrot 1935, p. 261.
32 *Ibid.*, pp. 250–68, 281, 283 and 146–55, for full accounts of both the reception given to Galsworthy's play and his correspondence with leading authors of the day about it. See also *Blackwell's*, April 1910, pp. 582–5. Consult further *The Times*, 21 February 1910, p. 11 and 22 February, p. 10.
33 Marrot 1935, p. 261.
34 Leslie 1938, p. 150.
35 PRO HO 45/13658/185668/4, Brise to Churchill, 25 February 1910 (all following quotes from this memorandum). Radzinowicz and Hood (1986, p. 594) describe Brise's reasons as 'all the worn out arguments which had been repeated over the last seventy years'. The Prison Commissioners and the Home Office senior officials had already deployed them on Gladstone when he was Home Secretary and wrestling with the problem of convict initial separate confinement. He had been relatively little influenced by them.
36 PRO HO 45/13658/185668/4, Troup to Churchill, 26 February 1910.
37 PRO HO 45/13658/185668/5, Churchill to Troup, 7 March 1910 (all following quotations are from this letter).
38 R. S. Churchill 1969, 2, pp. 1150–1.
39 Essex County Record Office, A5909 (part), Box 6.
40 R. S. Churchill 1969, 2, pp. 1150–1.
41 *Ibid.*, pp. 1151–2.
42 *Ibid.*, pp. 1152–3.
43 PRO HO 45/13658/185668/5. Also P Com. 7/309/17324/11M/XC 146779.
44 Galsworthy naturally disagreed with Brise on this point. In his diary for 5 April 1910, Galsworthy wrote: 'This is mere nonsense for Falder is by no means exceptional,

judging from what I have seen myself. And moreover, the ordinary governor would not be likely to take the notice of him that my Governor does' (Marrot 1935, p. 281). Galsworthy could be right. Cases of this kind do occur in prisons.

45 Galsworthy's play certainly aroused deep antagonism in the Home Office. The playwright's diary entry for 5 April 1910 records a lunch at which Masterman (Churchill's parliamentary under-secretary of state) was present. The latter told him that he 'had turned the Home Office upside down with Justice and that Ruggles-Brise was incensed with me' (*ibid*.). The Prison Commissioners, in paragraph 37 of their 1909–10 Annual Report to Parliament, vented their spleen on the portrayal of separate confinement in the play.
46 PRO HO 45/13658/185668/6.
47 *Ibid*.
48 See Chapter 3 of this book, n. 37.
49 Undated minute by Troup on a memorandum from Brise dated 10 March 1910 indicating that the information requested by Churchill was being assembled (PRO HO 45/13658/185668/5).
50 See Chapter 3 of this book, n. 37.
51 A distinguished French sociologist and criminologist, Tarde served as director of the Criminal Statistics Bureau at the Ministry of Justice in Paris. He pioneered the study of crime through statistics.
52 PRO HO 45/13658/185668/6.
53 See Chapter 1 of this book, n. 13. Mention should here be made of the impact on Churchill of Seebohm Rowntree's *Poverty*, an analysis of living conditions in York, on which he wrote an unpublished book review, probably in December 1901 (R. S. Churchill 1969, 1, pp. 105–11). Churchill referred to this book in a speech at Blackpool on 9 January 1902 (*ibid*., 2, p. 31.) He is quoted as saying that the poverty of people in York 'extends to one-fifth of the population; nearly one-fifth had something between one-and-a-half and three-fourths as much food to eat as the paupers in the York Union. That I call a terrible and shocking thing, people who have only the workhouse or prison as the only avenues to change from the present situation.'
54 Appendix 17C, p. 135, of the Prison Commissioners' Annual Report to Parliament for the year ended 31 March 1905.The appendix cites the statutory origin – regulations made under the Prison Act of 1898.
55 PRO HO 45/13658/185668/7.
56 PRO HO 45/13658/185668/7.
57 The minutes mentioned in this paragraph are in *ibid*.
58 *Ibid*.
59 *Ibid*.
60 *Ibid*.
61 *Ibid*.

Notes to Chapter 3

62 *Ibid.* It had to lie for no fewer than thirty days during which each House sat. However, after the presentation of the Rule the Lords sat for only fourteen days before the dissolution of Parliament. As the law required all the sitting days to be in the same session, the Rule had to be withdrawn, to be presented again in the next session of both Houses. A note on the file dated 24 March 1911 reveals that the represented Rule did not mature in due form until then. Only on that date, therefore, was it signed by Churchill and made operative. Since the rule had first been presented, there had been a general election, in late 1910. The new Parliament did not meet until early 1911.
63 Hansard, Fifth Series, 20 July 1910, vol. 19, cols 1327–64, especially col. 1349.
64 Marrot 1935, p. 283, diary entry for 12 July, in which Galsworthy records an interview with Churchill when the two men had discussed a wide range of prison issues.
65 R. S. Churchill 1969, 2, p. 1190.
66 W. Beveridge 1953, p. 66, whose verdict on Churchill's Presidency of the Board of Trule is applicable to Churchill's changes in separate confinement at the Home Office: a striking illustration 'of how much the personality of the minister in a few critical months may change the course of social legislation' (Rowse 1971 [1958], pp. 391–2).

Notes to Chapter 4

1 PRO HO 144/1067/189934/5 and PRO HO 144/926/ A49225/6 for all quotes and citations which follow, unless otherwise footnoted.
2 Prevention of Crime Act, 1908, which introduced the new sentence of preventive detention to be served in a special prison on the Isle of Wight. At the time Troup and Churchill were in discussion about aged convicts, the prison was still under construction and the Prison Rules relating to the regime for preventive detainees had not yet been drawn up or approved by Churchill. Section 12 of the Act enabled the Home Secretary to take the course of action suggested by Troup.
3 PRO HO/144/926/A49225/6.
4 *Ibid.* It will be recalled that it was on 27 May that Churchill issued his determination on initial separate confinement of convicts.
5 *Ibid.*
6 *Ibid.*
7 *Ibid.*
8 Aylesbury was a prison for female convicts. Only four prisoners satisfying the criteria for inclusion in the 'Old Guard' were held there, according to Brise's nominal role. It seems unlikely that Brise envisaged locating them in Parkhurst, a men's prison, of

9   PRO HO 144/926/A49225/6.
10 *Ibid*. See *The Times*, 8 January 2005 (News p. 35) for a description of today's arrangements at Norwich Prison for the regimes of elderly prisoners. The facilities compare very favourably with the best in community care homes and hospitals.
11 PRO HO 144/18869.
12 Churchill's idea of a 'special certificate of character' to help convicts to compete better for employment after their release, plus 'the money grant both to employers and workmen', was novel, and he deserves credit for it. Resettling discharged prisoners into regular employment in the hope that such employment would enable them to steer clear of crime in the future was ground-breaking.
13 PRO HO 144/18869, Brise to Churchill, 14 April 1910.
14 Brise has a point here. Churchill may have foreseen the problem and sought to avoid it by suggesting that the strenuous work party should be composed of volunteers. On the other hand, some selection or other would have been needed if there were more volunteers than places available, which would have been likely, as privileges were on offer. Trouble could then arise.
15 Borstals are dealt with in Chapter 5 of this book.
16 PRO HO 144/18869, Troup to Churchill, 25 April 1910.
17 Churchill was certainly aware of this because, in his memorandum of 28 March to Brise, he specifically mentioned extending remission by a further 25 per cent. Brise might have been expected to bridle at this, but he did not do so. Troup, however, picked up the point, significantly stressing the drastic effect it would have on the longest sentences and its implications for the courts. It was an issue which could not be casually ignored.
18 PRO HO 144/18869, Churchill to Brise, undated. The date could be 25 April 1910, because that is when Brise minuted to Troup about 'merit' marks, and that is on the same sheet as Churchill's comments to Brise. It will be recalled that by this date Churchill already had before him the data on convict crime which he had asked Troup and Brise to supply.
19 This subject is discussed at great length by Ruggles-Brise 1924, Chapter 14. There is, too, a useful historical prologue to aid for local prisoners as it had developed down to 1934 in Fox 1934, Chapter 11 and as it had developed at that date in convict and preventive detention prisons in Chapters 14 and 15. McConville 1981, pp. 362–3 and 419–25, and 1995, pp. 319–24, have modern assessments of these questions during the periods concerned. Radzinowicz and Hood 1986, Chapter 18, should also be consulted for the nineteenth-and early twentieth-century situation. Forsythe 1991 has a good study of the whole question up to 1939.
20 See pp. 56–7 of this book for the recidivism element at the heart of prison statistics.

Notes to Chapter 4

21 Churchill's aid scheme did not extend to prisoners serving terms of local imprisonment for whom other arrangements were already in being, which had long been the case.
22 Ruggles-Brise 1924, pp. 164–5. Convicts who graduated into the long sentence division of their sentences, having served more than five years of their terms, however, had special privileges which allowed them to spend part of their accumulating gratuities on 'articles of comfort and relaxation'. Most of the cash, however, remained in their discharge fund.
23 PRO HO 144/18869, Brise to Churchill, 14 April 1910.
24 The Royal Society was originally founded in London in 1860 by Samuel Whitbread. It attracted the patronage of the Duke of Westminster, gaining prestige as a result (Radzinowicz and Hood 1986, p. 605). Wheatley's Mission was officially St Giles's Christian Mission, whose superintendent was William Wheatley (McConville 1995, op. cit., p. 328).
25 PRO HO 144/18869, Brise to Churchill, 14 April 1910.
26 PRO HO 144/18869, Brise to Churchill, 13 May 1910.
27 PRO HO 144/18869.
28 Subsequently Churchill had taken part in a discussion with Lloyd George, Chancellor of the Exchequer, concerning the funding. 'He assured me', wrote Churchill, 'that he would be glad to agree to the expenditure, although, of course, the matter must be threshed out in the ordinary way with the Treasury. You may take this matter for settled provided that it is concluded during the tenure of the present Government' (Leslie 1938, 152–3).
29 R. S. Churchill 1969, 2, pp. 1183–6, correspondence between Hobhouse and Churchill from 'June' 1910 (Hobhouse to Churchill) and 26 June 1910 (Churchill to Hobhouse).
30 Gilbert 1991, p. 217.
31 PRO P Com. 7/413.
32 A young barrister and first director of the Borstal Association. He was later knighted and continued in office until his retirement in 1935 (Fox 1952, p. 266; Radzinowicz and Hood 1986, p. 384).
33 PRO HO 144/18869. This minute is one of Churchill's most important in the criminal justice field, because it marks the point when the focus of his interests shifts. During the early months of his Home Secretaryship he concentrated on what happened to people, especially convicts, inside prison. During his later months, however, his energies were concentrated on sentencing policies, his aim being to reduce the number of custodial sentences.
34 PRO P Com. 7/413.
35 The societies named in the minutes of Churchill's meeting on 19 July, above, with the addition of the United Synagogue Discharged Prisoners' Aid Society.
36 PRO P Com. 7/413.

37 Radzinowicz and Hood 1986, op. cit., p. 617.
38 Churchill 1989 [1900], pp. 69–70.
39 PRO HO 45/ 16483/192637/1, Churchill to Brise, 4 April 1910.
40 *Ibid.*
41 Prison Department Committee Report 1895, C-7702, especially paragraphs 23, 25 and 32.
42 Report of the Departmental Committee on the Education and Moral Instruction of Prisoners, 1896, C-8154.
43 *Ibid.*, paragraph 69 for the recommendation and paragraphs 70–6 for suggestions dealing with routine administrative matters relating to the organization of lectures. Paragraphs 65–8 deal with arguments against lectures in terms of the evidence given. While there was support for linking lectures to moral teaching, there was much evidence favouring secular subjects and here and there a desire for the latest teaching aid of the day, the magic lantern. Paragraph 77 is important historically because it is a reminder that lectures, certainly in convict prisons, were not necessarily as recent as Brise had suggested to Churchill.
44 The standing orders to governors of convict and local prisons which Brise sent to Churchill spell out the detailed central oversight of these events. A lecture could take place once a week in a convict prison. The prisoners had to 'proceed to labour direct from the Halls and ... cease labour earlier than the hour laid down ... so that attendance at the lecture or address may not interfere with the regular time allowed for dinner'. It was not labour that had to be sacrificed for the lecture but the morning chapel service. Labour was sacrosanct: it was part of discipline and had priority over every other regime activity.
45 See Chapter 5 of this book.
46 When, on 20 July 1910, Churchill defended his stewardship of the Home Office in the Commons, he informed the House that these events were eagerly anticipated by the prisoners, secured good conduct, and supplied people in prison with food for thought, 'and in regard to music a certain solace which cannot be injurious to the purpose the State has at heart'. On hearing these words, a Member momentarily interrupted, saying, 'The music will be an added punishment to some' (Hansard, Fifth Series, 1910, vol. 19, col. 1350). See also *Blackwood's* magazine, vol. 188, p. 397, where 'poor, simple folk' from Bermondsey and Bethnal Green, according to the author, were denied entertainment by a military band because they had not quickened 'the higher sentimentalism' and therefore had to remain 'without music and all unlectured until by theft or violence they have qualified themselves for Mr Churchill's sympathy'.
47 PRO HO 45 /16483/192637/1.
48 PRO HO 45/16483/192637/1, Churchill to Brise, 23 April 1910.
49 See Chapter 5 of this book.
50 PRO HO 45/16483/192637/1, Brise to Churchill, 5 May 1910.

Notes to Chapter 4

51 PROPCom. 7/550, Brise to Troup, 2 April 1910. Churchill's comments on this letter are on HO/190981, Churchill to Troup, 12 May 1910.
52 It is perhaps worth noting that at this time Maidstone Prison was increasingly being used for the imprisonment of young convicts, especially those less criminally sophisticated than the average run of the convict population.
53 Churchill's approach to this question fits in well with his general social philosophy, as declared in his speech to the House of Commons on 6 July 1908 on the Coal Mines (Eight Hours) Bill (Hansard, Fourth Series, 1908, vol. 191, col. 1330.) He spoke then about working people demanding 'time to look about them, time to see their homes by daylight, to see their children, time to read to think and to cultivate their gardens – time, in short, to live' (Churchill 1909, pp. 181–2). He took up the point again in his speech to the House on 20 July 1910, observing, 'It is forty years since the Education Act of 1870 was passed ... we have got a class of men in our prisons who need brain food of the most ordinary character' (Hansard, Fifth Series, 1910, vol. XIX, col. 1439).
54 PRO HO 45/16483/192637/1, Churchill to Brise, 6 May 1910.
55 PRO HO 45/16483/192637/1. Brise to Churchill, 11 May 1910.
56 We are probably entitled to read into the 'tiff' between Brise and Churchill the latter's desire to achieve public recognition for what he had done while he was still Home Secretary, given the uncertain lifespan of the Government at the time.
57 PRO HO 45/16483/192637/2.
58 PRO HO 45/16483/192637/3.
59 For the attacks on the scheme, see PRO HO 45/16483/192637/3, which contains a copy of a letter to *The Times* of 6 September 1910. The correspondent protests that a convict prison should not be regarded as a 'mere reformatory ... The prisoners are sentenced to be punished with hard labour, and the mitigation of such sentence as now sanctioned by the Home Secretary is in effect partly to nullify their effect, to the detriment of the community.' One particular bugbear was that a military band had performed in Verne Prison, thereby supposedly denigrating the King's uniform.
60 The foregoing is a summary of Prison Rule 65 (convict prisons) and Prison Rule 70 (local prisons), published in Parliamentary Accounts and Papers – 29 – 1899, vol. LXXIX.
61 *Ibid.* Prison Rules 45, 60, 62, 63 and 64 (convict prisons); and Prison Rules 50, 65, 67, 68 and 69 (local prisons).
62 This was one of the changes alluded to in Gladstone's hand-over notes. See p. 6 of this book, para 1.
63 Churchill employed the term 'brain-food' to signify books, lectures, concerts and education when he addressed the House of Commons on 20 July 1910 (Hansard, Fifth Series, 1910, vol. 19, col. 1349).
64 PRO HO 45/22702/168032/2a, 15 December 1909. She had been placed in the third division.

65 Meanwhile, we should note that Gladstone, on 15 February 1910, four days before Churchill took over, had minuted on a file concerning amendments to Prison Rules as they related to prisoners in the second and third divisions (forcible feeding) – PRO HO 144/1042/183256/17 – that 'I have often expressed the opinion that the Rules as regard library books should be reviewed and revised. I very much doubt that prison libraries should be left so completely as they are now to the discretion of Chaplains. Many Chaplains are well qualified for the duty. Several are not. I remain of the opinion that reading, and the uses of books, should be much more encouraged in prisons. This is one of the subjects I should have taken up had not our time been so much occupied by the futile and silly action of the "suffragettes".'

66 PRO HO 45/22702/168032 /2a.

67 A committee of inquiry into the regulations relating to the supply of books to prisoners was not new. In 1908 the idea was aired in a parliamentary question addressed to Gladstone, who sought the views of Brise as to a suitable reply. On 22 July 1908 Brise advised against such a committee and on this basis the Home Office's senior officials drafted a reply to the effect that all reasonable requirements were already met and there was therefore no reason to hold an inquiry. This draft, however, was not to Gladstone's liking and he altered it to read: 'The regulations are receiving my attention' (PRO HO 45/22702/168032/1). There the matter rested until the case of Violet Bryant reopened it.

68 PRO HO 45/22702/168032/2a. These terms of reference are set out in the report of the Library Committee, i.e., CD 5589, 1911. It seems strange at first sight that Churchill, bearing in mind the high value he placed on books in prisoners' regimes, should have allowed the progressive stage system to stand in the way of what prisoners could read. In this context, however, we need to remember his preliminary comment of 7 March 1910 on Brise's justification of the separate system of convict confinement (see p. 53 of this book).

69 Liberal Member of Parliament for Eddisbury, Cheshire, and related to Churchill by marriage (Soames 1999, pp. 698 and xxvi (family tree)).

70 Churchill's minute of 28 March 1910 (PRO HO 45/22702/168032/2a).

71 Char/12/4/18, Churchill College, Cambridge, dated 1 April 1910.

72 There was an unhealthy tendency in the Prison Commission to influence unduly the membership and terms of reference of internal Prison Department committees in order to ensure an outcome of their deliberations agreeable to the Commissioners (McConville 1995, p. 268). Brise was inclined modestly to leaven the official element, but he nevertheless attempted to ensure that in their outcomes there would be as little disturbance to established policies as possible (see *ibid.*, pp. 679–80 and 681–4). Brise's suggested membership and terms of reference for the Library Committee were well within this tradition. Unlike previous Home Secretaries, however, Churchill was not prepared to go along with traditions of this kind. He wanted to know the reali-

Notes to Chapter 4

ties of situations, palatable or otherwise, and had no compunction about challenging official advice.

73 CD5589, op. cit.
74 Something later emphasized by Waller in a personal letter of Gladstone on 9 October 1911 (Gladstone Papers, add. mss, British Library, 45994). Following the delivery of the committee's report, responsibility for the development of prison libraries was entrusted by the Commissioners to Waller, as recorded in their Minute Book on 14 December 1910.
75 CD5589, op. cit., paragraph 55.
76 *Ibid.*, paragraph 46. At the same time, however, in paragraph 48, the committee stoutly defended the progressive stage system in principle: 'firstly to concentrate prisoners' minds on serious and definitely improving subjects during the first portion of their sentences; and secondly to supply an incentive to industry and good conduct by reserving the privilege of the novel until the marks representing the first stage have been earned'.
77 *Ibid.*, paragraph 25.
78 *Ibid.*, paragraphs 13–27, especially paragraphs 15 and 26. This is an interesting analysis of prisoners' reading interests in the round.
79 *Ibid.*, paragraphs 22 and 23.
80 *Ibid.*, paragraphs 24 and 79, and Appendix III.
81 *Ibid.*, Recommendation XLIV and paragraph 127.
82 *Ibid.*, paragraphs 28–35.
83 *Ibid.*, paragraphs 31 and 35.
84 *Ibid.*, paragraphs 36–40.
85 *Ibid.*, paragraph 41.
86 *Ibid.*, paragraph 56–61.
87 *Ibid.*, paragraphs 65–70.
88 *Ibid.*, paragraphs 101–6.
89 *Ibid.*, paragraph 109.
90 *Ibid.*, paragraphs 62 and 71 and 101–8, 94, and 96–9.
91 PRO HO 45/22702/168032/7 for the committee's letter and /13 for the Treasury reply. The new capitation rules remained in being until 1978 when prison library arrangements were fully modernized.
92 CD5589, op. cit., paragraphs 77 and 80–90. See also Waller to Gladstone, 11 August 1910, where, in reference are the committee's recommendations on 'various improvements in distribution, selection, and the minutiae of librarians' work', he explains the need for them 'to avoid stupid mistakes'. Evidently the committee had not been impressed by the mechanics of library administration which had come to its notice (Gladstone Papers, add. mss, British Library, 45994, vol. X, f. 258). It would be interesting to know if the committee had been influenced in its recommendations by the observations on prison libraries made by Jabez Balfour in his book *My Prison*

Life (1907), Chapter XX, pp. 332–48. Shortly before the committee sat, Balfour emerged from a lengthy sentence of penal servitude inflicted on him for extensive fraudulent financial dealings (the 'Maxwell' of his day). He was an educated man and could write well (in his day he had been Mayor of Croydon and a Member of Parliament). During his imprisonment he had been employed helping prison chaplains and schoolmasters to run their prison libraries. He spoke highly of the libraries in which he worked and made sensible and practical suggestions for enhancing their effectiveness, of a kind set out in some of the committee's recommendations. Whether or not the committee read his book, however, is impossible to say.

93   PRO HO/45/22702/168032/6.
94   Fyfe 1992, p. xxii.

Notes to Chapter 5

1   8 Edw. 7 C. 59, Part I, sections 1–9. The Act was the Government's response to a recommendation in the 1895 Report (paragraph 84) that a penal reformatory should be established under government management for selected young offenders in the sixteen to twenty-three age group. 'Borstal', as a type of custodial institution, takes its name from a village in Kent, near Rochester, and in the beginning was a converted convict prison. It was the only centre for borstal detention in 1910. The second such institution opened at Feltham in 1911. A wing of Bedford Prison was used from 1900 to test an embryonic version of what later became the Borstal System and moved to Borstal itself a year later. By 1907 a small extension of this development was introduced at Lincoln Prison, but this was closed down in 1908 when the Prevention of Crime Act established the statutory Borstal System. Between 1911 and 1923 Canterbury Prison was used as a 'recall borstal'. See Hood 1965, pp. 1, 17 and 225.
2   *Ibid.*, sections 4 (1) and (2).
3   *Ibid.*, section 5 (1). The supervising authority in this case was the Borstal Association, a part of Churchill's new central agency for discharged penal servitude, preventive detention, and borstal inmates. It should be specially noted that the borstal sentence embodied the principle of indeterminacy. Generally speaking Churchill distrusted indeterminate sentences of all kinds – even borstal sentences – because he thought they could become 'an instrument of political oppression' (Radzinowicz and Hood, op. cit., p. 283).
4   PRO HO/144/18869, Churchill to Masterman, Troup and Brise, 30 June 1910.
5   Churchill sometimes described Swedish drill as 'defaulters' drills', presumably drawing on the vocabulary of his army days.
6   In his speech to the House of Commons on 20 July 1910 (Hansard, Fifth Series, vol. 19, col. 1347) Churchill contrasted the treatment of young offenders with the treatment

Notes to Chapter 5

of those from other social classes, whose similar offences committed in 'boisterous and exuberant moments, whether at Oxford or anywhere else', were punished 'less severely'.

7 PRO HO 144/18869.
8 How Churchill came to misunderstand the borstal system is difficult to fathom. It may be because he first came upon it in the course of his investigations into court calendars and on the strength of what he found there plunged straight into his two memoranda before he had been briefed on the system by either the Home Office's senior officials or the Commissioners. Maurice Waller, on the other hand, in a private letter to Gladstone of 18 August 1910, put the difficulties the senior officials and Commissioners were experiencing at Churchill's hands down to the fact that 'he does not know enough about these subjects yet and sometimes does not seem to take care to learn. He is exercising other Branches of the Home Office, too, greatly' (Gladstone Papers, add. mss, British Library, 45994, vol. X, ff. 250–60). Nevertheless, it is strange that Churchill slipped up in this way, because, between taking up his appointment as Home Secretary and writing his memoranda about the borstal system, he had been in close touch with Brise about structuring the education programme for borstal inmates (PRO P Comm. 7/550, 2 April 1910; and P Comm. 7/551). His interest, however, was not so much in the borstal regime as in the length of the borstal sentence, its indeterminacy, the offences to which it could be applied, and the question of proportionality.
9 *Ibid.*, Brise to Troup, 13 July 1910.
10 Of 1475 cases committed for trial from the time the Act came into operation, only 385 had resulted in sentences of borstal detention and of this number, only 58, or 15 per cent, carried sentences of three years.
11 But this statement is at variance with what he told the Budapest International Penitentiary Congress in 1905 (Brise 1924, p. 132), and it does not take into account the elaborate education programme that he and Waller were devising for the borstals in 1910.
12 PRO HO 144/18869.
13 Annual Report to Parliament of the Commissioners, 1909–10, Appendix 17, especially paragraphs 8a and 9.
14 One was, in fact, issued, unprecedentedly, to every magistrate in the Home Secretary's jurisdiction, as Churchill subsequently informed the House of Commons on 20 July 1910 (Hansard, Fifth Series, vol. 19, col. 1345).
15 PRO HO 144/18869, Troup to Churchill 14 July 1910.
16 Hansard, Fifth Series, vol. 19, cols 1347–8.
17 PRO HO 144/18869, Churchill to Troup, 21 July 1910. A handwritten note in Troup's handwriting on this minute, of the same date, addressed to Brise, informs him that, following a meeting with Churchill, it was agreed that a committee would meet to deal with the borstal questions. The Commissioners were also told in this note

that they would be responsible for processing all matters for aid to convicts on their discharge from custody.

18   All these matters eventually came to a head in Churchill's draft Abatement of Imprisonment Bill, subsequently retitled 'Draft Administration of Justice Bill, 8 April 1911', addressed in Chapter 7 of this book. In the event, his tenure at the Home Office was too short to enable him to put into practice his 'elaborate scale of minimum conditions' regulating the borstal sentence. But he had a long memory. When he was Chancellor of the Exchequer in Baldwin's administration (1924–9) the Home Office sought permission from the Treasury to insert provision in the Prison Commission expenditure estimates (£150,000) to cover the cost of a new borstal institution. He informed the Home Secretary that he remembered his own days at the Home Office, and that whilst he remained a supporter of the borstal system he still believed that there was 'a tendency to impose unduly long sentences in the belief that it is so bracing'. Nevertheless he believed that £150,000 was excessive for a new borstal in the light of the nation's economic difficulties at the time. Something less expensive should be considered. In the event he agreed to the inclusion of £13,000, leaving the Prison Commission to cover the remainder of the cost from elsewhere in its estimates, and using the borstal inmates to do the actual building construction under the supervision of the Commission's Works staff (Chancellor to Home Office, February 1928, PRO HO 45/1624/512613/2 and 14; also PRO P. Com. 9/55).

Notes to Chapter 6

1   8 Edw. 7 C. 59, Part II, sections 10–16.
2   Prison Department Committee Report, 1895, paragraph 85, and Recommendation X (4).
3   The circumstances are rehearsed in Radzinowicz and Hood 1986, pp. 268–73.
4   Sections 10 (4) and (5) of the 1908 Act. Moreover, in a Home Office circular of 1 September 1909 to all concerned with the application of the preventive detention sentence, it was stressed in paragraph 9 that the sentence applied 'only to criminals whose ordinary mode of life is criminal and not to offenders whose crimes are of an occasional character, even though they may be addicted to dishonesty and may have been repeatedly convicted'. To this circular was appended an extract from a circular issued to the police on this very point. It stressed it was the duty of the police to satisfy the Director of Public Prosecutions in the first instance that the case was a proper one for laying a formal charge of habitual criminality: 'The crimes must be of a serious character – such as burglary, housebreaking, coining, larceny from the person, robbery with violence, and the like; there must be evidence that the dishonesty is persistent and there must be good reason to believe that such dishonesty is

Notes to Chapter 6

part of the prisoner's mode of life, and is not due to drunkenness or destitution, or a mere aberration of intellect' (PRO HO 45/12905).

5   Section 12 of the 1908 Act. See also p. 65 of this book for an illustration of this section of the Act.
6   Section 13 (3) of the 1908 Act.
7   Hansard, Fifth Series, 1910, vol. 19, cols 1351–2.
8   Gladstone Papers, add. mss, British Library, 45994, ff. 259–60. Brise, too, voiced his anxieties about working under Churchill, in a private letter to Gladstone on 20 February 1911: 'We are still groaning under the domination of W.S.C. I could tell you stories of him which would make your hair turn white! but I must be silent on paper from the traditional loyalty of a public servant to his Chief' (*ibid.*, add. mss, British Library, 46070, ff. 215–6.)
9   PRO HO 144/670/106382A. See also Scriven [1931], pp. 26, 27, 34, 36, 50, 53, 55, 61, 65, 69 and 73. I owe my knowledge of this book to Shropshire County Record Office. The MP for Oswestry at the time Churchill was dealing with the Dartmoor Shepherd was William Clive Bridgeman, later Lord Bridgeman, destined himself to be Home Secretary 1922–4. Shropshire was plagued at the time by the Old Shepherd's depredations. Bridgeman kept a personal file on the Dartmoor Shepherd case which is now deposited in the Shropshire County Record Office. It contains a copy of Churchill's original narrative of the case, entitled 'The Old Shepherd Of Dartmoor' which he issued to Bridgeman on 26 January 1911, and which was published in *The Times* newspaper the following day. This file forms the basis of the account presented here.
10 Davies had submitted a petition to the Home Secretary on 19 October 1909, seeking a reduction in the length of his latest sentence on the same grounds of lack of proportionality between his offence and sentence length that Churchill had himself discerned. Churchill is here quoting from that petition.
11 Lloyd George had accompanied Churchill on a visit to Dartmoor Prison on 24 October 1910. Three days before Lloyd George delivered his speech on 21 November 1910, Asquith had announced the dissolution of Parliament to cut the constitutional knot in which the Liberal and Conservative Parties found themselves. In his rabble-rousing speech Lloyd George used the Davies case to illustrate the imbalance in the distribution of wealth in the community, an imbalance the Liberal Party was seeking to correct and, he claimed, the Conservative Party was seeking to maintain. A fair proportionality between offences and penalties was part of this correctional process (*Daily News*, 22 November 1910, pp. 1 and 2).
12 Hansard, Fifth Series, vol. 21, questions to Churchill, 8 and 20 February 1911, cols 274 and 1535–6 respectively.
13 *Ibid.*, questions to Churchill 12 and 23 February 1911 at cols 1900 and 2075 respectively; and 28 February 1911 at col. 198. Also 2, 7, 8 and 9 March 1911 at cols 554, 1029, 1211 and 1397 respectively; and in vol. XXIII, 6 April 1911, at cols 2432–3 and 2580

respectively; and in vol. XXIV, 11 and 19 April 1911, at cols 420 and 877–9 respectively. There are references to the case in *The Times* on 16, 19, 21 27 and 30 January, 18 February, 9 and 13 March 1911. Churchill's parliamentary critics, hardly surprisingly, included Members from Shropshire and the neighbouring counties, which had been the scenes of so many of Davies's nefarious activities.

14 See Scriven [1931], pp. 83–102 and 110–211 for a more detailed account of these proceedings and Davies's later history.
15 PRO HO 45/10589. The date and purpose of this meeting (on 8 June) is confirmed in a further letter from Matthews to Churchill on 7 November 1910 on the same file, but bearing the suffix reference /184160/25a.
16 This circular and draft memorandum are in PRO HO 45/10570/175865/19. See also Chapter 6 of this book, n. 4.
17 PRO HO 45/10589, memorandum from Churchill, 14 June 1910.
18 PRO HO 45/10589, 17 and 20 June 1910. Blackwell was a barrister of the Inner Temple recruited by the Home Office as an assistant under-secretary of state in 1906 to assist Troup. See also pp. 33–5 of this book.
19 *Ibid.*, Brise to Troup and Churchill, 27 June 1910.
20 *Ibid.*, Troup to Churchill, 1 July 1910.
21 Troup's underlining.
22 Sections 10 (2) and 10 (6) of the 1908 Act.
23 PRO HO/45/10589, 6 July 1910.
24 There is no record of an approach being made to the Law Officers. Presumably, it was subsequently deemed unnecessary.
25 PRO HO 45/10589, with the additional suffix /184160/25a. This is Brise's analysis of the statistical information requested by Churchill.
26 The number quoted by Churchill in his speech in the Commons on 20 July had clearly risen between then and 21 October 1910, the date of Brise's statistical analysis, i.e. from 174 to 193.
27 PRO HO 45/10589.
28 *Ibid.*, but also bearing a further reference, /184160/25a, 7 November 1910.
29 *Ibid.*, January 1911.
30 PRO P Com. 7/288, as suffixed by /17201/17BB for Churchill's signature, and P Com. 7/288 for the Rules, including the explanatory memorandum as laid before Parliament, and for the Standing Orders. The Rules and memorandum are also in the Appendix 17A, Annual Report to Parliament of the Prison Commissioners 1910–11, pp. 113–16.
31 Rules 2 and 7 include traces of Churchill's proposals for certificates of industry and conduct which he had mentioned in his earlier proposed scheme for a voluntary strenuous labour force; and of his scheme for the Zulu prisoners on St Helena to have plots for the cultivation of vegetables. At Camp Hill, arrangements were made

Notes to Chapter 6

32 for the prison to purchase at market prices the produce grown by prisoners, and to credit them with the proceeds. See also Chapter 1 of this book, n. 7.
32 As for Chapter 6 of this book, n. 30.
33 A point worth noting here is that between the date the sentence became operative in 1909 and the tabling of the Rules in 1911, the courts were sentencing prisoners to preventive detention without knowing the precise regime conditions under which those prisoners would be held. The opening of Camp Hill Prison is recorded in the Annual Report of the Prison Commissioners to Parliament, 1913–14, paragraph 21.
34 PRO P Com. 7/288.
35 Annual Report of the Prison Commissioners to Parliament, 1928, p. 13; pp. 12–18 tell the full story. These figures concern male prisoners. See also Chapter 9 of this book, n. 10.

Notes to Chapter 7

1 Hansard, Fifth Series, 1910, vol. 19, cols 1344–8. In the same speech he mentioned the amnesty accorded to prisoners on the accession of George V to the throne.
2 PRO HO 144/18869/196919, 13 August 1910.
3 Churchill had a preference for 'suspensory', whereas today the term 'suspended' is generally used.
4 See p. 45 of this book: Churchill's Prison Rule 243.
5 Blunt 1919, p. 281, diary entry for 5 September 1909. See pp. 4–5 of this book.
6 R. S. Churchill 1969, 2, pp. 1196–8. Blackwell at this time was an under-secretary of state at the Home Office. For his full career, see pp. 33–5 of this book.
7 PRO HO 144/18869/196919/4, Brise to Troup, 9 September 1910.
8 He represented the Home Office at the Eighth International Penitentiary Congress in Washington, USA, October 1910 (his report is in Parliamentary Papers 1911, vol. 39, CD5593, p. 621). See also paragraph 86 of the Annual Report of the Prison Commissioners to Parliament, 1910–11.
9 This statement should probably be treated with caution. Troup annotated it: 'I do not think this is accepted.'
10 Troup annotated this statement: 'How could the police be responsible?'
11 Brise stressed that in this substituted return he meant 61 per cent of 179,961, i.e., convicted persons, not persons committed to prison, and the sentences were not less than a fortnight but a fortnight or less. 'I am not clear', he wrote, 'how the Secretary of State arrives at the calculation that half of these were first offenders.' On this matter, see also Chapter 7 of this book, n. 13.
12 PRO HO 144/18869/196919/4, Troup to Churchill, 16 September 1910.

13 Troup's underlining. He is here referring to Brise's comment on the difficulty in following Churchill's figure of 61 per cent.
14 Churchill's minute is in PRO HO 45/10613, together with correspondence from Churchill's government colleagues, supporting his stance. Churchill, indeed, shortly afterwards expatiated further upon it. On 26 September he sought Prime Minister Asquith's approval for his proposals to abate the scale of imprisonment (R. S. Churchill 1969, 2, pp. 1198–1203, especially pp. 1199–1201). By a majority of just one vote, a parliamentary committee had reported in 1909 against the abolition of imprisonment for debt, so Churchill believed that he could press for abolition in his Bill. Churchill and those who thought like him believed that the law in its existing state was gravely weighted against the poor. Asquith replied on 2 October 1910 conveying his agreement in principle to Churchill's general plans, but counselling caution about abolishing imprisonment for debt (*ibid.*, p. 1204).
15 In a memorandum of 25 September 1910, PRO HO 45/10631/200605, Churchill indicated that for 'youths whose physique is not likely to be improved by physical exercises or for those who are actually at work under conditions which tax their strength to the full, there should be substituted some form of night school'.
16 PRO HO 144/18869/196919/2A. This document does not seem to have been printed until December 1910.
17 British Library Papers, BP 2/4 (15), 25 October 1910. Also Runciman Papers, WR/40, quoted by Addison 1992, p. 117.
18 PRO HO 144/18869/196919/5, Troup to Churchill, 1 November 1910.
19 PRO HO 144/18869, Brise to Troup, 29 October 1910.
20 Troup took exception to the use by Brise of the term 'draft Bill', annotating, 'there is no draft Bill yet'.
21 Troup's abatement headings specifically referred to the Commissioners having 'the widest powers of classifying prisoners, and assigning them appropriate treatment'. This statement was made in the context of second- and third-division treatment in the local prisons.
22 Closing prisons and determining the particular ones in which to locate particular prisoners was a vexatious question. For examples of the bitterness aroused when the local prisons were nationalized in 1877, see McConville (1995) op. cit., pp. 192 and 195–204, especially p. 200 for the intervention of Home Secretary Cross.
23 PRO HO 144/18869/196919/5.
24 PRO HO 144/18869/196919/5, Churchill to Troup, 2 November 1910.
25 PRO HO 144/18869/196919/6, Troup to Churchill, 17 December 1910. Brise had misgivings about Swedish drill on medical grounds and Henry doubted the suitability of police parade-ground facilities for the drill. He was even more concerned, however, about the pressures which would be placed on the finger-printing system, on which he was an internationally renowned expert whose scheme was in operation not just in the United Kingdom but throughout the world. Brise also thought that

Notes to Chapter 7

ordinary imprisonment could not be made harsher for prisoners, except by returning to discredited 'mechanical' practices.

26 PRO HO 45/10613 for the committee's report and PRO HO/10635/202187 for Churchill's instructions for setting up the committee and for the draft Bill. Churchill's draft circular was remitted to the committee as part of its terms of reference (PRO HO 45/10635/202187).

27 PRO HO 45/10635/202187. It would seem that Churchill also gave Blackwell some verbal, and so unrecorded, instructions on 2 January.

28 A prescient remark, if only because, in criminal justice, as Radzinowicz and Hood correctly point out, 'the final word belongs, more often than not, to social rather than to penal policy' (1986, p. 375).

29 PRO HO 45/10635/202187.

30 It should be noted here that, although ideas had been canvassed for the long-term detention of vagrants, habitual petty offenders and weak-minded offenders in special institutions in exchanges between Churchill and his senior Home Office officials and the Prison Commissioners, no place was found for them in the committee's report or in the draft Administration of Justice Bill. Churchill's interest in them, however, was profound. If feeble-minded persons likely to be a danger to the public had to be detained long term, he was insistent that their detention should be 'distinctly medical and non-penal' and that appeal facilities should be available to their relatives or friends, managed by 'a wholly unofficial medical authority independent of the Government of the day' (PRO HO 144/1085/193548/1, minutes of 9 and 20 April and 27 May 1910). For eugenical treatment, see Searle 1976, p. 107, quoting Box 12 of the Asquith Papers in the Bodleian Library for Churchill's arguments in favour of eugenical solutions which his senior officials, the Prison Commissioners and Masterman all discouraged him from advocating (PRO HO 144/1098/197900). His final comment on their advice, as it related to suppressing the procreation of children among the feeble-minded, in the file was: 'I think it is very evil to keep these wretched people cooped up all their lives when, in many cases – and there are cases on the border-line – where they desire freedom most they will be released after a simple operation.'

31 PRO HO 45/10631/200605, but also largely reproduced as Appendix E in the Blackwell Committee's report – PRO HO 45/10613.

32 Bills promoting the establishment of labour colonies were before Parliament in 1904, 1909, 1911 and 1912, but they all failed to make progress. The 1909 Bill attracted Churchill's attention during his Presidency of the Board of Trade. He wanted an arrangement under which no one convicted of vagrancy would be committed to prison unless he had been admonished three times within the previous twelve months. Thereafter he would be detained in a labour colony for at least a year (PRO HO 45/10578/179621/1). These matters are fully discussed in Radzinowicz and Hood 1986, pp. 367–75.

33 Under Section 6 of the 1898 Prison Act it was at the discretion of the court to direct that a prisoner, unless sentenced to hard labour, should serve his term in the first, second or third division, and if it did not exercise its discretion, the term had to be served in the third division. If the court specified the division, however, it was obliged to take into account the nature of the offence as well as the prisoner's antecedents. Under the draft Bill, the court now had to specify the division in place of the discretion it had enjoyed under the 1898 Act.

34 PRO HO 45/10613 for the report and PRO HO 45/10635/202187 for the draft Bill.

Notes to Chapter 8

1 See p. 11 of this book. See also Troup 1925, pp. 55–73, for a full discussion of the Royal Prerogative of Mercy as it operated in his time as Permanent Under-Secretary of State at the Home Office.

2 See Gardiner 1923, pp. 394–403, for exchanges of correspondence between Sir William Harcourt and Queen Victoria on the working of the Royal Prerogative of Mercy in particular cases where its application came before them for consideration.

3 A remission of this kind should not be confused with the remission which is earned by a prisoner who is serving a term of imprisonment and secures the remission by means of his or her good conduct.

4 Criminal Justice Statistics 1909, 1910 and 1911 published in *Accounts and Papers*, 58, vol. CII, 1911; 62, vol. CX, 1912–13 starting at p. 1; and 62, vol. CX, 1912–13, starting at p. 351. The figures mentioned in these official publications, however, should be viewed with caution. For example, Churchill in a speech to the House of Commons on 26 June 1911 (Hansard, Fifth Series, vol. 27, col. 252) put the remission figure at 436. Further, R.S. Churchill 1967, 2, p. 411, states that 43 death-sentence cases came before Churchill during the period he was in Office of which he recommended 21 for clemency under the Royal Prerogative. These figures have since been repeated by other historians, e.g. Jenkins, Best, Addison, and Radzinowicz and Hood, among others. Hansard, Fifth Series, vol. 28, cols 669–71, 17 July 1911 indicates that between February 1910 and July 1911 Churchill remitted 395 sentences. Part of the explanation for these differences in the figures may be that the Criminal Justice figures are calculated on an annual basis, whereas Churchill did not take office until 19 February 1910 and left on 24 October 1911. Action under the Royal Prerogative before the earlier date was therefore a matter for Gladstone, his predecessor, and after the later date for Churchill's successor, McKenna. Moreover there were occasions when Churchill was absent from the Home Office and his duties were performed by other ministers, notably, Sir Edward Grey, Lord Crewe and Lord Morley.

Notes to Chapter 8

5   Hansard, Fourth Series, vol. 172, col. 366, 11 April 1907. Churchill echoed Gladstone's and Harcourt's views: 'I am not prepared in any way to abrogate the full freedom of the prerogative of mercy, or to attach to its exercise either any obligation to consult or to be bound by consultation. No such obligation has been imposed on any previous occupant of this office, and if at any time in the due sequence of affairs the rt. Hon. Gentleman [a reference to the Member who had raised the point in debate] should find himself responsible for the duties of Home Secretary, I am quite certain that he would not consent to a general rule, and that the advisers to whom he would refer would not advise him to consent to a general rule that in no circumstances shall the prerogative be used unless there is a previous consultation with the court passing sentence. But, as a matter of fact, and of reasonable convenience in administration, in nearly every conceivable case the magistrates and the judges are consulted, and they will be fully and freely consulted on the subject in the future' (Hansard, Fifth Series, vol. 27, col. 254, 26 June 1911).

6   Writing in the *News of the World* on 7 May 1939, under the title 'Sombre Memories of the Home Office' (p. 12), he stated: 'Although I have seen a good many men killed in war and am a strong believer in capital punishment I cannot pretend for a moment that these responsibilities of life and death did not cast a shadow upon my life during the two and a half years that bore them.' Strong supporter of capital punishment he may have been, but at the same time he was haunted by doubt: 'Compassion wanders round the prison, seeking some window or loophole, however small, by which she can come to the aid of mortal suffering and fallible human retaliation.' The whole article concentrates on the sombre activities of the Home Office and at its conclusion he makes this view clearer still: 'Indeed, the Home Secretary's office is rightly considered a post of the highest dignity and honour, though it is certainly not one, which having held it, I would in any circumstances wish to occupy again.'

7   Details are in PRO P Com. 7/430. Churchill's reference to it is in his House of Commons address in Hansard, Fifth Series, vol. 19, cols 1353–4, 20 July 1910. Rather than release individual prisoners, he indicated that 'a general *pro rata* reduction of sentences over the whole area of the prison population' had been applied. 'The remissions which were granted on this occasion affected 11,000 prisoners and at a stroke struck 500 years of imprisonment and penal servitude from the prison population. I am glad to be able to tell the House that no evil results of any kind have followed from this. It is not at all true to say that a number of the men released have already returned to gaol.' But, he cautiously added, 'We must not allow optimism, or hope, or benevolence in these matters to carry us too far.'

8   Hansard, Fifth Series, vol. 27, cols 238–59, especially cols 254–6, for Churchill's response to the three cases concerned. On the Pentonville case, see also *The Times*, 3 October 1910, page 3a. The matter, prior to June 1911, had received an airing on 20 and 21 February 1911, when Churchill replied to parliamentary questions about it (Hansard, Fifth Series, vol. 21, cols 1533–5 and 1851–9). He explained that he had

deliberately gone to Pentonville Prison because he wanted to discover why young people in the juvenile division were detained there. He saw about forty of them and decided that the cases of sixteen deserved further consideration. He made small reductions in the sentences of seven, 'after a prolonged process of sifting on the spot and subsequently with the magistrates who convicted and the police authorities'. He described some of the cases in full, involving small fines or small terms of imprisonment in lieu for such offences as obscene language, bad language, travelling by rail without a ticket after walking fourteen miles to work (which the offender, who had no previous convictions, had failed to do), and a vague case of loitering. The *Law Journal* (1911), vol. 46, p. 411, has an interesting article on 'The Home Secretary's policies', which takes Churchill to task for not consulting with the judges when minded to use the Royal Prerogative to alter findings of the courts. Churchill was also challenged in the debate of 26 June 1911 on his attitude to the application of the Preventive Detention Act, a matter fully considered in Chapter 6 of this book. The debate saw Churchill's critics attempt to undermine his record as Home Secretary in the criminal justice field. He deflected their accusations with his usual vigour.

9   Hansard, Fifth Series, vol. 26, cols 238–59.
10 *Ibid.*
11 PRO HO 144/1087/194175.
12 *Ibid.* (emphasis in the original).
13 PRO HO 144/1144/209195. Cited in Ponting 1994, Chapter 6, p. 109. This chapter refers to a number of the cases on which Churchill cut his teeth.
14 *Law Journal*, vol. 46, 18 March 1911, p. 162. The journal continued to pursue this line of thought in further articles on 5 June and 10 June 1911 (vol. 46, pp. 349 and 374). The *Law Times* (3 June 1911, vol. 131, pp. 95–6) and the *Spectator* (3 June 1911, pp. 838–9) both took similar lines. By this time, however, there had been uproar in the House of Commons about these matters as is explained below.
15 Cited by Gilbert 1991, pp. 227–8; Hansard, Fifth Series, vol. 26, cols 1022–4.
16 Page 3 of this book.
17 *Law Journal*, vol. 45, 19 February 1910, p. 116: 'It is, perhaps, a little strange that in a Cabinet containing an unprecedented number of lawyers the office of Home Secretary should again be held by a layman. In view of his intimate connection with the administration of the law – his exercise of the Royal Prerogative of Mercy and the large amount of legal patronage at his disposal – there are obvious advantages in the Home Secretary being an experienced lawyer.' See also *Law Times*, vol. 128, 26 February 1910, p. 378: 'No reasonable person will desire to disparage the ability which the new Home Secretary possesses or question that it will be seconded by a rare capacity for hard work. It may, however, be justly and with reason urged that it would be more consistent with the nature of the duties assigned to the office were the holder to be equipped with a legal education ... Mr. Churchill will doubtless walk warily along the extremely slippery slopes to be traversed by a Home Secretary.' Constitutional

Notes to Chapter 8

niceties, however, as this book has indicated, were not exactly Churchill's forte, especially if they stood between him and the achievement of his objectives. In no way was he prepared to be deflected from his chosen policies.

18 *Law Journal*, vol. 46, 28 October 1911, p. 653. See Chapter 9 of this book for the circumstances under which Churchill transferred to the Admiralty.

Notes to Chapter 9

1 See Chapter 1 of this book: Lady Violet Bonham Carter, pp. 1–2, Scawen Blunt, pp. 4–5, and Galsworthy, p. 5. On the development of Churchill's reform programme, pp. 7–8.

2 See p. 9 of this book, and R. S. Churchill 1969, 2, p. 1153.

3 When Troup asked McKenna whether he would like to take over the draft Administration of Justice Bill where Churchill had left off, he replied bluntly: 'I cannot undertake to deal with the question at present' (Radzinowicz and Hood 1986, p. 773).

4 The tendency towards mildness in sentencing is rehearsed in *ibid.*, pp. 775–8. As far as prison treatment is concerned, the 1895 Report stressed the need to abate harsh and unfeeling treatment. In its place it recommended treatment 'more effectually designed to maintain, stimulate, or awaken the higher susceptibilities of the prisoners' (paragraph 25). By 1905, however, little progress had been made and it was only in that year, when Gladstone became Home Secretary, that progress began to be made. Gladstone himself was cautious, but he may be said to have set the stage for Churchill's accelerated pace in 1910 and 1911.

5 Churchill more or less confirmed this was his view when, in 1930, he reflected on his time at the Home Office: 'What it must mean for any man, especially an educated man, to be confined for years in a modern convict prison strains my imagination … when I was Home Secretary and had all the prisons of England in my charge I did my utmost consistent with public policy to introduce some sort of variety and indulgence into the life of their inmates, to give to educated minds books to feed on, to give to all periodical entertainments of some sort to look forward to and to look back upon, and to mitigate as far is reasonable the hard lot which, if they have deserved, they must none the less endure' (Churchill 1989 [1930], p. 274).

6 Sir Harold Butler, looking back on his days as a junior clerk in the Home Office during Churchill's tenure, offers chapter and verse for all of this in his memoirs (Butler 1950, p. 78). Instances of Churchill's interventions in court proceedings are in Forsythe 1991, p. 38, and in Radzinowicz and Hood 1986, pp. 770–1. See pp. 158–61 of this book.

7 See pp. 22–3 of this book.

8   Some recent exchanges of view between the Home Secretary and the Lord Chief Justice and others on the relationship between the executive and the judiciary suggest that these issues may be coming to the fore again.
9   Hansard, Fifth Series, vol. 19, col. 1345, 20 July 1910.
10 Other factors played their parts too, such as changes in the sentence practices of the courts. First World War exigencies accelerated the downward trend, as did a decline in the lengths of penal servitude sentences. By 1928, many offences which had previously attracted penal servitude and preventive detention sentences were being dealt with by sentences of ordinary imprisonment of up to two years' length. In 1931 Camp Hill became a borstal, and under the 1948 Criminal Justice Act the whole preventive detention system was subjected to a major reconstruction. See also Chapter 6 of this book, n. 35.
11 See p. 113 of this book and Chapter 5, n. 18.
12 Although currently there is some evidence of the executive seriously challenging the judiciary on its sentencing practices.
13 See p. 53 of this book.
14 PRO HO 45/10512/130921/6; Radzinowicz and Hood 1986, pp. 699 and 773–4; also p. 170 of this book and Chapter 8, n. 6.
15 R. S. Churchill 1969, 2, pp. 1152–3, Churchill to Galsworthy, 11 March 1910. This description tallies with his sombre presentation of the preventive detention Rules in the memorandum on them he laid before Parliament (see pp. 126–7 of this book), while at the same time indicating that it might be possible to alleviate further the regime conditions laid down in the Rules. From 1912 onwards, further alleviations were introduced. Prior to the end of the First World War there was some evidence to suggest that these contributed to reduced recidivism, but this was not borne out thereafter. (Paragraph 31 of the Commissioners' Annual Report to Parliament, 1918–19 for the encouragement; pp. 17 and 18 of their Annual Report, 1928 for the disillusion.) What was very encouraging, however, about the extended alleviation as practised at Camp Hill was the discovery that this produced both for staff and prisoners a more civilized atmosphere for life and work in the institution; and it did not undermine the law and order of the place. It may be said to have paved the way for the evolution of the open prison system in the late 1930s (Forsythe 1991, pp. 85–6 for the alleviations).
16 Hansard, Fifth Series, vol. 19, col. 1354.
17 Fox 1952, pp. 60 and 68.
18 This had already been reduced to fourteen days during the war, under the approval of the Home Secretary. The reduction had been made to satisfy the need for as large a prison labour force as possible to man war industries at a time when the prison population was falling.
19 Radzinowicz and Hood 1986, op. cit., p. 617.
20 PRO/HO 45/10601/189235/2.

21 Churchill 1989 [1930], p. 274.
22 *News of the World*, 7 May 1939, p. 12.
23 For a detailed explanation of Churchill's transfer to the Admiralty, see Jenkins 1964, pp. 241–2, and *idem* 2001, pp. 205–6. See also Ensor 1963, p. 436.
24 See Addison 1992 on 'The Two Faces of a Home Secretary'. The Home Secretary has to protect the quality of life in the nation, while suppressing tendencies which undermine it, forcibly if necessary. It is a difficult balancing act and some of Churchill's actions promoted public disquiet. Hence the reported remark of Home Secretary Morrison (1940–5) that 'the corridors of the Home Office are packed with dynamite'. Roy Jenkins was convinced that by the middle of 1911 Asquith had come round to the view that Churchill was no longer the right person to handle the Home Office portfolio and that the Admiralty would better suit his character (Jenkins 2001, pp. 189–206). See also Hansard, Fifth Series, 'Supply (Committee) Home Office', 26 June 1911, vol. 27, cols 238–305, for criticisms of Churchill's discharge of his criminal justice and law and order responsibilities.
25 Lady Violet Bonham Carter (1965, p. 236) recalls Churchill 'looking radiant' as he told her that her father, Asquith, had offered him the Admiralty. Later, he said to her, 'Look at the people I have had to deal with so far – judges and convicts! This is the big thing – the biggest thing that has ever come my way – the chance I should have chosen before all others. I shall pour into it everything I have got.' And, of course, he did. On Lloyd George's hand in securing the Admiralty for Churchill, see Lloyd George 2005, p. 87.

Bibliography

1. *Archives*

(a) Government Departments

Home Office
PRO HO 45
PRO HO 144
PRO P Com. (Sometimes Pri. Com.) 7

Treasury
PRO T1

Colonial Office
PRO CO 247

Cabinet Office
PRO CAB 37/108/178 (The feeble-minded). See also British Library Papers BP2/4 (15) which went before the Cabinet but are not indexed under a CAB reference. They concern the abatement of imprisonment.

(b) Private Papers

Asquith, H. H., Du Cane, E. and Harcourt, W. V. all at Bodleian Library, Oxford; Ruggles-Brise, E. at Essex County Record Office and held privately by Sir John Ruggles-Brise; Gladstone, H. at the British Library; Churchill, W. L. S. at Churchill College, Cambridge; Waller, M. L. held privately by Richard Waller; Bridgeman, W., at Shropshire Courts Record Office; and Prison Commissioners' minute books at the Public Record Office, Kew

2. Statutes

Convict Prison Act 1850, 13 and 14 Vict. C. 39. Directorate of Convict Prisons established.
Penal Servitude Act 1853, 16 and 17 Vict. C. 99
Penal Servitude Act 1857, 20 and 21 Vict. C. 3. Amendment to the 1853 Act.
The Prison Act 1865, 28 and 29 Vict. C. 126. Consolidation and amendment of the law relating to local prisons.
The Prison Act 1877, 40 and 41 Vict. C. 20. Amendment to the 1865 Act. (Creation of the Prison Commission.)
Probation of Offenders Act 1887, 50 and 51 Vict. C. 25.
Prison Act 1898, 61 and 62 Vict. C. 41. (Amendments to the Prison Acts of 1850 and 1877; amalgamation of the Prison Commissioners and Directors of Convict Prisons; divisional (local) imprisonment established; Secretary of State empowered to make Rules for the governance of prisons.)
Inebriates Act 1898, 61 and 62 Vict. C. 60. (Establishment, inter alia, of state inebriate reformatories under the Prison Commission.)
Probation of Offenders Act 1907, 7 Edw. 7 C. 17. (Act of 1887 repealed; probation system strengthened.)
Prevention of Crime Act 1908, 8 Edw. 7 C. 59. (Creation of borstal and preventive detention.)
Children Act 1908, 8 Edw. 7 C. 67. (Restriction of imprisonment for children.)
Criminal Justice Administration Act 1914, 4 and 5 Geo. 5 C. 58. (Notable, inter alia, for allowing offenders time to pay fines.)

3. Parliamentary Proceedings

Hansard, Fourth Series
'The Prerogative of Mercy Home Office': 11 April 1907, vol. 172, col. 366

Hansard, Fifth Series
'Treatment of Prisoners (New Rule)': 15 March 1910, vol. 15, cols 177–9; 31 March 1910, vol. 15, cols 1457–8; and 20 July 1910, vol. 19, cols 1348–9
'Supply (Report) Home Office': 20 July 1910, vol. 19, cols 1262–357, especially cols 1343–54 for Churchill's reforms
'Release of Convict David Davies': vol. 21, 8 and 20 February 1911, cols 274 and 1535–6; 22 and 23 February 1911, cols 1900 and 2075; and 28 February 1911, col. 198. Also

2, 7, 8 and 9 March 1911, cols 554, 1029, 1211 and 1397; and in vol. 23, 6 April 1911, cols 2432–3 and 2580; and in vol. 24, 11 and 19 April 1911, cols 420 and 877–9
'Supply (Committee) Home Office': 26 June 1911, vol. 27, cols 238–305, for criticisms of Churchill's conduct of his criminal justice and law and order responsibilities
'Sentences Remitted Home Office': 17 July 1911, vol. 28, cols 669–71

4. Official Papers

Parliamentary Papers

Report of the Departmental Committee on Prisons, PP 1895 [C7702], vol. 56
Report of the Departmental Committee on the Education and Moral Instruction of Prisoners in Local and Convict Prisons, PP 1896 [C8154], vol. 44
Report of the Departmental Committee on the Supply of Books to the Prisoners in H M Prisons and to the Inmates of Borstal Institutions, PP 1911 [CD5589], vol. 39
Annual Reports of the Prison Commissioners and Directors of Convict Prisons ended 31 March: 1909–10 [C5360]; 1910–11 [CD5891]; 1913–14 [CD760X7601]; 1918–19 [Cmd. 374]; and 1928 [Cmd. 3607]
Judicial Statistics – Introduction to the Criminal Statistics for the Year 1909 [CD5473]
Criminal Justice Statistics 1909, 1910 and 1911. Accounts and Papers 58, vol. CII, 1911; 62, vol. CX, 1912/13 starting at p. 1; and *ibid.* 1911 starting p. 351

5. Works of Reference

Annual Register
Boase, F. *Modern English Biography*
British Imperial Calendar and Civil Service List
Burke's Landed Gentry
Burke's Peerage, Baronetage, and Knightage
D.N.B.
Dod. *The Parliamentary Pocket Companion*
Kelly's Handbook to the Titled Landed and Official Classes
O.D.N.B.
University, Public School, and Inn of Court Registers

Who's Who
Who Was Who

6. Secondary Sources

(a) Works of Winston Spencer-Churchill

The Story of the Malakand Field Force. London: Longman, 1898
The River War, 2 vols. London: Longman, 1899
Savrola. London: Longman, 1900
The Boer War: London to Ladysmith and Ian Hamilton's March. London: Octopus, 1989 (originally published 1900)
Lord Randolph Churchill, 2 vols. London: Macmillan, 1906
My African Journey. London: Hodder and Stoughton, 1908
'The Untrodden Field in Politics', *The Nation*, 7 March 1908
Liberalism and the Social Problem. London: Hodder and Stoughton, 1909
My Early Life. London: Octopus, 1989 (originally published 1930)
Thoughts and Adventures. London: Thornton Butterworth, 1932
'Sombre Memories of the Home Office', *The News Of The World*, 7 May 1939

(b) Biographies of Churchill

Best, G. *Churchill: A Study in Greatness*. London: Hambledon, 2001
Birkenhead, Earl of. *Churchill 1874–1922*. London: Harrap, 1989
Blake, R. *Winston Churchill*. Stroud, Glos: Sutton, 1998
Carter, V.B. *Winston Churchill as I Knew Him*. London: Eyre and Spottiswoode and Collins, 1965
—— *Winston Churchill: An Intimate Portrait*. New York: Smithmark, 1994 (originally published 1965)
Churchill, R. S. *Winston S. Churchill, Official Biography. Vol. I: Youth 1874–1900*. London: Minerva, 1991 (originally published 1966)
—— *Winston S. Churchill, Official Biography Companion. Vol. I: Youth 1874–1900, Parts 1 and 2*. London: Minerva, 1991 (originally published 1966)
—— *Winston S. Churchill, Official Biography. Vol. II: Young Statesman 1901–1914*. London: Heinemann, 1967
—— *Winston S. Churchill, Official Biography Companion. Vol. II: Young Statesman 1901–1914, Parts 1, 2 and 3*. London: Heinemann, 1969

Gilbert, M. *Churchill: A Life*. London: Heinemann, 1991
Guedalla, P. *Mr Churchill: A Portrait*. London: Hodder and Stoughton, 1941
Jenkins, R. *Churchill*. London: Macmillan, 2001
Kemper, R. C. *Winston Churchill: Resolution, Defiance, Magnanimity, Good Will*. Columbia, MO: University of Missouri Press, 1996
Lukacs, J. *Churchill: Visionary, Statesman, Historian*. London and New Haven, CT: Yale University Press, 2002
Pelling, H. *Winston Churchill*. London: Macmillan, 1974
Ponting, C. *Churchill*. London: Sinclair-Stevenson, 1994
Rose, N. *Churchill: An Unruly Life*. London: Simon and Schuster, 1994
Scott, A. Mac. C. *Winston Spencer-Churchill*. London: Methuen, 1905

(c) Memoirs and Bibliographical Studies Relating to Churchill

Anderson, R. *The Lighter Side of My Official Life*. London: Blackwood, 1910
Asquith, H. H. *Fifty Years of Parliament*, 2 vols. London: Cassell, 1926
—— *Memories and Reflections 1882–1927*, 2 vols. London: Cassell, 1928
Blunt, W. S. *My Diaries, Vol. II, Part 2*. London: Secker, 1919
Butler, H. B. *Confident Morning*. London: Faber and Faber, 1950
Egremont, M. *The Cousins*. London: Collins, 1977
Gardiner, A. G. *The Life of Sir William Harcourt*. London: Constable, 1923
Grigg, G. *Lloyd George: The People's Champion 1902–11*. London: Penguin, 2002 (originally published 1978)
Guillemard, L. N. *Trivial Fond Records*. London: Methuen, 1937
Hassall, C. *Edward Marsh, Patron of the Arts*. London: Longman, 1959
James, R. R. *Lord Randolph Churchill*. London: Phoenix, 1994 (originally published 1959)
Jenkins, R. *Asquith*. London: Harper Collins, 1964
Lloyd George, R. *David and Winston – How a Friendship Changed History*. London: John Murray, 2005
Mallet, C. E. *Herbert Gladstone*. London: Hutchinson, 1932
Marrot, H. V. *The Life and Letters of John Galsworthy*. London: Heinemann, 1935
Scott, H. R. *Your Obedient Servant*. London: Andre Deutsch, 1951
Ward, C. H. D. and Spencer, C. B. *The Unconventional Civil Servant: Sir Henry H. Cunnynghame*. London: Michael Joseph, 1938
West, A. *Contemporary Portraits*. London: T. Fisher Unwin, 1920
Williamson, P. *The Modernisation of Conservative Politics: Diaries and Letters of William Bridgeman 1904–35*. London: The Historians' Press, 1988

(d) Other Books and Articles about Churchill

Addison, P. *The Political Beliefs of Winston Churchill*. Transactions of the Royal Historical Society, Fifth Series, vol. 30, 1980
—— *Churchill on the Home Front 1900–1955*. London: Cape, 1992
—— *The Three Careers of Winston Churchill*. Transactions of the Royal Historical Society, Sixth Series, vol. 11, 2001
—— *Churchill – The Unexpected Hero*. Oxford and New York, NY: Oxford University Press, 2005
Alanbrooke, Field Marshal Lord. *War Diaries 1939–1945*, ed. Alex Danchev and Daniel Todman. London: Weidenfeld and Nicolson, 2001
Cannadine, D. *Aspects of Aristocracy*. London: Penguin, 1995
—— *In Churchill's Shadow*. London: Penguin, 2002
Gilbert, M. *Churchill's Political Philosophy*. Oxford: Oxford University Press, 1981
Hyam, R. *Elgin and Churchill at the Colonial Office*. London: Macmillan, 1968
James, R. (ed.). *Winston S. Churchill: His Complete Speeches, 1897–1963*. New York: Chelsea House Publishers, 1974
Masterman, L. *C. F. G. Masterman: A Biography*. London: Nicholson and Watson, 1939
Soames, M. *Speaking for Themselves: The Personal Letters of Winston and Clementine Churchill*. London: Black Swan, 1999
Troup, E. 'Freedom Under The Law', *Evening Standard*, 22 April 1925

(e) Books Relating to the Home Office

Home Office. *The Home Office 1782–1982*. Layhill: HMP, Layhill, 1982
MacLeod, R. (ed.). *Government and Expertise: Specialists, Administrators and Professionals*. Cambridge: Cambridge University Press, 1988
Nelson, R. R. *The Home Office 1782–1801*. Durham, NC: Duke University Press, 1969
Newsam, F. *The Home Office*. London: Allen and Unwin, 1954
Pellew, J. *The Home Office 1848–1914: From Clerks to Bureaucrats*. London: Heinemann, 1982
Royal Institute of Public Administration. *The Home Office*. Callaghan's Bicentenary Lecture 'Reflections on Policy and Administration'. London: RIPA, 1982
Strutt, A. *The Home Office 'Peeps into the Past': Talks by Senior Officers of the Home Department*. London: Home Office, 1961
Troup, E. *The Home Office*. London: Putnam, 1925

Weiler, T. C. 'The Commissioners' Minute Books', *Prison Service Journal*, November 1996 and September 1997

(f) Books and Journal Articles Relating to Prisons and Criminal Justice

Balfour, J. S. *My Prison Life*. London: Chapman and Hall, 1907
Briggs, J., Harrison, C., McInnes, A. and Vincent, D. *Crime and Punishment in England: An Introductory History*. London: UCL Press, 1996
Clayton, E. G. 'The Home Secretary and Prison Reform', *The Nineteenth Century*, vol. CXIX, 1911
Cross, R. *Punishment, Prison and the Public*. London: Stevens, 1971
Du Cane, E. *The Punishment and Prevention of Crime*. London: Macmillan, 1885
Elmsley, C. *Crime and Society in England 1750–1900*. London: Longman, 1987
Forsythe, W. J. F. *Penal Discipline, Reformatory Projects and the English Prison Commission 1895–1939*. Exeter: University of Exeter Press, 1991
Fox, L. *The Modern English Prison*. London: Routledge, 1934
—— *The English Prison and Borstal Systems*. London: Routledge and Kegan Paul, 1952
Fyfe, J. *Books behind Bars: The Role of Books, Reading, and Libraries in British Prison Reform, 1701–1911*. Westpoint, CT: Greenwood Press, 1992
Garland, D. *Punishment and Welfare*. Aldershot: Gower, 1985
—— 'British Criminology before 1935', *British Journal of Criminology*, vol. 28, no. 2, Spring 1988
Goring, C. *The English Convict: A Statistical Study* London: HMSO, 1913
Green, T. H. *Lectures on the Principles of Political Obligation*. London: Longman, 1901
Grunhut, M. *Penal Reform*. Oxford: Oxford University Press, 1948
Harding, C., Hines, B., Ireland, R. and Rawlings, P. *Imprisonment in England and Wales: A Concise History*. London: Croom Helm, 1985
Hobhouse, S. and Brockway, F. *English Prisons: Report of the Labour Research Department*. London: Longman, 1922
Hood, R. *Borstal Reassessed*. London: Heinemann, 1965
King, J. *The Growth of Crime*. London: Hamish Hamilton, 1977
Leslie, S. *Sir Evelyn Ruggles-Brise: A Memoir of the Founder of Borstal*. London: John Murray, 1938
Lloyd George, D., 'Speech At Mile End', *Daily News*, 22 November 1910
McConville, S. *A History of English Prison Administration, Vol. I: 1750–1877*. London: Routledge and Kegan Paul, 1981

—— *English Local Prisons 1860–1900: Next Only to Death*. London: Routledge, 1995
Mannheim, H. *Pioneers in Criminology*. London: Stevens, 1973
Morris, N. and Rothman, A. J. (eds). *Oxford History of the Prison*. Oxford: Oxford University Press, 1995
Neale, K. *Her Majesty's Commissioners 1878–1978*. Maidstone: HMP, Maidstone, 1978
—— (ed.). *Prison Service People*. Newbold Revel: HM Prison Service Training College, 1993
Paterson, Arthur. *Our Prisons*. London: Hugh Rees, 1911
Radzinowicz, L. *Adventures in Criminology*. London, Routledge, 1998
Radzinowicz, L. and Hood R. *A History of English Criminal Law, Vol. V: The Emergence of Penal Policy*. London: Stevens and Sons, 1986
Rich, C. E. F. *Recollections of a Prison Governor*. London: Hurst, 1932
Rolph, C. H. *The Queen's Pardon*. London: Cassell, 1978
Ruggles-Brise, E. *The English Prison System*. London: Macmillan, 1921
—— *Prison Reform at Home and Abroad*. London: Macmillan, 1924
Rutherford, A. *Prisons and the Process of Justice*. Oxford: Oxford University Press, 1986
Scriven, A. *The Dartmoor Shepherd*. Oswestry: John Ainscow, n.d. [1931]
Searle, G. R. *Eugenics and Politics in Great Britain, 1900–1914*. Leyden: Nordhoff International Publishers, 1976
Sharpe, J. A. *Judicial Punishment in England*. London: Faber and Faber, 1990
Sim, J. *Medical Power in Prisons: The Medical Prison Service in England 1774–1989*. Milton Keynes: Open University Press, 1990
Thomas, J. E. *The English Prison Officer since 1850*. London: Routledge and Kegan Paul, 1972
Wiener, M. J. *Reconstructing the Criminal: Culture, Law, and Policy in England, 1830–1914*. Cambridge: Cambridge University Press, 1990
Williams, J. E. Hall. *Criminology and Criminal Justice*. London: Butterworth and Co., 1981

(g) Selected Other Books and Journal Articles

Bell, H. *Glimpses of a Governor's Life*. London: Sampson, Low, Martin and Co., 1946
Beveridge, W. *Power and Influence*. London: Hodder and Stoughton, 1953
Dangerfield, G. *The Strange Death of Liberal England*. London: Constable, 1936
David, E. *Inside Asquith's Cabinet*. London: John Murray, 1977

Elton, G. *The Tudor Constitution*, 2nd edn. Cambridge: Cambridge University Press, 1982
Ensor, R. C. K. *England 1870–1914*. Oxford: Oxford University Press, 1963
Faber, G. *A Portrait with a Background*. Cambridge, MA: Harvard University Press, 1957
Fulford, R. *Votes for Women*. London: Faber and Faber, 1956
Galsworthy, J., 'Solitary Confinement', *The Nation*, vol. 5, 1–8 May 1909
—— *Five Plays*. London: Methuen, 1984
Jenkins, R. *Mr Balfour's Poodle*. Kingswood: Heinemann, 1954
Mandelssohn, P. De. *The Age of Churchill: Heritage and Adventure 1874–1911*. London: Thames and Hudson, 1961
Pugh, M. *The Making of Modern British Politics 1867–1938*. Oxford: Blackwell, 1982
—— *Votes for Women in Britain, 1867–1928*. Historical Association Pamphlet (New Appreciations in History, No. 34). London: Historical Association, 1994
Read, D. *England 1868–1914: The Age of Urban Democracy*. London: Longman, 1979
—— (ed.). *Edwardian England*. Historical Association. London: Croom Helm, 1982
Rowse, A. L. *The Later Churchills*. London: Penguin, 1971 (originally published 1958)
Royle, E. *Modern Britain, A Social History 1750–1985*. London: Hodder Arnold, 1987

(h) Newspapers, Journals and Periodicals

Blackwood's, April and September 1910; February 1911
Daily News, 23 July and 22 November 1910
Evening Standard, 22 April 1925
Journal of Criminology, vol. 28, no. 2, Spring 1988
Law Journal, vol. 45, 19 February 1910; vol. 46, 18 March 1911 and 28 October 1911
Law Times, vol. 128, 26 February 1910; vol. 131, 3 June 1911
Manchester Guardian, 27 and 29 November 1954
The Nation, 7 March 1908; 8 May 1909
News of the World, 7 May 1939
Prison Service Journal, November 1996 and September 1997
Spectator, 30 July and 31 December 1910; 28 January, 11 February, 3 June and 28 October 1911
The Times, 21 and 22 February, and 23 July 1910; 11 and 27 January 1911; 20 August 1935

Index

Administration of Justice Bill (became Act 1914) 147, 153, 168, 170
Asquith, Herbert 18, 19–20, 25, 28, 141
 and WSC 1, 9, 25, 40, 141, 162, 166, 173, 174
 and Herbert Gladstone 28
 and Home Office 27, 30, 39
 and Ruggles-Brise 18
Aylesbury Prison 20, 69, 126

Balfour, A. J. 30
Beck, Adolph 33–4
beggars, tramps and vagrants and imprisonment 19, 146, 159
Birrell, Mrs Olive 93
Blackwell, Ernley (Assistant Under-Secretary of State) 15, 16, 33–5, 36
 and WSC's reform of sentencing 118, 132, 145
 on Troup 36
Blackwell Committee 146, 147–53, 170
Blackwell, James Hay 33
Blunt, Wilfrid Scawen 6
 and WSC 4–5, 31, 42, 46–7
Bonham Carter, Lady Violet 2
borstal system 20, 73, 85, 97, 102, 107, 133, 140, 150, 151
 establishment of borstals 6, 22, 101, 107, 111
 WSC on 8, 31, 32, 86, 102–3, 104–5, 108, 109, 131
 Galsworthy 54
 libraries in 93, 98
 official views of system 104

Ruggles-Brise on 73, 78, 79, 106, 133
 selection for 105–6, 107
 and sentencing policy 102, 107–8
 training at 86, 88, 89, 93, 98, 102, 106, 169
 Troup and 104–5, 108, 144
 see also preventive detention
Borstal 20, 94, 97, 102, 107, 140
Borstal Association 77, 78, 82, 83, 172
Bridewells 146
Brise, Sir Evelyn Ruggles *see under* Ruggles-Brise, Sir Evelyn
Bryant, Violet 91
Butler, Sir Harold 38–9
Butt, Clara 85
Byrne, William (Assistant Under-Secretary of State) 15

Camp Hill (prison), Isle of Wight 20, 33, 66, 78, 123, 126, 128
Campbell-Bannerman, Henry 25
Canterbury Prison 19, 20
Carter, Bessie 160–1
Catholic Aid Society 76, 82
Central Aid Association 123
Central Association 172
Ceylon (Sri Lanka) 2–3
Chamberlain, Joseph 24, 25
Chelmsford Prison 69
Childers, Hugh 27
Church Army 76, 82
Churchill, Lord Randolph 1, 24
Churchill, Winston:
 background 1–4

as prisoner in South African War 1–2, 84
attitudes towards his political stance 24, 25, 26, 40, 47, 172–3
explanation of change of party 24
in Colonial Office 2–3
as President of the Board of Trade 3, 5, 24, 49, 58, 71
appointment as Home Secretary 1, 3, 4, 6, 13
and adult offender system 32–3
and aged convicts 65–70, 171
Asquith 1, 9, 25, 40, 141, 162, 166, 173, 174
attitudes towards prevention of crime and sentencing policy 129ff, 167, 169, 170–1
and W. S. Blunt 4, 42–3, 46–7, 132
and borstals 102ff
codification of system 167–8, 169
committee on libraries in prison 93–4
convict initial separate confinement 53, 170
and David Davies case 114–17, 121
on Director of Public Prosecutions 122, 123
discussions with Treasury and Financial Secretary 79–83
on education and entertainment of prisoners 84–90, 171–2
policy development on ex-prisoners 53, 54, 74, 79–80–1, 83, 172
on employment of convicts (incentive labour scheme) 70–5
and Galsworthy 49–51, 54–5, 62–3, 171
and Herbert Gladstone 6, 34, 42, 102, 118, 127, 158
handling of recidivism and habitual criminals 53–4, 75, 58, 59, 80, 112–13, 117ff, 120, 124ff, 131, 168, 172
on Home Office 173

and House of Commons 12, 15–16, 26, 45, 62, 82–3, 88, 108, 112–13, 117, 122, 124, 126–7, 129, 148, 157, 158, 159, 161–2, 165, 168, 171
impact on reform of prison treatment 166
on imprisonment for debt 136, 139, 140
incentive labour scheme 70–5, 77, 172
and marks system 70–5
and Sir Charles Matthews 117, 123–5
memos to Troup and Ruggles-Brise 53, 54, 71, 88, 102, 120–2
and nature of criminal behaviour 54
on passive resisters 46
and police 113, 118
policy making 24–6, 126, 168
and political prisoners 42–5, 46–7
and preventive detention 66, 112ff, 124, 126, 127, 128, 168
on size of prison population 20, 58–9
prison and sentencing policies 157ff, 165ff
and Prison Commission 102, 118, 132, 147, 167, 173
prison reform programme 7–8, 9, 23–4, 31, 36, 44ff, 56
and prison regime 23–4
on prisoners' visits and correspondence 44–5
and prison as social reform 70–1
and Prison Rule 243A 45–6
and prisoners in British overseas territories 2
proposals for handling youth crime 32, 102–4, 106, 158–9, 168, 169
on proportionality of sentencing 102, 115, 118, 159–60, 167–8, 169
and provision of prison libraries 2, 90–9, 172
rationalisation of prison system 131–2
on recidivism 53, 59, 80, 122

Index

relations with judiciary 160–2, 168, 169, 170
on roots of criminal behaviour 54
and Royal Prerogative of Mercy 155, 158, 159
and Ruggles-Brise 16, 31–2, 50–2, 53, 59–60, 70, 71, 74–5, 76–81, 86, 117, 120, 122–4, 134ff, 141
sentencing proposals 2, 26, 102–4, 129, 130–2, 146–7
sentencing policy 159–60, 169–70
on short sentences 131–2, 140
and suspended sentences 129–30, 168, 171
and suffragettes 46, 47, 170, 171, 173
on Trade Unions 161–2
and Treasury 75, 81, 82, 88, 89
and Troup 39, 40, 42, 43, 44, 52–3, 60, 61, 65, 66, 74, 82, 83, 109, 117, 119, 120, 121–2, 136ff, 160
visit to Dartmoor 116
visit to Pentonville 158
and volunteering for incentive labour scheme 74
transfer to Admiralty 8, 9, 152, 162, 166, 168, 173, 174
see also Home Office
Connolly, Annie 160
Court of Criminal Appeal, establishment of 34
Criminal Justice Act (1948) 18
Criminal Justice Act (1967) 169, 172
criminology, development of 57–8
Cross, R. A. 27
Cunynghame, Sir Henry (Legal Under-Secretary of State) 15, 35

Dartmoor Prison 69, 87, 94, 114, 116
Davies, David (the Dartmoor Shepherd)
and issue of preventive detention 114–17, 121, 124

death penalty 34, 170, 173, 174
and prerogative of mercy 155, 156
debt and imprisonment 17, 133, 152
WSC on 136, 139, 140
Director of Public Prosecutions 112, 113, 117, 118, 119
and WSC's reforms 120, 122, 123–4, 127
and habitual prisoners 118, 120, 123
see also under Sir Charles Matthews
Directorate of Convict Prisons 17, 18, 134
see also Prison Commissioners
discharged prisoners' aid societies 76–7, 79, 80, 81
WSC on 74, 75ff, 81, 105, 106, 132
gratuities paid to 76, 79, 80, 81
Home Secretary and 112
Ruggles-Brise and 74–5, 76–7, 77–81, 82, 105, 123
Donkin, Horatio 18
Dorchester Prison 69
drill, penal 140, 145, 148, 149, 168
defaulters' drill 104, 130, 135, 141, 158
Swedish drill and imprisonment 103–4, 108, 109
Dryhurst, Frederick 18, 19–20
Du Cane, Major General Sir Edmund 27–8, 29

Eardley-Wilmot, Captain Cecil 18–19
education in prisons 84–90
committee on libraries 93–8
prison libraries 90–9
Edward VII 81
Elizabeth I 12
Exeter Prison 69

Faunt, Sir Nicholas 12
Fawcett, Henry 19
Feltham Borstal 88, 20
fines 103, 137, 140, 141, 147, 148, 149, 150, 151, 152, 157, 168

fingerprinting, use of 136, 138, 141, 145
flogging 170
Fox, Charles James 10

Galsworthy, John 6, 47
  and reform of prison system 5, 49–50, 54–5
  and WSC 5, 31, 32, 49–50, 54–5, 62–3, 171
  and ending of separate confinement 49, 54, 55
  play *Justice* 50–1, 53, 55
George V 81, 157
Gladstone, Herbert 1, 8, 27, 102, 107, 158, 170, 172
  and Asquith 1, 28, 174
  circular on habituality 117–18
  convict classification 48
  and WSC 6–7, 28, 34, 42, 46, 102, 118, 127, 158
  and Ruggles-Brise 31
  First Commissioner of Public Works 28
  and Home Office 1, 5, 6, 9, 14, 28, 30, 55
  and prerogative of mercy 156
  and preventive detention 111, 113, 117–18, 127
  Prison Department Inquiry Committee 30
  and Prison Commissioners 6, 9, 170, 174
  and prison libraries 91
  and prisons 28, 30, 36, 44, 170
  reform of prison system 6–7, 36, 42, 48–9, 53, 58, 59, 167
  on separate confinement 5, 53, 59, 60
  and suffragettes 6, 42, 47
  and treatment of prisoners 46, 49, 172
  and Troup 37–8, 59, 60
  see also Prevention of Crime Act
Gladstone, W. E. 11, 19, 25
Gloucester Prison 69

Goring, Charles 29
Green, T. H. 27, 29
Guillemard, Sir Lawrence 38

habitual criminals 111–12, 122, 124–6, 144
  defined 112
  and preventive detention 118, 127
  see also under recidivism
Harcourt, Sir William 11–12, 27, 38, 156
hard labour 7, 41, 48, 54, 130, 133, 140, 151, 159
Harris, S. W. 14
Henry, Sir Edward (Metropolitan Police Commissioner) 144, 145, 146, 148
Holloway 93, 94
Home Office 9
  described 10–16
  origins and responsibilities 10–13
  organisation and staffing 13–16
  administration of criminal justice system 161
  and borstal system 104–5
  and WSC 9, 113, 132, 165, 166–7, 168–9, 173
  Criminal Justice Department 33
  and Herbert Gladstone 9
  and judiciary 160
  nature of business 166
  Parliamentary and Industrial department 37
  and police 122, 127
  and Prevention of Crime Act (1908) 117
  and preventive detention 113, 117, 118, 120
  and prisons 16, 17, 49
  and prisoners' access to library books 92
  and Prison Commission 36
  and Prison Commissioners 9ff, 54, 101–2, 104, 113, 114, 130

Index

reform of prison system 36, 54
and separate confinement 54
Royal Prerogative of Mercy 33, 35, 158, 160
Superintendent of Convicts 17
Home Secretary 10–11, 12
and borstals 101–2, 104
and Borstal Association 77
case for legal background in the appointee 162
and petitions 155
and prerogative of mercy 156, 157
and preventive detention 6, 112, 113, 126, 127
and sentencing policy 7, 122, 129, 130, 135, 144, 151
Hopwood, Sir Francis (Permanent Under-Secretary of State, Colonial Office) 3, 162
Hornby, Admiral 27

Identification of Habitual Offenders 145
Imprisonment Abatement Committee (chairman Ernley Blackwell) 34
inebriates and prison/reformatories 20, 131, 134, 136, 140, 141, 146, 147, 148, 157
Isle of Wight Prison *see* Camp Hill

Jowett, Benjamin 29
juvenile crime, treatment of 158, 168, 169

larceny, punishment of 57, 118, 119, 120, 122, 124, 137, 140
Lewes Prison 69
Lincoln Borstal 88
Lincoln Prison 19
Liverpool Prison 93
Lloyd George, David 3, 26, 116
Local Government Board 39

McKenna, Reginald (WSC's successor as Home Secretary) 153, 162–3, 166, 174
Maidstone Prison 87, 88
Marsh, Eddie 14, 93
Masterman, C. F. G. (Parliamentary Under-Secretary of State) 14–15, 16, 39, 82, 129
Masterman, Lucy 39, 40
Matthews, Sir Charles (Director of Public Prosecutions) 117–18, 122
on preventive detention 123–5
Matthews, Henry (Viscount Llandaff) 27
mitigation and sentencing 56, 124, 127, 128, 171
Morrison, Herbert 12

National Insurance Act (1911) 3
North, Lord 10

pardons
types 155–6
WSC's views on 157
and prerogative of mercy 155
Paris International Penitentiary Congress (1895) 27, 29
Parkhurst Prison 19, 66, 67, 68, 87
and aged prisoners 67, 68, 69–70
passive resisters 46, 47, 171
Paterson, Alexander 83
Pearson, Carl 29
Pentonville Prison 158
police:
and DPP 113, 118, 119, 121, 122, 123
and habitual prisoners 124, 127–8
and Home Office 12, 13, 83, 118, 122
and probation 104, 140, 143
and sentencing 119, 120, 121, 122, 123, 125, 127, 148, 149

and supervision of ex-prisoners 48, 76, 77, 78, 80, 81, 103, 106, 113, 172
Ruggles-Brise on 57, 77, 123, 135, 136, 141
Portland Prison 87
prerogative of mercy 33, 34, 155ff
Prevention of Crime Act (1908) 6, 8, 20
  establishment of borstals 6, 101, 111
  Herbert Gladstone and 170
  and habitual criminals 111–12, 126
  and preventive detention 114, 119, 120, 124, 126
preventive detention and habitual criminals 66, 78–9, 80, 111, 112, 117, 118, 122, 123, 124
  WSC on 66, 112ff, 124, 126, 127, 128, 168
  Ruggles-Brise on 119
Preventive Institutes 81
Prison Act (1865) 47
Prison Act (1877) 21, 27
Prison Act (1898) 7, 41, 152
  and Prison Rules 112
  and suffragettes 42
prison chaplains 84, 90–1, 95, 96, 97
Prison Commission 16–24, 54, 83, 94, 165
  origins 16–18
  Annual Report 88, 89,
  and borstals 101–2, 104, 105–6
  and changes in confinement procedures 61
  and WSC 102, 118, 132, 147, 167, 173
  classification of prisoners 41, 44
  and confinement system 48–9
  education and entertainment of prisoners 84–5, 88
  ex-prisoners' gratuities 80
  and Herbert Gladstone 6
  and HMSO 97–8
  and Home Office 130
  management 21–2
  organisation 18–20
  preventive detention 113, 118
  and prison libraries 90, 98
  prison reform 35–6
  and prisoners' gratuities 76, 79–80
  and recidivism 53
  reorganisation 16–17
  responsibilities 20–1
  and Treasury 80
  see also Directors of Convict Prisons, preventive detention
Prison Commissioners 6, 15, 132, 134, 140
  WSC and transfer of powers 46
  and classification of prisoners 41
  and ex-prisoners 75, 76–7
  and habitual criminals 118–19, 123
  and Home Office 130, 167
  preventive detention 113, 18
  reform of prisoners' illegal conduct 140
  and suffragettes' illegal conduct 47
  and young offenders 101, 102
  see also Home Office, Sir Evelyn Ruggles-Brise
Prison Department Committee (1895) 17, 21, 22, 27–8, 35, 170
  Report 30, 49, 58, 84, 172
  Report and habitual criminals 111, 119–20
  Asquith and Inquiry 174
  Galsworthy and 49
prison libraries 90–9
  categorisation of prison books 2, 42, 44, 45, 46, 51, 91, 94–6
  committee on prison libraries 93–7
  and periodicals 96
Prison Rule 243A 45–6
Prison Rules
  (1898) 112
  (1905) 51, 62, 90
  and aged prisoners 67, 69
  WSC on 43, 45, 67

Index

and library books 90, 91–2
preventive detention 112
and separate confinement 51
prison warders (now Prison Officers) 21–3
interactions with prisoners 21, 22–3, 167
prisoners
  classification 7, 48, 54, 140, 142, 151
    first, second and third division defined 41–2
    First Division 44, 45, 46–7, 48–58, 130, 151
    Second Division 41, 44, 45, 46, 47, 130, 140
    Third Division 45, 46, 140, 151
    intermediate classification 48, 60, 62
    'star' system 41, 46, 48, 58, 60, 61, 140, 142
  access to library books 42, 90–9
  aged prisoners 65–70, 134, 171
  aid to ex-prisoners 74–83, 172
  arrangements with ex-prisoners pre-Churchill 76
  attempts to reform 21
  contacts with outside world 96
  earning of privileges 21, 23, 48, 72
  education of *see under* prisons
  employment of prisoners 70–5, 97, 172
  hard labour 41, 48, 54
  license system after release 76, 77, 105, 108
  marks system 71–2, 76
  prisoners' petitions 34
  privileged prisoners 131
  political prisoners 42–5, 46–7
  recidivists and habitual criminals 48, 56–60, 61, 111, 112, 120, 131, 150
  remission of sentence 2, 48, 70–2
  separate confinement 47ff, 52, 58, 60, 61, 171
  treatment of political prisoners 42–3

release on licence (ticket-of-leave) 48, 53, 59, 71, 77, 78, 83, 102, 105, 108, 116
  see also under sentencing
prisoners' aid societies *see under* discharged prisoners' aid societies
prisons, life in 21–4
  collecting prisons 48, 106, 143
  convict prisons 16, 17, 18, 47ff, 59, 60, 70, 76, 79, 85, 86, 88, 95, 98, 170
  correctional 133
  development of prison system 47–8
  education and entertainment in 84–90, 171–2
  hard labour 7, 41, 48, 54, 130, 133, 140, 151, 159
  incentive labour 70–5, 77
  libraries in 90–9
  local prisons 7, 16, 17, 18, 48, 52, 59, 68, 76, 79, 86, 90, 95, 98, 106, 130, 133, 171
  penal servitude prisons 48, 133
  reform, origins of onset of 22–4
  Ruggles-Brise on 136
  see also under preventive detention
Probation and After-Care Service 172
Probation of Offenders Act (1907) 103, 130, 152, 168
probation 106, 108, 135, 140, 144
  Probation Officers 104, 135, 143–4
prostitutes and criminal justice system 129, 134, 137, 138, 140, 147, 148, 150, 151

Raleigh, Professor Walter 93
Reading Gaol 160
recidivism 48, 51, 60, 75
  WSC on 80
  views of 58
reformatories 103
  see also borstals, inebriate reformatories

remissions:
  of fines 157, 159
  of sentence 155, 156, 157
respites of sentence 155
Rosebery, Lord 27, 174
Royal Prerogative of Mercy 155ff
Royal Society 76, 82
Royal Society for the Assistance of Discharged Prisoners 116
Ruggles-Brise, Sir Evelyn (Prison Commissioner) 15, 16, 18, 19, 20, 27–33, 43, 53, 171
  background 27–8
  appointment to Prison Service 27, 174
  and aged prisoners 67–9
  on aid to ex-prisoners 74–5, 77–9
  attitudes towards prison reform 43, 56–7
  and borstal system 105–6, 108
  and WSC 31–2, 43, 50–1, 54, 55, 57–8, 59–60, 71, 76, 77, 81, 82, 83, 84, 105, 106, 117, 119, 121, 129
  and WSC's reform of sentencing 118–19, 122–3, 132–8, 141f
  discussion on aid to discharged prisoners 76–81
  education and entertainment of prisoners 84–90
  and Galsworthy 50–1, 55–6
  and Herbert Gladstone 31, 58
  and marks' system for prisoners' remission 71–4
  and Matthews 122
  memorandum to WSC (14 April 1910) Central Government Association to oversee and aid discharged prisoners 76–8
  on penal drill 148
  and political prisoners 43, 44
  and preventive detention 118–19, 122–3

Prison Department Inquiry 28
  on prison libraries and prisoners' reading materials 92, 93
  on recidivism 58, 123
  and reform of prison system 32, 50–2, 54, 55, 57–8, 60–2
  on separate confinement 51–2, 55
  on transfer of prisoners between prisons in public view 142–3
  and Troup 43, 59, 60, 75, 83, 104, 132, 141–2
  views on prison service 16, 52
Runciman, Walter 141

Salisbury, Lord 30
Salvation Army 76, 82
Scott, Sir Harold 38, 39
Scott, McCallum 24
sentencing policy 129–30, 59–60, 140, 146–7
  abatement headings 143
  WSC on 129–30
  and debt 139, 152
  detentive imprisonment 133–4
  disciplinary detention 151–2
  Herbert Gladstone on 7
  indeterminate sentences 111, 134
  non-custodial sentences 158, 168
  penal servitude 16, 18, 60, 112, 122, 126, 133
  preventive detention 122
  and probation 130
  short sentences (under a month) 129–30, 131, 136, 137–8, 140, 142, 143, 151
  suspended 129–30, 136, 150, 168
  and young offenders 101–4
Shelburne, Lord 10
Simpson, Revd C. B. 93
solitary confinement 5, 47ff
  Ruggles-Brise on 51–2

St Giles's Christian Mission (Wheatley's) 76, 82
Stafford Prison 69
Stanley, Hon. A. L. 93
suffragettes 6, 41–2, 46, 47, 170, 171, 173
Superintendent of Convicts (Home Office) 17
Sydney Street Siege 40, 173

Tarde, Professor 58
Thomson, Basil 18, 83, 93–4
ticket-of-leave system (release being conditioned by parole rather than licence) 48, 53, 59, 71, 77, 78, 83, 102, 105, 108, 116
Trade Unions and judiciary 161–2
Treasury:
    WSC 75, 81, 82, 88, 89
    and education and entertainment of prisoners 86, 89, 98
    and financing of prisoners' release scheme 75, 79–80, 81
    and Home Office 14
    Ruggles-Brise and 79, 86
Troup, Sir Edward (Permanent Under-Secretary of State, Home Office) 14, 15, 16, 35–40, 50, 54, 160
    and aged prisoners 65–9
    attitude towards reforms 74
    and borstal system 108, 109
    and WSC 39, 40, 42, 44, 52–3, 60, 65, 66, 74, 82, 83, 109, 117, 120, 121–2, 136ff, 160
    and WSC's reforms of sentencing system 59–62, 118–19, 126, 136–40, 141ff, 146
    education of prisoners 89
    impact on Home Office 36–7
    and management of political prisoners 42–5
    penal drill 148
    and preventive detention 118, 119–20, 126
    and prisoners incapable of reform 66–7
    on reform of prison system 42–4, 52–3, 56, 61
    retirement 36
    and Ruggles-Brise 59–60, 74, 75, 83, 105, 108, 136, 141, 144
    on separate confinement 52–3

vagrancy 136, 137, 138, 140, 141, 146, 148, 158
1906 committee on vagrancy 19
Vagrancy Acts 147

Wall, A. J. 94
Wallace, Sir Robert 113, 114
Waller, Maurice 18, 19, 20, 93
    on borstal system 107–8
    on preventive detention 113–14
Walsingham, Sir Francis 12
Wardle, Mr, MP 161
Warwick Prison 20
'weak-minded' and prison 66, 131, 134, 140, 141, 142
Wheatley's Mission (St Giles's Christian Mission) 76, 82
White, alias Smith (prisoner) 65–6
Wills, Sir Alfred (High Court Judge) 116
Wilson, Wemyss Grant 82, 83
workhouses 66, 68, 147, 148
Wormwood Scrubs 94

youth crime 6, 103, 106, 108, 130, 141, 169
    WSC on 8, 32, 86, 102ff, 130, 158, 168
    Ruggles-Brise on 32, 105–6, 107, 108, 135
young offenders and imprisonment 22, 28, 96, Chapter 5
    see also Borstal, borstal system